D0859830

Checkerboard Square

CHECKERBOARD SQUARE

Culture and Resistance in a Homeless Community

David Wagner

f∂/3

Westview Press

BOULDER • SAN FRANCISCO • OXFORD

Copyright © 1993 by Westview Press, Inc.

Published in 1993 in the United States of America by Westview Press, Inc., 5500 Central Avenue, Boulder, Colorado 80301-2877, and in the United Kingdom by Westview Press, 36 Lonsdale Road, Summertown, Oxford OX2 7EW

Library of Congress Cataloging-in-Publication Data
Wagner, David.
    Checkerboard Square : culture and resistance in a homeless community / David Wagner.
        p.   cm.
    Includes bibliographical references and index.
    ISBN 0-8133-1585-9. — ISBN 0-8133-1586-7 (pbk.)
    1. Homeless persons—United States—Case studies.   2. Homeless persons—Services for—United States—Case studies.   3. Homeless persons—United States—Attitudes—Case studies.   I. Title.
HV4505.W23   1993
362.5'0973—dc20   93-3744
                                                                                             CIP

Printed and bound in the United States of America

The paper used in this publication meets the requirements
of the American National Standard for Permanence of Paper
for Printed Library Materials Z39.48-1984.

10   9   8   7   6   5   4   3   2   1

To the memory of
Sam Wagner
and Janice Reiss

Contents

Part Two: The Social Organization of the Streets   119

Acknowledgments

This book and the research it is based on could not have taken place without many other people. Although praise or blame for this account of "Checkerboard Square" lies solely with the author, there are some unindicted co-conspirators.

First, Marcia B. Cohen of the University of New England, who is also my wife, was a co-researcher in the first phase of this study (see Chapter 2) and a continual source of advice, an unofficial editor, and a sounding board throughout the years involved in this project. My debt to her covers the gamut from her work with the research team in phase one of the study, to her help in the conceptualization of many of the ideas, to her constant emotional support.

Second, as in all ethnographic studies, only "informants" among the people studied allow the author in. "Katherine" and "Mitch" served as the primary contacts with the homeless people of "North City" in 1990 and helped me gain initial access to records (such as those of the Coalition for the Dignity of the Homeless and Poor) and, most importantly, to the people of Checkerboard Square, enabling members of the research team to gain the trust of street people. They assisted in many aspects of the study, from going over lists of people, to escorting us in the streets, to constantly answering a myriad of questions. A large number of other homeless and formerly homeless people gave of their time and energies for this project. I particularly want to remember "Nina," who spent so much time giving us the benefit of her near photographic memory about the whereabouts of street people and patiently reviewing lists of names, and "Eric," who I came to know well as the study went on and whose enthusiasm for the book has been unrivaled. "Larry," a worker over the years at several North City agencies serving the homeless, gave unstintingly of his time to help me interpret the subcultures within the street population and the social connections between different social networks.

Third, several students at the University of Southern Maine served as research assistants and wandered the streets, soup kitchens, parks, and agencies to find and talk with street people. Most exceptional was Barbara Reed, who let no obstacle stop her from engaging strangers and writing field notes about what she saw and heard. Laura Madigan also conducted a good number of interviews, and Michelle Raschack was extremely helpful in organizing work with informants and coding. I owe them, and several others who did more limited work, a great debt.

Dean Birkenkamp at Westview Press has been an author's dream of an editor. Dean has been consistently complimentary and supportive as well as thorough and thoughtful. Diana Luykx and Michelle Asakawa of Westview Press also helped me through all the stages of getting this manuscript into a book, and they have been a pleasure to work with.

A number of people read parts or all of this manuscript, and their support and comments were extremely helpful. I wish to thank particularly Joel Blau, Richard Cloward, Dan Cress, Luisa DePrez, David Forbes, Herbert Gans, Bob Hayes, Peter Marcuse, David Snow, and Ida Susser. Finally, I want to thank all the subjects of this book for their time and patience with our intruding into their personal lives, and also the staff of a large number of social agencies, political organizations, and government offices in North City who gave of their time and were always tolerant of our presence and many questions.

David Wagner

1

Beyond the Conventional Wisdom on the Homeless

"Pauperism is the consequence of wilful error, of shameful indolence, of vicious habits. It is a misery of human creation, the pernicious work of man, the lamentable consequence of bad principles and morals."
    —*Charles Burroughs, "Discourse," 1834 (as quoted in Katz, 1986:19)*

"The underclass ... urban knots that threaten to become enclaves of permanent poverty and vice ... their chronic lawlessness, drug use, out-of-wedlock births, non-work, welfare dependency and school failure."
    —*Myron Magnet, FORTUNE, (1987:130)*

This book is about what used to be called the *rabble*. The poor, once labeled *paupers, vagrants, rabble, the dangerous classes, vagabonds, tramps*, and *bums*, today are the *underclass* and *the homeless*. As the quotes above—written 150 years apart—indicate, little seems to have changed. The very poor have long been objects of fear and loathing in Western society. Their existence is not new, nor are attempts to control them or to limit their political and social rights (see Piven & Cloward, 1971, for the best historical treatment). The poor are stigmatized and blamed for being poor, and they are held responsible for nearly every existing social problem.

Of course, not all poor people are equally stigmatized. Some groups among the poor arouse pity and sympathy and, in modern times, receive some social welfare benefits and charitable aid. Conceptualized as early as the fifteenth century (see Michielse, 1990) and transplanted to America with the English Poor Laws, the historical distinction between the "deserving" and the "undeserving" poor allowed certain groups among the poor to be singled out for particularly harsh treatment, whereas others were given alms and sustenance. As is documented in histories of social welfare (Abramovitz, 1988; Katz, 1986; Piven & Cloward, 1971), compliance with the major shibboleths of bourgeois society has been the primary condition for receiving minimal aid from both the state and private charity: In

1

brief, this includes compliance with the work ethic (e.g., the poor person is working or strongly affirms his or her desire to work) and with the family ethic (e.g., the poor person is in a traditional family constellation and accepts his or her role within it).[1]

Although widows and orphans and later the elderly came to be classified as the deserving poor, men who had no visible means of support were considered vagrants. In colonial and nineteenth-century America, they were singled out for the workhouse or for unceremonious "dumping" at the edge of town. Women who failed to marry or to stay with their families of origin were also considered undeserving and were, at best, excluded from all aid or, at worst, ostracized, institutionalized, and separated from their children. As recent historical analysts have argued, even relatively progressive reforms in social welfare, such as the Social Security Act of 1935, have remained consistent with these ideological themes, with eligibility for aid being contingent on workplace participation and family status (Abramovitz, 1988).

In the contemporary United States, many view all homeless and very poor people with disdain. Newspaper accounts and television shows often reveal stereotypical and hostile views of the very poor (see, for example, Hope & Young, 1986:26–28), and there are widespread "not-in-my-backyard" movements against shelters and even against soup kitchens. Many cities responded to the huge increases in poverty and homelessness in the 1980s with repressive measures, including street sweeps of homeless people and the provision of bus tickets to send the homeless elsewhere (Schmalz, 1988; Uzelac, 1990). Conservative theorists have conceptualized the very poor as an underclass and have portrayed this ill-defined group as pathological. They fault the generosity of the welfare state, blame the urban poor for failing to follow middle-class values, and cite "nonwork," welfare dependency, crime, illegitimate births, and single-parent families as examples of deviant behavior (Auletta, 1982; Mead, 1986; Murray, 1984).

However, campaigns by charities and homeless advocates, sympathetic books and movies, and human interest stories had an effect on the U.S. public in the 1980s (for example, a 1989 Gallup poll found that the majority of Americans blamed homelessness on "circumstances" rather than on lack of individual effort; see *New York Times*, Aug. 23, 1989). Books like Jonathan Kozol's *Rachel and Her Children* (1988) and films like *God Bless the Child* (ABC television movie, 1988) depict families with small children who became homeless through no fault of their own—usually because of eviction or unemployment—who want to work and lead a normal life. Sympathy and charity became so prevalent in some circles by the late 1980s that an expert on social welfare could suggest that the public distinguishes between the term *underclass* when speaking negatively about the poor and the term *homeless* when speaking more positively about the very poor (Katz, 1989:185–186).

In actuality, the line between the *deserving poor* and the *rabble* has remained fairly consistent from colonial times to today. Advocates and social service workers intentionally seek to portray the poor as deserving to arouse sympathy, focusing particularly on homeless families. The homeless family with small children pictured huddled under a bridge arouses pity. No such sympathy usually extends to the single, adult woman who looks like a "bag lady," the elderly man who looks like he belongs on skid row, or to the young male (particularly a minority) who conjures up fears of criminality. Not only is there no tradition of sympathy for the single male or the childless couple that is poor, but in keeping with the colonial tradition, most Americans feels sympathy only for those who comply with behavioral codes. Street people who are unruly, who do not seem to want to work, who panhandle or engage in illegal activity, or who act in a strange manner are variously condemned, diagnosed, or ignored even in the social science literature. As the public became more aware of poverty in the 1980s, it seems to have continued to subdivide the poor between deserving families—presumably suffering temporary setbacks—and others, particularly nonfamilies, who are perceived to be more permanently entrenched in poverty. The public's limited tolerance for the poor extends perhaps to charitable appeals for emergency aid based on pathos, whereas simultaneously it blames the poor for long-term poverty, deviancy, and laziness.

Within both this public debate about poverty and the social science literature, the voices of the poor are noticeably absent. This is not surprising. The poor, particularly those who cannot be found at workplaces and those who have no housing, have little access to the media. Even the most resourceful social scientists have had extreme difficulty locating those with the least structure when they have attempted to count or to interview the homeless. Only a small ethnographic tradition within the social sciences and an occasional militant protest by the poor serve to give voice to their views. How do people at the bottom of society live, and what are their viewpoints about poverty, work, the family, and social institutions?

In this book I examine—from their own perspective—a group of street people[2] who would be considered by most to be nondeserving poor. Although many of these people have relatives on the streets and do have children, our subjects generally are categorized as homeless individuals rather than as deserving families.[3] Neither isolated nor dependent as portrayed by most advocates and social scientists, they implicitly or explicitly challenge many of the norms of society. By giving voice to part of the rabble in the ethnographic tradition of William Whyte (1966), Herbert Gans (1962), Elliot Liebow (1967), and Carol Stack (1974), I question the dominant portrayal of the homeless as vulnerable and dependent people worthy perhaps of sympathy but judged to be socially disorganized, disaffiliated, and disempowered. Second, by examining the understandings and cultural values of a group of street people, particularly regarding the dominant cultural norms of work and family, I suggest that the nexus of values sustaining the modern United States is deeply at stake in the issues of homelessness and poverty. The dominant beliefs in the work and family ethics are ideological constructs that essentially fail the very poor, if indeed they actually work for others in U.S. society.

Advocates and the Politics of Compassion

Charles Hoch and Robert Slayton (1989) have described the efforts made by advocates, professionals, researchers, charities, and others to assist the homeless in the 1980s as a "politics of compassion" in which the homeless were presented as "vulnerable victims." Because the rise of the "new homelessness" and the growth of poverty occurred during an era of dominant conservative national administrations bent on denying the problem, advocates fought bitterly to secure government recognition on state, local, and federal levels, as well as public support. Such efforts often presented the homeless as helpless victims of social policies, in particular the Reagan cutbacks in social services, the escalating cost of housing, unemployment and deindustrialization, deinstitutionalization, and other causes such as the breakdown of the family (Baxter & Hopper, 1984; Blau, 1992; Hopper & Hamburg, 1984; Marcuse, 1988; Ropers, 1988; Rossi, 1989). Faced with at least the perception of a hostile public and the lack of a social movement by the poor themselves, the politics of compassion contrasted with movements staged by workers, the unemployed, and the elderly in the 1930s and by minorities, women, and antiwar protesters of the 1960s. Unlike these social movements, the politics of compassion was generally led by advocates, not by the poor, and was hardly a politics of confrontation or militancy.

As is well summarized by Blau (1992), the movement for the homeless made some notable gains during the 1980s. Major lawsuits won dramatic increases in the number of shelter beds, in food programs, in civil rights (the right of the homeless to vote, for example) and in eligibility for social benefits (for example, prior to the late 1980s, an address was usually required before a person could receive benefits). The legal strategy, as well as efforts by charities, churches, social welfare professionals, and social science researchers, influenced the government to enact limited federal reforms, such as the McKinney Act (1988), as well as a host of local and state plans for affordable housing, transitional housing, aid to the mentally ill homeless, and so forth.

Yet as Hoch and Slayton note (1989:208), the "politics of compassion" has come at a cost. Whereas the view of the homeless held by advocates, social scientists, and liberals "relieved the homeless of moral responsibility for their condition" (unlike the conservative view), it did so "at the cost of portraying the homeless as dependent, isolated, and different from the rest of the population." Hoch and Slayton blame this approach for the policy of "shelterization," which in their view turned the issue of homelessness into one of containment and treatment and re-created the poorhouses of old. Whether advocates can be blamed for shelterization is debatable, but certainly the dominant social science approach (as well as the approaches of the advocates and of social service) to homelessness has overdetermined the very poor as being helpless.

Because of the perceived political-social need to appeal to a public audience, to government, and to the nonprofit sector for recognition of the problem of homelessness as well as for funding and legislation on behalf of the homeless, researchers as well as advocates have sought to portray the homeless as the deserving poor, either by focusing on sympathetic people and ignoring nonsympathetic individuals among the poor or by reframing a potential nondeserving group into a deserving one (for an excellent discussion of how to achieve this, see Wright, 1988). This strategy, whether consciously or not, led social scientists to emphasize diagnosis and differentiation of the poor and the necessity for making political appeals for the poor based on dependency while simultaneously couching these appeals within the liberal opposition to Reaganism during the 1980s rather than challenging the conventional wisdom of either conservatism or liberalism.

I argue that despite the positive accomplishments of the advocates for homeless people and the poor, the emphasis in the 1980s on pathos and pathology on the streets has obscured the strengths of the homeless and the very poor and has tended to portray the very poor as "judgmental dupes" (Garfinkel, 1967) who lack political and social awareness of themselves and of their conditions. Moreover, in order to gain maximum political attention for the problem, advocates minimize both the historical consistency in the treatment of the poor throughout U.S. history and the radical changes that would be necessary to eliminate poverty and homelessness.

Social Scientists and the Homeless

Throughout the 1980s many social scientists defined, counted, and analyzed different subgroups of the homeless. The research literature contains many accounts of and disputes about how many or what percentages of the homeless are mentally ill, substance abusers, veterans, criminals, and so forth (see, for example, Fisher & Breakey, 1986; Rossi, 1989; Roth, Bean, & Johnson, 1986; Shinn & Weitzman, 1990; Struening, 1987). It is frequently concluded that a large percentage of the homeless is mentally ill or abuse substances. Regardless of the validity of the various claims, this approach of "specialism" assumes that the various individual characteristics of the poor are somehow involved in causing homelessness or are helpful in solving the problem of poverty. This misleads the public, as Peter Marcuse (1988) has noted:

> Akin to blaming the victim is specialism, or calling a general problem the sum of a number of different special problems, defined in this case by the characteristics of the victims ... thus much research connected with homelessness focuses on ascertaining the precise characteristics of the victims rather than the causes of their victimization. (p. 88)

As Marcuse and Hoch and Slayton note, specialism turns the political and economic problems of poverty and homelessness into a mental health, substance abuse, or criminal justice problem. Also, as with all labeling, such categorization tends to deny the potential social consciousness, political power, and humanity of the actual people involved. Henry Miller's study (1991) of the very poor throughout U.S. history suggests that the composition of today's homeless population is in many ways very similar to those of the nineteenth-century rabble, of the transients during the Depression, or of homeless populations in other periods (the homeless remain primarily young males; see in particular Marin, 1991). Moreover, the problems of drinking, aberrant behavior, and mental illness among the destitute have been noted since the eighteenth century. And yet diagnosis was not entertained among the tramps and bums organized by the Wobblies (International Workers of the World, a radical labor union) at the turn of the century or by the demonstrating crowds of the unemployed in the 1930s. The key point about such social scientific and psychiatric labeling is that it serves as a "neutralizing" strategy (Marcuse, 1988), disempowering the homeless and minimizing the potential political issues at stake.

Most social science literature has also accepted the assessment of the homeless population and many members of the marginal poor population as suffering from disaffiliation, isolation, vulnerability, and disempowerment. This assessment dates from the old "skid row" studies of the 1960s in which the structural functionalist sociologists saw the skid row bum "as detached from society ... characterized by the absence or attenuation of the affiliative bonds that link settled persons to a network of interconnected social structures" (Theodore Caplow, cited in Watson & Austerberry, 1986:17).

Although some of the negative stereotyping connected with the disaffiliation label has receded with social scientists' shift in focus to the new homeless and away from the old skid row bums, the term *disaffiliation* and others such as *isolated, vulnerable,* and *disempowered* still pervade the literature (see, for example, Bachrach, 1984; U.S. Alcohol, Drug Abuse, and Mental Health Administration, cited in Fisher & Breakey, 1986; Hudson, 1988; Ropers, 1988; Rossi, 1989). Recent ethnographic evidence has now challenged the notion that homeless people are isolated from each other as well as from other social networks (Cohen, Teresi, Holmes, & Roth, 1988; Grigsby, Baumann, Gregorich, & Roberts-Gray, 1990; La Gory, Ritchey, & Mullis, 1989; Rosenthal, 1989; Snow & Anderson, 1992; Snow & Anderson, 1987). As I discuss later in this section, most social scientists, particularly those involved in survey research, continue to find detachment and isolation among the very poor for reasons related to their methodology and their own values.

Also, although in the 1960s and early 1970s the dominant social norms of work and family were under attack from the counterculture, the New Left, and the feminist movement, liberal observers and social scientists took great pains in the 1980s to criticize what they regarded as unacceptable conduct or pathological behavior even when their research uncovered and explained such behavior. For example, in the best-known liberal–social democratic social science response to Charles Murray and other conservatives, William Julius Wilson (*The Truly Disad-*

vantaged, 1987) argues against the conservative interpretation of the causes of pathological behavior but agrees with its diagnosis. Specifically, he identifies as social pathologies nonwork, welfare dependency, illegitimate births, crime and delinquency, the decline in the traditional family, and teenage pregnancy. Wilson's highly acclaimed book combines clearly deplorable behavior (violent crime) with legal behaviors that in many cases are widespread social trends extant throughout society and that are arguably appropriate and functional behavior (e.g., collecting social welfare benefits, forming single-parent families, having children as teenagers).

Another sympathetic account of the poor, which at the same time condemns street life as pathological, is Kornblum and William's study *Growing up Poor* (1985). In their many interesting interviews, the authors find poor children who are growing up with solid and productive norms because of exposure to strong families, other adult role models, and church and voluntary groups. However, "the lure of the streets and the risk of violence cannot be kept from young people who insist on making their own way to adulthood" (p. 9). Kornblum and Williams eloquently identify the many reasons poor youngsters find themselves on the streets, in the underground economy, or having children in their teen years, yet they affirm the pathology of the streets as the problem and condemn this as deviant behavior. Like Wilson, they believe that work (particularly through more government youth jobs programs) will resolve the problems of these poor kids. Paradoxically, the data in books such as Wilson's and Kornblum & Williams's actually suggest that in a society dominated by deindustrialization and broad social changes in the family and community, the norms of work and family are becoming less relevant, but they still insist that liberal reforms—particularly the provision of jobs—will somehow promote major changes for the millions of poor people.

I suggest that social science researchers' support for the politics of compassion by urging others to give sympathy and support to the homeless and the very poor while at the same time finding them victims of serious personal problems, vulnerable and isolated, and engaged in pathological behavior is explained by three factors: the research methodologies used by social scientists; the self-interest of professionals in certain formulations of social problems; and the ideological preconceptions and political strategies of most advocates and researchers.

Almost all research on the homeless has been survey research consisting of one-time interviews or of counts of the poor conducted at places that serve those in crisis: shelters, hospital emergency rooms, clinics, soup kitchens, or missions (see, for example, Arce, Tadlock, Vergare, & Shapiro, 1983; Johnson & Kreuger, 1989; Lipton, Sabatini, & Katz, 1983; Struening, 1987; Struening & Susser, 1986; Weitzman, Shinn, & Knickman, 1989). It is of course not surprising that researchers would find people recently evicted from their homes or just admitted to emergency rooms to be vulnerable and in distress. Few studies have had any longitudinal dimension, and few have followed groups of the very poor past their personal crises. Like the charity workers discussed in a book first published 90 years ago by Jane Addams (1961), social workers, social scientists, and others observing or working in homeless shelters or in crisis centers are in a sense caught in an eco-logical fallacy by dealing with the poor only at their point of greatest vulnerability:

> The difference between the relief-station relation to the poor and the Settlement re-lation to its neighbors [is that] the latter wish to know them [the poor] through all the varying conditions of life, to stand by them when they are in distress, but by no means to drop intercourse with them when normal prosperity returns. (p. 125)

Yet if social scientists or mental health workers see the poor only at times of acute crisis, they may miss the forest for the trees. For example, the few longitudi-nal studies conducted have noted that much homelessness is episodic and that when people are followed over a period of time, many do secure housing (Piliavin & Sosin, 1987; Rossi, 1989; Sosin, Piliavin, & Westerfelt, 1990). Based on data that covered a 4-year period, the majority of a group of homeless people studied for this book also found housing. Numerous changes in the lives of our subjects oc-curred over the years that researchers or crisis workers would never see based on their snapshot views of the homeless.

Researchers and service providers may also miss the social strengths and cohe-sion of the long-term homeless when they are no longer in acute crisis and are no longer frequent users of shelters, clinics, or emergency rooms. Snow and Ander-son (1987) found a high degree of "role embracement" (identification and relative comfort with the homeless role and life-style) among some long-term homeless, and Grigsby et al. (1990) found that the long-term homeless (who they catego-rized as "outsiders") were strongly affiliated and socially organized as opposed to the newly homeless.

A second reason for the findings of vulnerability, disaffiliation, and pathology involves the self-interest and professional training of researchers, advocates, and social service providers. As C. Wright Mills (1943) described so well, "social pa-thologists" are likely to define a social problem in terms in which only they can resolve the problem. Hoch and Slayton (1989) have also noted how the ideology of professionalism has assumed that the homeless can only be helped with the aid and through the guidance of professionals. This is not to argue that service pro-viders and social scientists are not sincere and well-meaning; rather, it suggests that because of training and middle-class ideology, social pathologists interpret social problems as requiring treatment, assessment, and intervention. It is highly unlikely that a social worker or a psychologist would decide to do nothing about a homeless person who is acting strangely or is seen drinking from a liquor bottle. It is also extremely rare for even the most radical social worker or psychiatrist to urge street people to foment revolution. In a parallel fashion, social scientists—whose livelihood is reliant on government and foundation funding, university largess, and outlets for publication—are unlikely to either say that the problem is intractable or simply write a tract on the need for revolution.

Because of their disciplinary training and self-interest, social scientists will seek to define a social problem that is critical, newsworthy, and amenable to some active form of reform intervention. This critique, then, relates not only to the more individual "causes" of homelessness, such as substance abuse and psychiatric disorders, that many experts—particularly mental health professionals—always "discover" among the poor but to the social causes as well, such as housing reform and employment reform, which are often presented as new and profound by each generation of reform social scientists. Unlike members of professions that are often conservative politically, social scientists have a vested interest in reform (see McCarthy & Zald, 1975, for a similar point). Reform movements present opportunities for professional leadership, administration, program development, direct care staffing, and program evaluation. As McCarthy and Zald (1975) note, however, reform is not revolution, and strong disincentives exist against "organizational intellectuals" (social scientists, government bureaucrats, social workers) advocating extreme radicalism.

In fact, the political and ideological perspectives of most social scientists and advocates prevent an examination of the broader crisis that lurks when poverty is examined as a social issue. It is well-known that the bulk of studies on the poor and the homeless were undertaken and often funded by researchers, institutes, and sponsors that were opposed to the conservative political direction of the 1980s. The growing homeless social problem was among the most visible and dramatic manifestations of the Reagan and Bush eras. With few exceptions, however, social scientists and advocates looked not to radical transformations but to liberal or Democratic victories in the next election for solutions. The modesty of most proposals for change—Wilson's proposed macroeconomic policy changes and job creation, for example, or calls for a higher minimum wage, public service jobs, more day-care centers, or a family leave policy—suggests a convergence of the advocates, social scientists, social service professionals, and Democratic party agendas.

Whether a liberal political program can solve the problem of poverty cannot be definitively ascertained, but we should note that to sustain itself, the liberal view—as with conservative ideology—relies on upholding traditional normative values and slogans. Liberal slogans would be weakened if they portrayed homeless or poor people who in some way do not accept work when jobs are made available. A defense of nonwork does not fit well with calls for full employment policies anymore than it would with conservative calls for workfare. Life in the streets is pathologized by most social scientists and advocates, as well as conservatives, either because the former also believe that the media reports of crime, vice, and drugs are the only reality in low-income communities or because they fear that any defense of the low-income community's behavior would weaken their political agenda. Liberals uphold "family values," at least since the popularity of the New Right in the 1970s, and condemn the dissolution of the family. Presumably this desire to reunite separated poor families or to minimize the incidences of divorce or runaway children would be challenged by examples of poor people who fare better outside of families. Strong elements of consensus on the potential pathologies of the poor greatly explain the fact that liberals and conservatives actually *do* agree on most social welfare policies as exemplified by the bipartisan Family Support Act of 1988, which conditions the receipt of welfare benefits on workforce participation, and by proposals of recently elected President Bill Clinton to condition the receipt of welfare on behavior and to place time limits on receiving aid.

Paradoxically, it might be suggested that at the very time that liberals and conservatives were reaching a consensus about the poor, the traditional slogans and ideological constructs that undergrid their policies were losing ground. That is, I suggest that the crisis of homelessness represents the continued failure of the work and family ethics and of traditional state services to hold much legitimacy. To support this view, I discuss the radical implications of homelessness as they reflect the major social changes of the past decades.

Homelessness and the Limits of Bourgeois Order

One of the few writers to note the broader cultural meaning of homelessness is Peter Marcuse. In a 1988 article, Marcuse asks not just why there are so many homeless people but also why there is so much concern about them in U.S. society. After all, Marcuse notes, most intractable structural problems are avoided by the media, but stories on the homeless and the very poor proliferated in the 1980s. Marcuse (1988) notes that the shock that results from the growing numbers of homeless people everywhere points to a broader crisis in bourgeois society:

> Just as the hippies of the 1960s deeply shocked conventional citizens by their rejection of bourgeois values and goals, the homeless shock those with a conventional view of the world, if in a deeper and less conscious way. The rewards of society have not proven attractive, or available, to them. But neither have the penalties: jail holds no fear for them, humiliation, cold, and hunger are part of their daily lives. The system has no power over them. ... Homelessness inspires not only the intellectual realization that the machinery of the system has failed somehow to produce basic shelter everyone needs, *but even more the social realization that the system has come up against some limits it cannot exceed, has created a world it can no longer control.* (pp. 83–84; emphasis added)

Homelessness can be seen as both causing and being reflective of a broader legitimation crisis in modern society, a crisis not subject to quick reform, or to a return to the prosperity of the 1950s and 1960s. As Marcuse notes, the very concept of millions of people on the street not dividing their lives between a public and a private sphere of existence and apparently living independent of social institutions strikes at many people's basic conception of the bourgeois social order. But homeless and street people are not only causes of a legitimation crisis: They are reflective of a social breakdown. When millions of Americans are not dependent on the workplace, have left their families, and cannot be controlled by police or the government, this is indeed reflective of disorder and unrest within U.S. society.

If we accept Marcuse's idea that homelessness may reveal some limits of bourgeois society, what are these limits? How do these limits affect not only poor people but other Americans as well?

Whither the Work Ethic?

Although experts have estimated that at any one time as many as one-third of homeless people are engaged in some work (Rossi, 1989), for most Americans the image of thousands of people filling their local streets, plazas, and transportation centers (whether they are actually homeless or are simply unemployed urban residents who do have homes) raises public consternation and leads to the question, Why don't they get a job? Historically, the pauper was stigmatized because of his or her presumed failure to abide by the work ethic. Paupers and beggars were deemed to be vicious and indolent because of their alleged preference to survive on alms rather than through labor. Consistent throughout history—having been applied to the 1960s hippies, to the homeless and street people of today, and to the welfare mother with young children—is the assumption that the poor are lazy, dependent, and feeding at the public trough.

Commitment to the work ethic seems hegemonic among political, social, and academic leaders of all political orientations. It is manifested by conservatives, who favor repressive measures to ensure work-force participation, and liberals, who seek ameliorative policies to assist disenfranchised people in securing jobs.

Yet in other times, social critics have attacked the work ethic. Bertrand Russell (1935) noted that the work ethic served the wealthy classes by forcing the poor to work while the rich enjoyed their leisure. As recently as the 1960s, in a time of relative prosperity, images of "beatniks" and "hippies," as well as some New Left literature, popularized a critique of work. For many youth, working for the "Establishment" was viewed as meaningless and filled with drudgery (see Aronowitz, 1973, on the contested meaning of work at that time; see also H. Miller, 1991, Chapter 4). The call to drop out influenced millions of youths for at least short periods of time in the 1960s and 1970s. The rise of the feminist movement also led to some radical critiques of work. Radical and socialist feminism revealed the tendency to equate men's labor in the marketplace with productive work in contrast to women's domestic roles as caretakers and housewives, which were nonpaying. Radical feminism questioned the traditional public-private split by developing such slogans as "wages for housework" (see, for example, Coulson, Magas, & Wainwright, 1975; Dalla Costa & Dalla Costa, 1973; Eisenstein, 1979). Some feminists and New Left–influenced radicals still maintain opposition to forcing mothers to work for welfare and support guaranteed income proposals, which had brief support in the two major political parties in the late 1960s and early 1970s (Aronowitz, 1985; Jones, 1992; Lefkowitz & Withorn, 1986; Macarov, 1984, 1988).

Just as the champions of dropping out in the 1960s and the more radical feminist critiques of work seemed to fade from consciousness, changes in the economy and in the nature of work were actually challenging the effectiveness of the work ethic. Beginning with the recession of 1973, large-scale unemployment and underemployment became prevalent throughout the nation. With the loss of 40 million industrial jobs through plant closings, relocations, and overseas moves, the possibility of well-paid industrial jobs became all but a dream for a new generation (Bluestone & Harrison, 1982). The loss of industrial jobs coupled with concessionary bargaining and the demise of the trade union movement meant that new or existing jobs—primarily in the service sector—would be low paying, nonunion, often temporary or seasonal, and without fringe benefits. Most jobs in the 1980s and 1990s—particularly for youth, women, and minorities—are as waiters and waitresses, hotel and motel clerks, janitors, convenience store clerks, security guards, or housekeepers, and all are at or near minimum wage. The employment contract is literally "at will" since there is no countervailing power at the workplace to limit employers' ability to hire and fire, to reduce benefits, or to impose grueling working conditions.

The work ethic secured its legitimacy in part because of a work bargain that functioned to some extent in the growing U.S. economy during most of our pre-1973 history. For example, in the post–World War II economy, work was widely available. Although much work was alienating and unfulfilling, wage rates for industrial and other blue-collar workers were sufficient to meet the promise of acceptable levels of consumption and sufficient leisure time. Except for professionals and upper-income workers, fulfillment through work was not a social expectation. Blue-collar and white-collar workers accepted a trade-off between working 8-hour days and earning enough to purchase suburban homes, television sets, boats, and cars and to take vacations (Aronowitz, 1973; H. Marcuse, 1964). Moreover, in the era of Pax-Americana after World War II, the industrial sector was characterized by strong trade unions that exerted a powerful constraint on employer domination and on deteriorating working conditions.

The bargain failed by the 1970s, and the limits of the work ethic may have arrived by the 1990s. Work no longer offers a guarantee of wages that even surpass the government's poverty line (nearly half of those who fall below the abysmally low government poverty level *do* work; see Levitan, 1990) let alone provide the basics of consumption and leisure. The beacon of attaining upward mobility through work is weak, if it exists at all, for most working-class and poor people. Dreams of finding fulfilling work are rarely met in an age of deindustrialization and widespread poverty, except within the highly privileged sectors.

The work ethic continues its presumed dominance among the majority of citizens because of its ideological omnipresence and the brute force of the labor market. Most working-class people not only see work as an obligation, but they do not have the option of not working, and they must submit to an unfair job bargain that robs them of leisure and pleasure. Having accepted this bargain, many working-class people are inwardly angry and bitter about the toll work takes over their lives; they then direct this anger toward the poor or others deemed to be rebelling against work (see Rubin, 1976; and Sennett & Cobb, 1973, on the psychology of the working class). The concept of work is often supported not because it has been rewarding or pleasurable but because—like a tribe enforcing an arduous initiation rite—workers believe that since they endured it, everyone else should suffer as well.

As labor historians have noted (Edwards, 1979; Gutman, 1976; Roedlinger & Foner, 1986), workers *do* resist work on a day-to-day basis. They do not usually do so with visible banners but rather by struggling over the hours of labor and over productivity requirements and by resignations, absenteeism, lateness, and even sabotage. The need for income and the dominance of the work ethic allow for little ideological awareness of the struggle over work, but much contemporary behavior can be explained as such. For the middle and upper classes, delaying work to engage in extended schooling, becoming an artist or an academic with discretionary time, or leaving the work force to raise children (increasingly as house husbands as well as housewives) are socially sanctioned alternatives to the working 8-hour days.

For the poor and the working class, economic coercion only offers the choice among low-paid work, living on welfare, or implementing innovative survival strategies such as turning to the underground economy or to crime in order to survive. Resistance is almost never socially sanctioned, and approval is withheld even from those who are forced to go on disability benefits. The people described in this book have all worked, usually in the low-paying service sector. Their jobs as security guards, fast-food workers, fish cutters, janitors, waiters and waitresses, hotel workers, or convenience store clerks did not pay them enough to survive. Their resistance to being exploited caused many of them to be fired or to repeatedly quit jobs. For the subjects studied, it was not only low wages but also their "penetrations" into the work world that led them to resist employer authority. Few subjects set out to be rebels or nonconformists, but almost all of them came to view work as oppressive, at least on the terms of the current job bargain. Contrary to the belief of conservative and liberal theorists who live in the middle-class world, most low-income work provides neither upward mobility nor respectability to the very poor; it has minimal or in some cases no tangible benefits.

Finally, in the new era of deindustrialization, the limits of the bourgeois order in resolving the issue of poverty through familiar slogans such as "jobs" are quite limited. One wonders how the old solutions of liberals—full employment, public service jobs, or human resource development and job training—will work in the

1990s. Will public works jobs that pay well be provided for the poor in an era in which low-paying service work is the norm for millions of working-class people? Can the poor simply be "upgraded" through skill development in a society that can barely employ its more affluent and well-educated members? Moreover, policymakers almost universally ignore issues of control and authority in the employer-dominated work world in favor of a narrow focus on employment or wage rates (for a similar argument, see Jones, 1992; Macarov, 1984, 1988).

The Collapsing Family Ethic

Homeless or visibly poor families arouse sympathy and pity, but a crowd of single homeless or street people invokes fear, disgust, and contempt. The public often wants to know not only why they do not get jobs but also why the street youngsters are not at home with their families or why the older, disheveled bums or bag ladies are not at home being cared for by their children. In this sense, homelessness and street life are shocking to conventional society since the people seem not only to be nonworkers but to be detached from the traditional family life-style.

Poor people are punished for not being in families. Along with the work ethic, the family ethic dominates the treatment of the poor by the state. As Abramovitz (1988) notes, benefits are conditioned on family status. No group receives as few services as do single men and women or childless couples. Whereas widows at least get survivor benefits from Social Security and women with young children get Aid to Families with Dependent Children (AFDC), singles are denied even these. In some cities, only families are eligible for shelter and services, and in some states, there is no income assistance for nonfamilies (Levitan, 1990:58).

As with the work ethic, few, if any, political leaders, policymakers, or social scientists challenge the dominance of the family ethic. Both liberals and conservatives tend to see youngsters who are separated from their families as candidates for delinquency and crime; both groups deplore runaway and incorrigible children. Middle-aged singles or nontraditional couples on the streets tend to be viewed as mentally ill. The elderly homeless man is classified as a "skid row" type, and the middle-aged or elderly woman is labeled a "bag lady." On the broader political level, liberals compete with conservatives to embrace the mantle of family issues. For liberals, reforms such as the Family Leave Bill are ways to preserve the family.

Of course, starting in the 1960s, a number of social movements have consciously resisted the family ethic. The youth, hippie, and countercultural movements led millions of people to try collective living arrangements and nonfamily forms in the 1960s and 1970s. The rise of feminism led to support for women living alone or remaining unmarried, for living in groups, and for developing matrifocal families. The rise of the gay and lesbian movements led to awareness of alternative social and sexual relationships, and indeed gays and lesbians wage a daily struggle to maintain their social arrangements against an often hostile state. It is ironic that in the late 1980s, when liberals, leftist advocates, and social scientists who have generally supported these movements turned their focus to the issue of poverty, they saw only the need to "stabilize the family" (see, for example, Edelman, 1987; Schorr, 1988; Sidel, 1986). It is not clear whether such rhetoric simply reflects a politically convenient way to appeal to the public and to legislators or whether it actually presages a rejection of alternative life-styles for the poor (as opposed to the middle class).

The rhetoric about families obscures the reality of deep trouble within the family. As many as one out of every two women is battered within the family, and at least 4 million children annually are victims of abuse within the family (Armstrong, 1983). In a recent study, one in six adults stated that they had been sexually abused as children (Patterson & Kim, 1991). Despite widely publicized information about family violence, the social service system and liberal ideology, as much as conservative ideology, aim at keeping family together. The tremendous social changes since the 1960s—influenced greatly by the women's movement, increased female work-force participation, and the gay and lesbian movements— have transformed the family. Nearly one in two marriages ends in divorce, and the typical "Cleaver" family composed of a female housewife, a male breadwinner, and children no longer exists. Single women with children, homogenized families composed of children from many marriages, gay couples, and a rising number of singles fragment any notion of an "average" family.

As with the work ethic, people do resist the family ethic, although usually in private and unconscious ways. Both sexes are staying single longer and divorcing more often. Millions of children run away from home, and even middle-class kids spend time on the streets in peer groups, to the dismay of their parents. Millions of couples live together without being married. For many people, both the family bargain and the work bargain have failed in recent years. The old male-dominated nuclear family rested on an economic trade-off between a male breadwinner who provided economic security and protection and a female housewife who managed the household and affective needs. The decline of the sexual division of labor, as well as changed gender roles, have left millions of people disoriented and confused.

Poor people face special family problems. Families have little to offer in the areas of economic support, stability, and security. The impact of poverty, substance abuse, and family violence often creates chaos and fear among the children. Yet successful adaptations to family life do occur, and ironically, the less they resemble the traditional middle-class family, the more successful they seem to be. For example, Stack (1974) found highly functional black families with extended kinship patterns, including a wide network of relatives, friends, and neighbors who shared child care duties, bartered, and shared their possessions. The poor family is either attacked as being pathological (for example, Moynihan, 1965) or exhorted, even by ghetto leaders, to follow perceived middle-class family norms.

The street people interviewed for this book, like millions of other Americans, are victims of the limits of the family ethic. Overwhelmingly from abusive families of origin, and often also victims of spouse abuse and divorce, they fled from these families into a social welfare system that denied them social benefits and sometimes even shelter because they were no longer part of a traditional family unit. Some were bankrupted and emotionally devastated by divorce and separation, which sometimes led to substance abuse and psychiatric problems. Each subject faced a daily struggle to survive and to supplant the family. Rather than return to their families of origin or to re-create a new nuclear family, the street people often formed friendship communities, engaged in serial relationships, or formed partnerships without taking formal marriage vows. They also engaged, as did Stack's subjects, in considerable mutual aide among nonrelated people such as fictive "mothers of the street" who assisted the homeless in gaining shelter. Many street people, unlike political leaders or social scientists, were openly critical not only of their own families but also of the family ethic.

Limits of the State

The third institution deeply entwined in the crisis of homelessness is the government. As the public watches a crowd of street people or a group of seemingly rootless "underclass" youth, it wants to know why nothing is being done. This usually means government involvement, whether state, local, or federal. In an angry or fearful mood, the public will want police repression, arrests, or street sweeps. In a more generous mood, the public may want the very poor to be given shelter, food, or clothing and possibly even social services and job training.

As the homeless issue reveals the limits of work and family, it also reveals the limit of state intervention (as do many of our current crises such as drugs, teenage pregnancy, crime in the streets, declining schools, and similar problems). For conservatives and the fearful public, the crisis is the failure of social control. Social control is very expensive, paradoxically raising the taxes of and resulting in government intervention for those who least want them. More important, social control is notoriously unreliable. In spite of the many street sweeps that have been undertaken, the many prisons that have been built, and the many wars on drugs that have been declared, crime has continued to rise. People seem to find new ways to resist social order. Unless conservatives could turn the country into a garrison state and eliminate civil liberties, it appears that such approaches will always be primarily symbolic rather than being effective public policy.

The dilemma is different for liberals, social democrats, and socialists who often see the state as a key instrument in regulating unbridled market forces, redistributing social resources, and alleviating the social problems of the poor. Advocates and political leaders call for state intervention, yet passing legislation or winning court suits does not guarantee success and, ironically, sometimes leads to simply changing the locus of the oppression of the poor. The history of U.S. reform is a history of tragic results stemming from reformers' good intentions. For example, in the nineteenth century, institutional care for the poor and the dependent was urged by the social reformers; this led only to overcrowded and inhumane alms-houses, mental hospitals, orphanages, and other institutions (Katz, 1986; Rothman, 1971). The institution came to replace the family as a key instrument of social control over the poor. One hundred years after Dorothea Dix, the new re-form was to "deinstitutionalize" the dependent poor. Again, the humanitarian impulse created a host of new problems, new tragedies, and new victims of state policy (see, for example, Morrissey & Goldman, 1984). The development of large municipal shelters seems historically to echo the 1830s campaign by reformers to provide "indoor relief" for the poor (which had horrible results, including over-crowding and spreading of diseases) (Jansson, 1988).

The "success" of the advocates' campaigns for the homeless is often lost on the homeless themselves, who see the huge shelters built to house them as vehicles to strip them of individuality and dignity. They resent rigid controls over their be-havior and the personal surveillance necessary just to receive bed and board. Whether it is in the form of shelter, food, welfare benefits, counseling, or other services, state aid to the poor is conditioned on behavioral controls. Unlike advo-cates, many poor people, including the subjects of this book, are antibureau-cratic, and they resist the intrusion of the state into their lives. Rather than be stigmatized and submit to "degradation rituals," they often avoid shelters, child welfare agencies, welfare offices, and mental health offices.

The dilemma of state intervention raises the question of whether paternalism and social control built into the government can solve a social welfare problem (for a good discussion, see Gaylin, Glasser, Marcus, & Rothman, 1981). If people demand a "solution" to homelessness (or drug use or teenage pregnancy), despite the rhetoric of good intentions, they are not demanding that the "clients" be con-sulted or that the affected people have self-determination. Rather the "state as parent" is licensed to control the "clients," presumably for "their own good" (Gaylin et al., 1981).

In such circumstances, the differences between liberals and conservatives are greatly diminished. True, liberals would rather use the carrot than the stick: They would rather see the drug user receive treatment than be sentenced to prison, and they would rather have the homeless person go into a shelter than be arrested for vagrancy. But behind any policy lies the possibility or probability of enforcement and control, of which poor people are well aware. Their choice is between "help" or repression. Beneath the veneer of benevolence, "solving" a social problem means making it go away, peacefully or by force. In this paradigm, neither liberals nor conservatives really want to debate with the client (homeless, drug user, and the like) about his or her rights or choices. When poor people do not do what they should, liberals are as likely as conservatives to enforce social control. New York City's recent history regarding homelessness is indicative: When Billy Boggs, a woman said to be homeless and mentally ill, refused to be forced off the street and sued the mayor of New York, liberals were as uneasy as conservatives; and when a large number of homeless people took over Tompkins Square Park, David Dinkens's administration quickly arrested them, leading to violence.

I am not at all, however, arguing against the need for state intervention to redistribute wealth, which is sorely needed. However, redistributory reforms (as occurred in the 1930s) seem only to occur at times of dramatic social unrest and rising political power among poor people (Piven & Cloward, 1971, 1977). Further, only when the state can guarantee a service as an entitlement to all citizens rather than as a solution to a "social problem" among a despised population can true social change occur. On this issue, Wilson (1987) is correct: Only a universalistic approach to poverty can work. This is true not only for the practical political reasons Wilson emphasizes (e.g., the public and government will not support programs tailored to groups they suspect or despise) but also because without a majoritarian entitlement, whatever minimal benefits the poor do receive will be at the cost of social control and will result in stigmatization.

The street people portrayed in this book want housing and income. They are either overtly or instinctively radical on the issue of redistribution. Even more than most Americans, however, they are hostile toward bureaucratic control and resist complying with state edicts. They question government benevolence that enforces behavioral codes before they can receive shelter, that would force them to work for a welfare check, and that forces them to surrender their children if they are judged unfit parents. Their experience leads them to be anti-state.

Overview of the Book

This book is based on an ethnographic study of a cohort of street people (currently homeless or formerly homeless), ranging in age from 16 to 77, in "North City" (see Chapter 2), and it involves in-depth interview data and 2 years of participant observation (see Chapter 2). In this book I provide a different view of the poor from that found in much of the literature. I support the perspective that poor people are not just acted upon or just passive victims of society, and I show how street people develop their own self-consciousness, culture, and alternative community. My focus represents a radical departure from other accounts of the homeless.

Resistance

I suggest that street people struggle to survive resisting the dominant institutions of society—the traditional family forms, the demands of employers, and the rules of the state bureaucracy—while at the same time developing alternative forms of social organization. I build on the analysis of several sociologists who have explored a "culture of resistance" among youth (Giroux, 1983; MacLeod, 1987;

Willis, 1977) to interpret the "Checkerboard Square" community (see Chapter 2) as a subculture in which participants have made penetrations into the dominant culture and consciously or subconsciously developed their own identities in opposition to the dominant norms. Unlike researchers who portray the very poor as accepting the traditional values of family and work in order to present them as "deserving poor," I reveal a far more complex reality.

The subjects in this book have been robbed of the dignity of work, not only because of a lack of job opportunities and low wages but because of hostile treatment in the service industries. Rather than affirm the work ethic, they often downgrade the importance and status of work and replace traditional work roles with innovative strategies. Overwhelmingly from abusive families of origin, subjects sought to replace the family with street friends and street partners. Thwarted by the hostile reaction of courts, police, the welfare system, and other systems, subjects resisted submitting to the bureaucratic institutions of government. Such resistance is never complete, and at times accommodations are made with the work world, families, and government institutions. Awareness of such resistance also varies within the community. Some subjects claimed to be revolutionaries or visionaries, and others dreamed of a more stable conventional life.

Social Organization and Community

Although resistance and the struggle for survival do take their toll (deaths and frequent tragedies occur on the street), most subjects in this book participated in an intricate and cohesive alternative community. That is, homeless and formerly homeless subjects relied on considerable social networks of friends and companions, and some participated heavily in political action groups, self-help groups, church groups, a mental health club, and social service organizations (the latter were geared toward control of the poor and were nonstigmatizing, such as the Drop-In Center). Complex forms of social organization connected the very poor with certain elements of middle-class culture (for example, ministers and social workers). I challenge the prevailing view of the homeless as disempowered (Blau, 1992:179–185; Hope & Young, 1986:242). Over the years the Checkerboard Square community developed a community of intense solidarity that maintained dense social networks and that sustained a degree of political and social cohesion despite changes in its composition as people came and went. I raise the possibility that street communities can develop into loosely organized social movements.

Finally, I question the dominant social policy prescriptions of most of the current literature. Whereas the prevailing approach of service providers and advocates is to individualize the poor and provide them with housing, social welfare benefits, or case management, the strong ties within the street community suggest collective approaches to poverty that build on existing social networks to assist poor people in obtaining housing and other benefits *collectively*. I conclude by raising questions about the prevalent strategies of advocates for the poor and suggest a number of alternative directions.

Notes

1. I use the term *family ethic*, as does Abramovitz (1988) and other feminists, to describe the legal, cultural, and social nexuses upholding the nuclear family, giving rights to partners in a heterosexual marriage and to married parents over their children. Historically, the family ethic has disenfranchised single parents, single men and women without children or with children born out of wedlock, children or adolescents living without adults, and gays and lesbians.

2. The issue of labeling the poor is complex. There are strong definitional arguments over the meaning of the word *homeless*, for example. Advocates take a broad view of the term and apply it to people who are doubled up or staying with others and even to those who are institutionalized or in group homes or prisons. Social scientists (see Rossi, 1989) prefer the more literal definition in which the person is sleeping on the street or in a shelter and has no place indoors to sleep.

In many ways, because literal homelessness is often episodic and many of our subjects move in and out of housing, the term *street person* seems more accurate. It stresses identification with the symbols and label of homelessness and continued participation in the street community even if the person temporarily has a place to sleep. Although I use this term, for more theoretical and comparative statements I return to the term *homeless* and the recent literature on homelessness since *street person* is still a very imprecise term and remains less recognized as a social science term.

3. This book was based initially on a cohort that participated in a "tent city" protest staged primarily by those who were not homeless families and hence were excluded from benefits based on their family status. Ironically, however, as I describe, many indeed were related (sisters, father and adult son, and similar relationships), were parents of young children (some of whom the state took into custody and some of whom were staying with others [see Chapter 3], were unmarried partners (sometimes with children), or were members of gay partnerships. This makes the role of the family ethic (based on age-old definitions of the family) even more dramatic in dividing up the homeless and labeling some homeless people as deviants and undeserving poor.

2

Voices from
Checkerboard Square

In this chapter I briefly introduce the settings of this ethnography, "North City" and "Checkerboard Square," where the study's subjects spend much of their time. I also introduce a number of homeless or formerly homeless subjects who contrast sharply with most stereotypes about street people. I also discuss the methodology of the study, which was conducted in two phases between 1989 and 1991.

"North City"

The events in this book take place in a medium-sized New England city (metropolitan area 270,000) that typifies the contrast between the economic decline of the Northeast throughout most of the twentieth century and the facade of the "economic miracle" and gentrification of the 1980s. Like many New England cities, North City has a proud history that includes colonial landmarks and nineteenth-century factories and mills. New England experienced a decline from the 1920s onward as industry moved south (and then overseas) to pursue cheaper labor, lower taxes, and lower energy costs. By the 1970s, North City's traditional New England main street appeared bereft of business and consumer activity because of competition from suburban malls and the decline of a stable urban population base of working-class and middle-class consumers.

Paradoxically, like most of the Northeast, North City experienced both "boom" and "bust" in the 1980s. As the high-technology, banking, and real estate industries flourished in that decade, the city gained new jobs, and its regional location as a tourist center and a desirable place to live led to a dramatic real estate boom. Building occurred everywhere; housing costs soared dramatically; and the city—once avoided by upper-middle-class consumers—became an attractive haven because of the development of a new historic district complete with boutiques, fancy restaurants, bars, and discos. Affluent businesspeople and professionals moved to North City, expanding the tax base and creating a class of new, "hip" consumers previously unknown to the area and often the subject of hostile "yuppie" jokes invented by long-time residents.

The economic miracle in New England, touted by 1988 presidential candidate Michael Dukakis and others, never reached the poor or even the average working-class citizen. In fact, in the 1980s these groups' living conditions worsened. A steep rise in housing prices (in the desirable downtown area, some rents shot up 300 percent in the 1980s) made it almost impossible for the poor to pay rent. At the same time, cuts in social benefits emanating from Washington, D.C., reduced the levels of Aid to Families with Dependent Children (AFDC), food stamps, and unemployment insurance. Many recipients were dropped entirely from social programs, particularly Social Security Disability, Supplemental Security Income (SSI), and food stamps. Deindustrialization, the process of plant closings and un-planned conversion from a manufacturing economy to a low-paid service econ-omy, had been well underway in New England for decades. The continued closing of factories and defeats for trade unions (exemplified by a nationally publicized strike that after a year and a half ended in defeat for the union and a loss of 2,000 union jobs), as well as the freezing of the minimum wage, meant that the 1980s represented hard times for working-class and poor citizens. Laid off by industry or facing wage freezes or rollbacks, blue-collar workers did not benefit from the thousands of new jobs touted by the national administration and by local politi-cal leaders. Most new jobs paid poorly ($4–6 an hour) compared with the old, higher-paying industrial jobs; were often part-time, seasonal, or temporary; and lacked fringe benefits.

Homelessness in North City

During a seeming boom period, then, homelessness became a crisis in North City. In addition to such factors as the housing crisis, deindustrialization, and benefit cutbacks, social factors caused North City to become the center of homelessness in the region. As it became known that North City was booming and that jobs were available there, a large number of people from small towns and rural areas of the region came to North City looking for work. Teenagers not only sought work but were also looking for a semblance of urban life. North City had become a "hip" place, whereas the rural areas were lacking both diversions and jobs. The city's access to public transportation in a state in which a car is a neces-sity, and its relatively more advanced provision of social services, were also factors in attracting the rural poor. Deinstitutionalization and other factors related to the decline of public social services were additional causes of homelessness, as large numbers of mentally ill homeless people and runaway kids came to North City.

By the late 1980s, advocates estimated that in North City as many as 2,000 peo-ple were homeless over the course of a year. If this figure is accurate, the number of homeless per capita would be as high as that in the largest urban areas in the nation.[1] According to studies conducted in North City, the local homeless population resembles the demographic profile of the national homeless population in terms of age, gender, education, marital status, rates of mental illness and substance abuse, percentage receiving social benefits and income from work, and birthplace (like most homeless groups studied, the homeless of North City are predominantly people from within the state). The one demographic characteristic that somewhat distinguishes North City from many major cities is its racial composition. Like much of New England, North City has few racial minorities; hence, its homeless population is predominantly white, although the homeless include a greater percentage of American Indians than in other cities.

From the early days of the 1980s, the homeless of North City displayed militant political behavior. Each small step taken by the city to deal with homelessness on an "emergency" basis (see Lipsky & Smith, 1989, for a cogent analysis of how government responds to crises defined as "emergencies") was criticized as inadequate by the protesters. As early as 1984, street protests and sleep-ins were held. In 1987, over 100 homeless people began a protest at City Hall sparked by the closing of two temporary shelters. After being threatened with arrest, the group moved to a public park where it established a tent city encampment. About 3 weeks later, homeless activist Mitch Snyder arrived in North City to help the protesters. After about 4 weeks, the demonstrators received most of their demands: more city shelters, the waiving of various categorical requirements in order to receive shelter, the liberalization of city welfare, and a voice for homeless people as consumers on boards and task forces within the city.

Although the level of homeless militancy had declined when this book was completed, at the time the study began, North City had three competing groups of homeless advocates that acted as grievance committees for the homeless, generating considerable publicity. At one point in 1989–1990, as many as 30 homeless and ex-homeless peer advocates roamed the city, carrying beepers and cajoling and threatening city officials.

"Checkerboard Square"

When the New England weather is warm enough, large numbers of street people cluster in "Checkerboard Square." Checkerboard Square is emblematic of the paradoxes of the 1980s. A plaza in the heart of downtown North City, the square faces an elegant new hotel built in the 1980s, one of the largest buildings in the city. The plaza is the epitome of the new architecture designed to highlight North City's appeal to tourists and to the "yuppies" who replaced much of the older population in the 1980s. The focal point of the plaza is a large antique clock, which formerly graced the now-defunct railroad station. The clock is now enclosed in glass so tourists can view a relic of nineteenth-century New England history. Antique replica cobblestones formed in squares (hence the designation "Checkerboard Square") mimic the historic look of nineteenth-century New England. It is ironic that this new plaza with its trees and benches and historic "cuteness," which was built to attract tourists and hotel visitors, often serves as a center for street people.

Of course, anyone can use the square. At times it becomes crowded with teenagers throwing frisbees, tourists resting on benches, mothers passing through with baby carriages, and busy downtown workers walking through. But more often one sees a variety of street people congregating and conversing and others sitting alone, reading the paper or simply waiting. Although Checkerboard Square does not have a particularly threatening look, it is filled with enough people who appear down on their luck so that most passerbys walk by the perimeter and do not enter the square. Those who enter might be asked for spare change or may occasionally see a particularly disorderly homeless person or a group of street youth.

Street people like the square because of its central location (there are nicer and more spacious parks elsewhere in the city). Located near one of the busiest intersections in the city, it provides a center for socialization and a meeting point and is near many service agencies and soup kitchens. Unlike actions taken in the new historic district about a half a mile away, police do not sweep the area and harass street people, except during special campaigns by the police chief.

While doing research for this study, the research team and I combed North City looking for street people. We often stopped at the plaza to meet new acquaintances and to ask where they thought we might find someone. I was often surprised not only by how up-to-date everyone was on the whereabouts of others, but how total strangers (to me) entered the conversation to help me find someone. "Oh, you're looking for Larry? ... I'm Sally, I used to go out with him."[2] Housed or homeless, single or family member, mentally ill or emotionally stable, anyone could become part of the scene at Checkerboard Square. Although not all street people spend most of their time at the square, and it is hardly the only stop during a street person's day, Checkerboard Square is the center of North City's street community, its most reliable center for the homeless conversing and "checking in" with one another.

Of course, people do not *live* in the square. Yet Checkerboard Square is a graphic representation of the non–spatially organized community that street people inhabit and that is a major subject of this book (see particularly Chapters 6 and 7). Linked not only by residential location but by dense friendship networks, socialization patterns, social service and self-help networks, and political and religious affiliations, in many ways members of the street community rely more on the traditional face-to-face interaction that characterized the old U.S. neighborhood than is true in most residential areas today.

Voices from Checkerboard Square

The six profiles below capture some of the range of extraordinary people who are part of the Checkerboard Square community. In their strengths, self-consciousness, and cohesion, they present a striking contrast to the dominant portrayal of street people as dangerous, pathological, or simply tragic and pathetic.

Joel: '60s Child

Joel is a 43-year-old child of the 1960s whose cocked beret, army jacket bedecked with a variety of political and countercultural buttons, and long, graying beard remind one more of someone from Berkeley than a person from New England. Indeed, when I met Joel at the apartment at which he had been staying for several months (like other street people, Joel goes in and out of housing) with an artist girlfriend, the place was scattered with leaflets, posters, and political memorabilia from a variety of causes. It resembled a crash pad or college dormitory, with several mattresses randomly thrown down amid the clutter of art and literature.

Joel is a self-proclaimed throwback to earlier times. After going absent without leave from the army in the late 1960s, Joel went to Haight-Ashbury and "got the love message." His eyes glittered as he talked in 1990 about "the magic in the air" in the late 1960s and how he learned to live by "foraging" in a variety of cities. For the past 20 years, Joel has alternated among apartment living, living out of a van (which he has parked in a variety of places), and, at a number of points, "literal homelessness."[3] A key organizer of the tent city protest and of other homeless political efforts in North City, Joel believes he has remained loyal to the causes of the 1960s, whereas others have been coopted. When I interviewed Joel, he was about to leave for the Earth First summer in northern California, and he also talked about spiking trees in northern Maine. In addition to his involvement in homeless and environmental causes, Joel receives a small stipend as a client advocate for a consumer-run mental health group, the North City Coalition for the Psychiatrically Labeled.

Joel is an example of a self-conscious street person who draws on a tradition of street life that is quite different from that depicted in discourses in the 1980s and 1990s. He reminds the interviewer of the long U.S. tradition of "tramping" and "hobos" going back to the nineteenth century and combines this image of the Wobblies with that of the late-1960s–early-1970s street youth.

> I regard myself as a visionary. There is beauty on the streets in the way people help each other. There is beauty in the sun coming up in southern California, which I saw sleeping there in the dunes ... everywhere I go I meet interesting people and I get involved with some kind of nonconformist folk, some kind of subculture that doesn't accept society as it is.

On the one hand, Joel represents the small minority of people who could be classified as street people who chose the streets, but he also typifies the inadequacies of academic and social service classifications. Joel is both a product of countercultural rebellion, at times choosing to be homeless (he told me he expected he would soon leave his temporary quarters to live out of his van), and a victim of unfortunate circumstances. Since becoming alienated from his family and receiving a less than honorable discharge from the army in the late 1960s, Joel has had severe economic problems, for which his childhood in a relatively middle-class family did not prepare him. His many difficulties with work and income are in part a product of the difficult times experienced since the 1970s by babyboomers who lack technical or professional skills. Moreover, since the mid-1970s, Joel has suffered several psychiatric breakdowns, although he was hospitalized only once, evidently just overnight. Is Joel, then, to be classified as an economic victim, a disabled veteran, a member of the mentally ill homeless population, or a voluntary street person? As Joel says, no single label totally fits:

> You could consider me a voluntary street person. … But only to an extent … because a lot of things have happened along the way. It's very different [being on the streets] now than in 1969 … and then disappointment as the years went by, and some feeling, yeah, that I have a lot of limitations. I'm coming to accept some of them, that I have a lot of personal problems too … and a lot of what I hoped to do I can't … but I don't regard myself as a victim either, not a typical person who was evicted or something.

Mitch: Advocate for the Homeless

Mitch, a 31-year-old, square-shouldered man with short hair, looks very "straight" compared to Joel. Indeed, Mitch evinces little countercultural influence. But Mitch is a newly politicized street person with a mission: Get Mitch into a conversation and he verbally attacks the city and a variety of public officials in the strongest terms. Like a militant union shop steward, Mitch indignantly states the case of whichever homeless person he is currently fighting for:

> The city is guilty of neglect and we've got to get the public to know that. … Like [Joe] this guy we're helping, they keep saying, "Yeah, we're dealing with it … we'll get him shelter," and it's bullshit; without us [advocates] he'll get nothing … and they know it. We're [advocates] the only ones forcing the issues of homelessness.

Mitch carries a beeper and numerous scraps of paper with the names of "clients" and telephone numbers of city officials, and he was one of the leading advocates for a self-styled group called Let's Talk, the successor to the Coalition for the Dignity of the Homeless and Poor, which led the 1987 tent city protest.

Like Joel, Mitch is from a middle-class background and is an army veteran. In the service, he developed severe neurological problems, then lost a clerical post to which he had been transferred. Through a series of circumstances, Mitch lost several jobs and then went through a difficult divorce. He ended up in a New England veterans' hospital. Mitch felt he was being overmedicated and abused; he left the hospital and ended up wandering the streets of rural northern New England. Mitch can also be viewed as mentally ill.[4] Other subjects remember him

claiming to be Jesus Christ during the tent city encampment and alternately or-
dering people around and forgiving them. Although Mitch places far more emphasis on the physiological causes of his disability, he does not reject the psychiatric label, as shown by his involvement with the Friendly Center, a self-help club
for psychiatrically labeled people.[5]

Also like Joel, Mitch fits few stereotypes. Agitated at times and rehospitalized
for several weeks in the summer of 1991 due to seizures, Mitch is also a part-time
university student who has spoken to students in social science courses about
homelessness. He is a very capable advocate and is known to make city officials
wary. He is an active member of the Friendly Center and is now employed by the
center part-time to assist with its new computers. He is a member of a religious
group and has been active in a local political campaign.

Of course, given Mitch's neurological and psychiatric problems, he occasionally has trouble functioning and has had help in maintaining housing over the
past year and a half. His girlfriend Katherine, a social worker and homeless
leader—once homeless herself—often puts her arms around Mitch when he is agitated and says something like, "Come on Mitch, it's time to go." Like other marginally housed people, Mitch spends a good part of his day at Checkerboard
Square and at other locales where the homeless spend time. "These are my folks,"
says Mitch. "I identify with the homeless whether I have a place or not."

Cora: Runaway to the City

Cora, an attractive 21-year-old woman with long black hair, typifies a large number of homeless and formerly homeless people interviewed in North City: young
runaways from rural areas who fled abuse or neglect to join the street culture in
"the city." Cora grew up in a poor family in a rural town characterized by poverty.
When Cora was 7 years old, her father died and her mother "could not cope at
all." Cora's mother—a heavy drinker—along with a succession of her boyfriends,
began to abuse Cora and her sister, both of whom were ultimately removed to
foster care by the state child protective system. Thus began a rather typical odys-
sey of being shunted among a large number of foster homes—many of them
abusive—and teen shelters, with Cora eventually running away from the foster
care system. Cora's comments reflect a high level of awareness of the combination
of negative and positive factors that lead youth into the city streets:

> I was a very pissed off kid. I mean I was fed up, fed up with abuse, with being abused,
> with being shuffled from one place to another by [state social services] … and then
> again, yes, met these friends in [North City], drank, had a lot of fun and partying
> with these older kids. [North City] was the place to go, to grow up, [to] be around
> these cool kids.

Cora has spent nearly 5 years on and off the streets, living in abandoned houses
and in shelters and staying intermittently with friends and with her sister, who

also fled to North City. Like many other runaways, Cora became heavily involved with alcohol and received convictions for minor charges such as trespassing, criminal mischief, and disorderly conduct. I met Cora at Checkerboard Square, where she spent time until noon every day with her sister Cheryl and Cheryl's boyfriend, Brad. Cora was about to go "make a scene" at the city welfare department because she had recently been evicted from a small, one-room apartment the city had placed her in:

> This guy [the landlord] was a bastard. ... The place was caving in, the roof leaked, there was lead paint, and as you can see, I'm pregnant. I called City Hall and reported him [the landlord] ... and what do I get, I get evicted for the trouble, and the city, my social worker, they say, "Well, Cora you're right, but you shouldn't have acted this way so quick."

Cora and her sister were active in the tent city protest, and as relatively verbal and appealing homeless youths, they attracted a wide range of attention from social service and charitable organizations and obtained housing. But remaining housed has proven difficult; only a variety of low-paying service jobs have been available to Cora, and she has held each for less than a few months at a time. Her only assistance between jobs (when she is approved) has been city welfare for her rent and $50 a month in food stamps. Cora "takes no gruff" from landlords or from welfare workers, and her fierce independence gets her into trouble. She is fully aware of this problem:

> I know I have a temper, and this gets me into trouble with the city, [with] landlords, [with] bosses ... but I can't see staying quiet and meek.

Cora stayed with Cheryl and Brad for a while and then spent a week at the Porthouse Shelter, a private shelter for adolescents. She was placed in new housing several weeks later. Homeless and pregnant, Cora maintained a regular schedule of activities, which, in addition to socialization, included being a regular participant at the drop-in center where she received counseling and participated in a women's group. She has also participated in another youth program (where she maintained close friendships with several workers as well as with other clients) and in Alcoholics Anonymous (AA) groups.

Cora was strongly connected to a network of street people and was a valuable source of information; she knew where everybody was at any given time, who was dating whom, who had left town, and who was in jail. Throughout the study, Cora helped me contact homeless subjects. "Just give me the name. I'll tell you where to find them," Cora insisted.

Harry: On the Borders of the Law

I first met Harry at breakfast at the Drop-In Center for the homeless. After a social worker pointed him out to me and I introduced myself, Harry jumped with excitement: "I'm going to be interviewed!" he yelled. As often happened during the course of this study, however, before a time could be arranged for an interview, Harry was no longer in his usual habitat but was in jail. After calling first, I arrived at the county jail and was greeted with enthusiasm by Harry, who remembered our conversation.

Harry, a stocky, pudgy-faced, muscular 21-year-old man, has a background similar to Cora's. Born in an extremely poor Massachusetts family, he was a victim of repeated physical and sexual abuse by both his natural parents and his adoptive parents. But like many male street youth, he expressed more defiance toward the social institutions and more involvement in criminal activity than women displayed (see Cloward & Piven, 1979, for an important exploration of differences in how men and women deviate from social norms). Harry was being held in jail for 45 days for violating his probation. He had been arrested for stealing a record player from a car.

Harry had been on and off the streets for 4 or 5 years. He denied that he was homeless during our jail talk; he told me he was staying with friends before being arrested and that they would always have him back. But like others interviewed, his residence was highly impermanent, and 2 months later I met Harry in the line for a city shelter bed. Harry alternates among living with different friends, living on the streets, and living in apartments; and as with other street people— particularly young men—for him the jail is as much a place to be housed as it is a punishment.[6]

To much of the public, Harry would fit the "undeserving poor" label. He is arrested sporadically for petty theft and minor drug raps and is contemptuous of the police and the various infractions of which he is accused. He admits to drinking heavily and to using the system. For example, Harry was going to try to get Supplemental Security Income (SSI) for a psychiatric disability, although he admitted to me that he really did not have a psychiatric history ("It's all head games! To survive, I can convince them I'm crazy"). As is the case regarding most of the long-term homeless, the local police had a somewhat nonchalant attitude about Harry. "Oh, yeah, we'll have him back here I'm sure soon. He's really an all right kid," said one of the police at the jail's booking desk.

Harry is engaging and articulate. I soon learned he was among the favorite clients of several social workers at the drop-in center. Part of this is explained by his youthful excitement and openness, and part is because of his relatively clear perceptions of the marginal role of poor people in society. Harry was apparently influenced strongly by a 2-year stay at an Indian reservation in Canada after running away from his adoptive home at age 16:

> They were the best people I ever met. It was cool, they took me in and I cut lumber with them. I was accepted for the first time. I mean, you have to understand—I never felt accepted anywhere. The Indians have a different sense of equality, really of all life, than the whites. It was weird, there I was with 2,000 Indians and this one honkey.

Harry was active in the tent city protest and remains highly involved in political protests. Unlike Joel, he does not speak of ideology, and although he strongly agrees with Mitch about government mistreatment, he finds the minutiae of grievances to be boring. Rather, Harry's activism comes from gut feelings:

> I know that the rich, the city, could care less about [the homeless]. Yeah, they have money to bail out the banks or some foreign country. … That's why it was so cool to march on Washington [Harry was one of about 30 homeless or ex-homeless North City people to travel to Washington, D.C., in October 1989 for a demonstration for affordable housing and aid to the homeless]. It was the first time I saw a whole bunch of people just like me. It was mobbed. … I felt like, yeah, maybe so many of us can change things. We could have an effect.

Harry, like others interviewed, makes no secret of his personal problems, including substance abuse, and does not hold himself up as a role model. For example, when asked about the homeless in North City, he said:

> Kids keep coming on the street, more and more of them. They think it's cool at first … some of them even think I'm some sort of hero. Because I've been out there and take some drugs and stuff. I tell them the last thing they want to be is to be like me. They don't know what it feels like to be on the streets so long.

Amy: A Mental Health Consumer

Perhaps no group is as stigmatized and misunderstood as those labeled *mentally ill homeless*. They often appear to be feared by the general public and to be stereotyped by the mental health and social service providers as "chronic cases" who are uninteresting or beyond help. When one gets to know a person in a more normal environment than a treatment center or a service agency, labels such as *mentally ill* become less meaningful and are easier to discard.

For example, I met Amy—a friendly, grandmotherly looking woman, whose gray hair and worn appearance make her seem much older than her 38 years—at a church that had a street ministry. Amy immediately began laughing and flirting with a student researcher and me. Over the next months, it seemed as though I saw Amy everywhere I went: at the supermarket, at the drop-in center, at Checkerboard Square, or on the street helping an elderly person across the street. It turned out that Amy led such a busy life that she was hard to schedule for an interview.

When interviewed, Amy described her typical daily schedule to a student interviewer:

7 A.M. Breakfast with her boyfriend at soup kitchen
8 A.M. Meeting with her social worker
9 A.M. AA meeting
10 A.M. Church group meeting

12 NOON Lunch at soup kitchen
1 P.M. Meeting of North City Coalition for Psychiatrically Labeled
3 P.M. Meeting of the newsletter committee of the Friendly Center
5 P.M. Dinner with boyfriend at soup kitchen
7 P.M. Church services

Amy was a social dynamo, and most of the service providers knew her. She could often be found joking with them. For example, the director of the drop-in center left a bowl of condoms (used to encourage safe sex) near Amy, joking, "I'm sure you'll need them!" Amy laughed and replied, "No, not this many. You're embarrassing me!" The banter between the administrator and Amy continued for several minutes.

Amy's strong involvement with social service and self-help groups make the academic stereotype of "disaffiliation" almost laughable. She maintains a more active social and organizational life than do many middle-class people. She counts large numbers of street people, as well as ministers, social workers, and other middle-class people, as her friends. She is an engaging and humorous person.

Of course, Amy's life does contain severe problems; during the course of the research study, she became homeless again, at times staying with her family and her boyfriend and then at a private shelter for the mentally ill. She is on tenuous terms with her family, who, according to Amy, threw her out of the house when she became pregnant at age 18. Although her family lives nearby and is evidently willing to help her, Amy says, "It's a real last resort for me. It's not a case of being wanted there, really, it's humiliating. No, I avoid it unless I'm really just out here freezing."

Nina: Mother of the Street

Early in the study an informant told us, "If you're trying to locate people, go see Nina." This was good advice. Nina, a 38-year-old overweight woman who also looks somewhat older than her age, held court in a crowded apartment in a low-income neighborhood. As the telephone rang incessantly, children crisscrossed the room, the television blared, and an assortment of people dropped by to say hello, I reviewed the list of tent city participants with her name by name. Blessed with both a photographic memory and extensive contacts with street people, Nina proved to be a key informant for the study.

I initially failed to realize that many of the people we were looking for stayed at Nina's. Only when others started to tell me that "so-and-so" was staying there and another researcher found three or four subjects staying at Nina's house did we realize that Nina served as a "mother of the street," sheltering and sustaining a variety of homeless people. Nina began this role when she got an apartment 3 years ago and as many as 10 people stayed with her. She has less room in her new apartment, but she never turns people away. Asked about this, Nina responded:

I take them [the homeless] in and help them because no one did this for me when I was on the streets. I felt cheated. I don't want them to be cheated. The kids, they all call me nanna, they see me as their mother or grandma, and that's OK with me.

As the study progressed, we found at least three or four other mothers of the street who sheltered the homeless in their small apartments, called social agencies for them, and helped feed and clothe them. Like Nina, these were middle-aged women who had been homeless themselves. Often they had been battered wives. They felt naturally obligated to help those in distress at a time when they were somewhat more fortunate. Nina and the others took no money nor any other tangible good for their aid. They also occasionally suffered for their hospitality, as when Nina had things stolen by a street person, who has also been telephoning her collect from Arizona for the past year.

Nina has been on and off the streets since late adolescence. Her father and a former husband suffered violent deaths; she was sexually abused by her mother's boyfriend while a teenager in an impoverished household; later, she was abused physically in several marriages. At the time of the tent city protest, Nina's son, Del—then 15 and already a street kid—urged Nina to join him at the encampment. Tired of being beaten by her abusive boyfriend, Nina packed her belongings and moved to the tent city, serving as a cook for the protesters. Nina has now been housed for about 2 years. She was married 1 year ago to her fifth husband, Ben, who until recently was also a street person.

Despite a myriad of personal problems, Nina finds time to be a dedicated helper not only at her apartment but through volunteer work at the Friendly Center and at a local AIDS agency (her brother has AIDS). Intelligent and self-assured, she told me she had taken a lot of notes at an earlier point so she could write a book about her experience with homelessness.

Subjective Elements of Homelessness

These profiles raise several themes that are developed throughout the book. Each subject was strongly affected by the major macro-level causes of homelessness documented by social scientists: the housing crisis, the economy, and social benefit cutbacks. Yet the subjects' own accounts of how they became homeless stress personal issues and often their own actions in deciding to live in the streets. The study of subjective behavior among the homeless and the very poor has been limited by the narrow range of the debate on poverty, as noted in Chapter 1, which consists of blaming the victim on the conservative side of the debate and the embracing the politics of compassion on the liberal side. When conservatives argued that people "choose" to be on the streets, as typified by former President Reagan's famous comments on the homeless (Roberts, 1988), liberals and most social scientists responded by stressing the macro-level causes of homelessness. This made sense in the context of the widespread American tendency to view public issues as personal troubles, to trivialize and individualize social problems (Mills, 1959), and to ignore economic causation.

Yet the macro-level, or social structural, approach holds the danger of "overdetermining" social causation to the point at which social actors become only "judgmental dupes" (Garfinkel, 1967). First, the reality of homelessness is usually far more complex than any single-cause explanation can address. Most often there is an interaction between the opportunity structure (the economy, the housing market, social benefits) and the particular social location of the family or individual. Second, if the poor are people with no choices, there is little room for resistance or social change. The poor are then only passive victims of social policies and the economic system. Third, as Hoch and Slayton (1989) note, if all choices are equally bad for the poor and all effects of poverty are seen as only pathological, then policymakers and analysts can be inactive as different aspects of low-income life are intruded upon. For example, in Hoch and Slayton's study, the tendency of liberal policymakers to support or ignore the destruction of single-room occupancy (SRO) hotels and their distinctive community is cited. Finally, the social structural arguments ignore all effects of culture and norms in low-income communities.

One way to explain the situations of the six street people described above is to argue that the macro-level social changes of the 1980s interacted with personal problems and had their greatest impact on those most vulnerable to homelessness—such as the mentally ill, the physically ill, those isolated from family, and those with criminal convictions (Rossi, 1989, Chapter 6). This is a more sophisticated treatment than viewing all of the poor as equally affected by social policies, but it still does not address the subjective and cultural elements of life in low-income communities.

For example, although Mitch, Cora, Harry, Amy, and Nina can be understood to have been vulnerable to homelessness due to family problems, mental illness, or physical disability, it was their own resistance to institutionalization, family abuse, the foster care system, and landlords that caused each of them to incur periods of homelessness. Had Cora, Harry, and Nina tolerated physical abuse, as millions of Americans evidently do, they could have remained housed (although I cannot comment on their chances of physical survival). Had Joel and Mitch returned to their middle-class families of origin when they developed financial, health, or mental health problems, they may have never experienced homelessness. Yet as we have seen, Joel has at times chosen to live in his van (only in part because he cannot afford housing); Mitch left a veterans' hospital to live on the streets; Cora, Harry, Amy, and Nina all left, and refused to return to, their abusive or hostile homes. Cora's resistance to a slum landlord, to various low-paying employers, and to the city welfare department has also extended her periods of homelessness, as have Harry's criminal acts and refusal to apply for welfare because of its workfare (forced work in order to receive welfare benefits) requirement.

The key difficulty in explaining subjective processes centers around the understanding of the word *choice*. As social scientists know well, few people choose to become poor, and this is the best counterpoint to the extreme voluntarism of Reaganite individualism. To be poor is to be without the options of daily life that are available to middle-class citizens, including securing an apartment separate from parents, getting away from home to work or to go to school, obtaining a divorce from an abusive spouse, and moving with one's children to a new household. Yet to acknowledge the closing off of options for the poor is not the same as denying that *any* choice exists among the socially structured alternatives available to the very poor. Street life must always be compared to the *actual alternatives* available to the poor. Although some subjects found the streets and the homeless experience to be devastating, others—fleeing family abuse, institutional arrangements, and other dysfunctional situations—told researchers they preferred the streets to their prior living arrangements. Of the six individuals profiled, Joel preferred the streets to shelters and institutions; Cora, Harry, Amy, and Nina preferred the streets to living with their families (Nina even left her apartment to live in tent city). Only Mitch described the streets as a completely negative experience to which under no circumstances would he ever return.

Sociological thought (Merton, 1968) is based on the notion that the social structure limits and constrains choice to structural alternatives. It is a disservice to the poor to also deny them any choice within these structural alternatives. For example, the horrible alternatives of living literally on the streets, living within the shelter system, staying with friends or family, or living out of a car represent choices. So do decisions to stay in one city or region or to move, to lie and receive benefits or to be honest, to steal for food or to submit to institutional degradation in order to receive food, and so forth. Since all of these choices seem bizarre to a middle-class observer, these important realms of subjective behavior of the very poor are often misunderstood or completely ignored.

Replacement of Traditional Family-Work Roles

The six profiles of study subjects illustrate the relative decline of family and work ties among North City's street people compared with involvement in alternative pursuits and socialization patterns. Of the six, only Amy was in regular touch with her family of origin, and, as noted, this is a highly conflictual relationship. Nina was married, but Joel and Mitch had girlfriends, and Mitch had no contact with his children from two previous marriages. Cora was pregnant with no plans to marry or to live with the baby's father. Harry and Amy also had lovers and had no plans to marry them. All mentioned love interests and social lives, but these were outside the traditional bounds of marriage and family (except for Nina's fifth marriage).

These six people are very active and productive. Joel works for several political cause groups, Nina volunteers with AIDS patients and the mentally ill, as well as homeless people. Mitch serves as a peer advocate for the homeless and takes university classes. Amy attends self-help meetings and is active in church organizations. Of course, these are not paying jobs. Mitch speaks of his guilt about not working more, although he receives disability benefits. He feels he is not carrying his weight. All six subjects had extensive experience working in the service sector but in various ways had opted out of the usual low-paying job market.

The subjects differ in their aspirations. Amy and Nina seem relatively content with their current pursuits. Joel has had roughly 50 jobs ranging from caretaking on a farm to being a tax assessor. He feels alienated from the work world but would like to earn more money working with an "alternative organization." Mitch speaks of taking more university courses if he could afford them. Harry is probably the most troubled by his situation; He lives primarily on underground earnings and money borrowed from friends and wants to get a "construction job or something skilled where I can make money." But Harry's lack of skills and the regional collapse of the construction industry make such aspirations extremely unlikely to be realized in the near future.

For the foreseeable future, these six street people (and many of the other subjects interviewed) are participants in an alternative culture that is relatively hidden from public view. Some attend political demonstrations or serve as advocates; some attend self-help groups, work as volunteers, or receive counseling at service agencies. Many just spend time with friends on the streets. These alternative activities result in a use of time and energy that differs drastically from that of the traditional work world.

Methodology

In order to truly understand street people, their lives, and their community, it is necessary to become an insider and to gain legitimacy. Initial contacts for this study were made beginning with a contact at the university who had once been homeless and who served as a leader of the tent city protest, as well as contacts made through the drop-in center, a major service provider for low-income people in North City. Fortunately, leaders of the Coalition for the Dignity of the Homeless and Poor, which had led the tent city protest, were extremely interested in the possibility of finding and following those people who were homeless at the time of tent city in 1987.

This book came about as a result of two phases of research. In late 1989, Marcia B. Cohen of the University of New England and I became interested in locating a cohort of homeless people in order to do a longitudinal study. As noted in Chapter 1, most research on the homeless has consisted of single counts and survey data of those who use shelters or soup kitchens *at one point in time*. As a result of data kept by the Coalition for the Dignity of the Homeless and Poor, we were able to develop a list of people who were homeless in the second week of July 1987, and we began to contact them nearly 3 years later. In the fall of 1990, after 65 in-depth interviews were completed, I was led into further participant observation of street people, which resulted in numerous group interviews and field notes.

Phase One

The rather unique effort to secure a cohort of people who were homeless at one point in time (July 1987) had much support among activists, homeless people, and service providers. Contrary to stereotypes of isolation and tragedy, the streets of North City constituted a community, and many service providers are a part of that community, although they sleep at home at night. Many service professionals immediately asked us to "tell [me] if you find so-and-so" or exclaimed, "I'd love to know how so-and-so is doing."

The coalition had collected some basic data from tent city participants in 1987 and also kept a list of names of street people who had signed up the first night of the protest. Neither the list nor the data were complete. Moreover, some of the 63 names on the list were first names, nicknames, or initials. Over the course of the study, through meetings with homeless activists, indigenous leaders, ministers, social workers, and the subjects themselves, I was able to accumulate a list of 105 people who were homeless and active in tent city, which advocates believe approximated the number of people who stayed at tent city over the 4-week period of the protest. Surprisingly, through discussion with people on the streets, many of the people identified only by nicknames or first names were also found. Of course, given the fact that the protest was in many ways a spontaneous event, I do not claim that the list was 100 percent accurate.

Few researchers had tried to locate homeless people on the streets at an earlier date. The research team developed a wide variety of methods for finding people. Some were easily located through informants at shelters, at the drop-in center, at the Friendly Center, and on street corners. Some were located through mothers of the street who were in touch with many homeless people. Some were located through arrest records; others were found at soup kitchens; some were located through advocates and some through a low-income ministry. Based on leads provided by street people at Checkerboard Square, researchers telephoned possible relatives (sometimes only people with similar names) as well as agencies and government offices that were willing to cooperate. Interviews took place in parks and on street corners, at shelters and service agencies, at subjects' homes (if they were housed), in jails and prisons, and at the university offices and cafeteria. A number of subjects were located out of the region and were interviewed by telephone or by meeting them in their new locales.

The first phase of the study was based on an in-depth interview with each homeless or formerly homeless person. Subjects were asked to give detailed information about their lives, how they became homeless, how long they were homeless, and what had happened to them over the past 3 years, and they were asked a variety of questions about the politics of homelessness. Interviews lasted from 45 minutes to, in a couple of cases, 5 hours over several sessions. As is common with ethnographic studies conducted with the very poor, some people disappeared over the course of the study. For example, a man was interviewed for an hour and a half, but by the following week, when the research assistant went to meet him to complete the interview, he had become homeless again and left the city. We were unable to locate him. A few homeless people who were well-known to us kept agreeing to be interviewed but on each occasion would tell us the time was "not right." These people frequently turned out to be refusals, even though we had often spent a great deal of time with them chatting informally. Between February and September 1990, the research team found 81 of the 105 people on the list, but due to deaths, refusals, and failure to complete interviews, a total of 65 full-length ethnographic interviews were completed. Although supplemented with the second phase of the study (discussed in the next section), the material in Chapters 3–5 is drawn primarily from data from personal interviews conducted with and survey sheets completed by homeless people in 1987.

Phase Two

Social scientists have historically conceptualized ethnography as consisting of the expert researcher departing from his or her home culture and living among natives of a different culture, traditionally in far-removed, exotic places. In this case, I was drawn into continuing an ethnographic study by my location, which is close to the culture being studied. In the fall of 1990, after the completion of the first study, informants who had helped us locate subjects continued to telephone my office and home asking if I was looking for a particular person, on walks or drives through the city I inevitably encountered homeless subjects I knew; and my service on some committees at the Drop-In Center caused me to hear various news flashes and stories of the social workers and to socialize with homeless or formerly homeless subjects.

It had become obvious that the first phase of research had resulted in many contacts and insights but that individual interviews were limited in what they could reveal about group interaction, about the nature of conversation and of truths that were known among the whole community, and about trends within the community that personal accounts might deny or obscure. In the fall of 1990, a research assistant and I began to systematically talk with, spend time with, and observe the dense social networks existing on the streets of North City. Whereas field notes were not systematically recorded in phase one, between the fall of 1990 and the end of the summer of 1991 we developed pages of notes on interaction within the homeless community. Often we returned to sites familiar from phase one to gather more information. In many cases, we found subjects who had been interviewed in phase one and talked with them again. In other cases, we met homeless people who had not been tent city participants. Some had been homeless for a long time but had not been at the protest; most were homeless people who had ended up on the streets since the time of tent city or even since the first study. Of course, in some cases, original cohort members had left the city or had died. So although my initial impetus was the tent city project, the 2 years spent observing people on the streets of North City led to numerous contacts and informal interviews with street people who were not at the 1987 tent city protest. We met a total of approximately 110 different subjects. It should be noted that neither I nor my assistants participated in the homeless life in the sense of living on the streets or sharing the hardships; we were always clearly identified experts who went back to a middle-class life. In this sense, we obviously recorded the daytime experience more than nighttime street experience, and in some ways we documented the easier parts of the lives of the homeless than would have been the case if we had actually lived on the streets.

In addition to interviews and participant observation, extended conversations with two key informants were invaluable. Katherine, a leader of tent city and other homeless movements, and Larry, a worker with a number of homeless programs, spent many hours talking to me and my assistants about their memories of different people and events and commenting on interpretations.

Chapters 6 and 7 of this book are drawn primarily from this second phase of the study.

Questions of "Representativeness" and Interpretation

Research findings have become more complex in the social science world of the 1990s. Although empirical canons still dominate social science research, competing postmodernist and radical interpretive views have increasingly come to question the existential validity of any work. Traditional social scientists ask how any sample of subjects empirically represents a larger population; however, some observers believe all work should be considered more of an interpretation based on the context of the study and of the researcher's social characteristics (see Clifford & Marcus, 1986, for an excellent critique of all ethnographic research as essentially interpretive fiction).

Further, virtually all discussions of the homeless population by empirical researchers begin with the caveat that is almost impossible to count, develop a coherent sample of, and generalize about this group (Rossi, 1989; Shinn & Weitzman, 1990). Unlike students, employees, homeowners, or welfare recipients, the homeless are not listed in official records, and no acceptable census figures are available. Not only does the social location of the homeless make them hard to find and to count, but—at least for some long-term homeless—the very definition of their situation resists enumeration as well as contact with any officials.

However, since I believe there is some validity in conducting empirical research on the poor yet am also strongly persuaded by recent critiques of empiricism, I briefly locate this work within both contexts: the empirical and the subjectivist-postmodern critique. From an empirical viewpoint, this sample has some limitations: I cannot make statements on homeless families, for example, because the subjects were not defined as traditional families; nor can I suggest that my subjects' actions reflect the homeless populations of New York or Los Angeles because this group did not contain large numbers of Afro-Americans and Latino Americans. Also, special local conditions always exist. Perhaps it is easier to be homeless in a smaller city than in New York or Chicago, although I have no evidence on either side of this argument. Perhaps some subjects' involvement in the tent city protest made them more "political" than other homeless, although interviews and contact with nonparticipants did not reveal sharply different patterns, nor could the vast majority of the tent city participants be considered politically militant or radical.

Despite these limitations, there are strong reasons to uphold the study's validity, at least for the large numbers of unattached homeless men and women. First, as noted, the North City homeless reflect the same demographics as do other national studies in all aspects except numbers of minorities. Second, those subjects interviewed even in phase one constituted an evident majority of *all* homeless people in North City at the time of tent city, an accomplishment that, despite the relatively small size of the group, is unique.[7] When these elements are combined with the failure of most research efforts in the 1980s to locate a cohort of subjects who were homeless, to follow them over time, and to participate intensively within their community, the study's data provide us with a fuller, richer sense of street life than do those of many other studies. In terms of the points made here, there is every reason to believe that samples including more Afro-Americans or Latinos would likely share more rather than less of the culture of resistance discussed in Part One, as was true of the many American Indians in this sample.[8]

Indeed, a new wave of documentary films and research on the homeless in the late 1980s and early 1990s is changing some of the portrayal of the homeless as being isolated and pathetic. Two films based on the homeless of New York City— *Inside Life Outside* (1989) and *Sidetracks* (1991)—for example, focus on the community, the dense social networks, and the politicization of the homeless. Several new books have recently appeared (Golden, 1992; Snow & Anderson, 1992) or are scheduled to appear (Liebow, 1993) that present aspects of homeless people's communities or that reinterpret homeless people's actions as being innovative rather than deviant or tragic. Social service workers also have increasingly noted the strong social networks of the poor and the development of community among street people, a point I stress in Chapter 6 (Cohen, 1988; Glasser, 1986; Silverman, Segal, & Anello, 1989).

However, the argument that the social context of the researcher and the contingent reality of time and place make all research, including ethnography, as much subjective as objective is persuasive. For example, a recent special edition of the *Journal of Contemporary Ethnography* (1992) debated the reality of William Whyte's classic *Street Corner Society,* a virtual canon among U.S. ethnographies originally published in 1943. A researcher who is critical of Whyte and other ethnographers (Boelen, 1992) returned to Cornerville and charged that Whyte had misrepresented certain aspects of the community; almost all respondents, however, argued against Boelen that any researcher returning to Cornerville would bring forth a different account since no objective reality exists in Cornerville but only *interpretations* of the reality of Cornerville based on the time of the study and on researcher judgment, class, gender, age, race, political viewpoint, and personal relations with particular subjects.

Like Cornerville, North City is constantly changing, and just as Whyte's work holds a different contextual meaning in 1992 than it did when it was originally published, the reality of North City differs in 1992 than it did even in 1990. Moreover, not only the "realities" of the city and of homeless life change almost daily but the readership of academic and other work constantly changes. For example, had this study been conducted and written in 1983 or 1987 or even 1989, the need to document the presence of homelessness in American society or to bring to light the pathos and tragedy found on the street might have been primary. Yet, as noted in Chapter 1, by the 1990s many books exist on these subjects, and the questions framed by politics and by social science had changed by 1990. For this reason, in this book, despite the many anecdotes about the cold, hunger, and fear on the streets, I do not give primacy to those topics. Moreover, the researcher's approach is always influenced by ideology and personal characteristics as framing forces in what he or she will find. For example, a radical feminist interviewing our subjects would undoubtedly frame a study around a gender perspective. Interviews did give voice at times to a gender story; they also give voice to stories about alcohol, drugs, and psychiatric trouble. Experience is so vast and so rich that neither interviews nor observation can be limited solely to one textual meaning. Yet within the social science tradition the author must take "authority" over the meaning system of interviews and observation, and in this sense, the organization of meaning is only the author's.

The ethnographer's authority is almost scary. He or she always translates the lives of others from a vast number of spoken words and visual cues into an organized reality to be presented to others who have no personal experience of the subjects. Subjects of social science research, with few exceptions, have no access to readerships and hence are dependent on those researchers' goodwill in presenting their accounts of their reality. Often we cannot be clear about what the subject is saying or ultimately meant to say. In my contact with the poor and the homeless in North City, a large number of people said to me, "Tell them who we really are" or remarked, "They just don't understand us." A point was often reached in conversation or interviews at which the subject became silent after such remarks; this may have indicated pain and sorrow or perhaps been the realization of an unbridgeable reality between his or her experience and that of a middle-class audience.

Who are the *they?* What exactly is it they do not *understand?* My interpretation of these entreaties to represent the homeless of North City as "they are" to those "who do not understand" takes this to mean that virtually all of the public does not understand (although this may not have always been meant) and that the "who they are" means not just the obvious (they are homeless; their lives are filled with tragedy and pain; they are victims of unfortunate economic circumstances). Rather in reflecting on these dozens of comments, I formed a latent meaning: These subjects have suffered unfair humiliation and suffering inflicted by those who have power over their lives (see Chapters 3–5), and despite all the pain, their lives reflect all of the essential human ingenuity including organizing their communal lives in innovative ways (Chapters 6–7). Again, subjects may not have meant for this interpretation to be taken; I was forced to interpret and then to generalize based on individual or small-group contact made at one time and in one place.

Some observers, then, will take issue with aspects of the interpretation, and perhaps even some subjects will. This is as it should be because the reality of life is far too complex to have only one interpretation, and at its heart, the book is one of interpretation, not of cold data.

Notes

1. Estimates are from the Coalition for the Homeless in the state in which North City is located. It should be noted that all estimates regarding homelessness are extremely inexact due to methodological arguments and a particular lack of longitudinal data on how many different individuals are homeless over the course of a year. National estimates have ranged from a low of 250,000 to a high of 3 million people being homeless at one point in time (Blau, 1992). If my estimate is close to accurate, and if estimates from other coalitions of the homeless in major states such as New York and California are true, proportionally a similar number of people are homeless in the North City area as is true in New York City or Los Angeles.

2. Throughout the book, all names of subjects have been changed to ensure confidentiality. Although some street people urged me to use their real names, there were enough instances in which this would have created problems for those interviewed that no actual names have been used.

3. As noted in Chapter 1, note 1, I distinguish between living literally on the streets or in shelters and various kinds of staying with others, doubling up, and other forms of homelessness, which social scientists such as Rossi (1989) do not judge to be "literal homelessness."

4. No attempt was made to verify psychiatric diagnoses for subjects for a variety of reasons, including confidentiality. Had we done so, some form of checking official records and developing a working definition of *mentally ill* would have been necessary.

Nevertheless, the findings of this research study support the arguments of Snow et al. (1986), Marcuse (1988), Johnson (1990), and others who have questioned the prominence of mental illness and deinstitutionalization as primary causes of homelessness; in the study I also question whether the construct of "mental illness" is useful in explaining the homeless experience. Only a tiny percentage of the sample members had ever been institutionalized or found to exhibit psychotic symptoms, and it was the experience of the research team that regardless of whether psychiatric problems were present when the subject became homeless, the majority of subjects developed severe personal problems as a result of being homeless. Since personal problems are so endemic to the homeless experience, it is very difficult to classify the degree to which a psychiatric problem relates to the etiology of homelessness.

Moreover, although Joel and Mitch can be labeled *mentally ill,* I do not find the label particularly useful because they are capable of a wide range of activities and of involvement in community, vocational, and other life activities. Thus, if they are labeled *mentally ill,* they are no more so than millions of Americans who suffer from depression, manic-depression, or other symptomatologies and who successfully maintain their roles in life. However, this is not to argue that mental health services and social services that are offered within the culture of the poor cannot have a very positive impact, as was clearly the case with Mitch and Amy.

5. In 1992, Mitch's own assessment of his problem seemed confirmed by a large, retroactive award from the Veterans' Administration (VA) (for which he had fought for 12 years); the VA agreed that his neurological disability was service connected (and presumably that it superseded any psychiatric diagnosis).

6. A number of street people interviewed stated that they intentionally did things in order to get arrested so they "would have a bed and the three square [meals]." The popularity of the now-defunct jail shelter in North City is also a reflection of the very different meanings of institutions to the poor. Whereas most people would avoid such a place, the street people gave the jail shelter very high marks, particularly in comparison with other shelters (public and private) in New England. The jail shelter—evidently because of its security— was safer than most shelters, and the surroundings and food were better, according to informants, suggesting perhaps that the care given prisoners is better than the care provided by most homeless shelters.

7. A caveat must always be raised about the "softness" of data on the homeless. The Coalition for the Dignity of the Homeless and Poor surveyed North City in July 1987 and found 174 homeless people, of which 105 are in our cohort. Yet the number appears small, particularly in light of the state Coalition for the Homeless's estimate for the North City area. One reason may be seasonal variation (this survey was conducted in the summer), and second, I believe the coalition surveyed only the literal homeless, missing those who were doubled up and those in group homes, institutions, and halfway houses. One informant I spoke to also implied that the surveyors missed the family shelters in North City since they were not a major focus of the protest.

In the summer of 1987, however, city officials took the position that the coalition exaggerated the numbers, so again, we will never have a definitive number.

8. In this study, the more than one in seven subjects who were identified as American Indians were generally both more politically militant and more resistant to government and other controls than were white homeless people. Although it is speculative, a strong case can be made that the added elements of racial consciousness and the awareness of oppression among many minority people combined with the experiences of poverty and exclusion most homeless people encounter, as documented in this book, are hardly likely to make them more passive or isolated but generally cause them to be more self-consciously resistant.

Part One

Homelessness and the Culture of Resistance

Middle-class people, even journalists or academics who write about the poor, conjure up a very different vision of family, work, and government than fits the experience of very poor or homeless people. Although problems with the institution are acknowledged, symbolically, in media and expert representations the "family" remains a Norman Rockwell replica: Sentimentality and pathos are predominant themes in describing homelessness and poverty and the family. Work remains the basis for respectability and citizenship and is proposed by middle-class observers as the solution to any and all of the problems of the very poor. Government aid, despite the ambivalence of many Americans, generally receives media and expert support as help for those who need it, who—if they are wise—will use such aid to further "pull themselves up" and to get ahead.

In the chapters in Part I, I argue—based on my experience with the street community in North City—that these institutions have a totally different meaning for some Americans. Far from reflecting the platitudes of the media or others, subjects often fled family life, felt humiliated and oppressed by employers, and resisted government controls.

"Culture," as Wilson (1987) notes, became a dirty word to some in the 1960s as a result of the "culture of poverty" debate. This is unfortunate because in one way or another, culture is at the heart of the social science enterprise: Without understanding the meanings people impute to their surroundings and the collective interpretations of society they hold, we have no chance of understanding people. Further, without this inquiry, by default we have only a middle-class, or "official," view of the reality of the poor.

I do not, of course, argue that the subjects in Checkerboard Square are homeless because of culture or of any actions they have taken: They are poor and homeless because of social structural conditions and the way the "system" operates. What I focus on, rather, is the culture that develops *once people become homeless*, usually after some period of time. But to understand how these subjects function on a day-to-day basis, how they perceive their world, and how they act—sometimes in spite of the expectations of middle-class people—we must turn to their subjective interpretations based on their own experience. When poor people do not always accept the media and expert entreaties to get a job, to preserve the family, or to go to a shelter, these are indications that the understandings of some poor people lead to resistance rather than compliance with middle-class norms.

The term *resistance* is used not in a psychological or a political sense (although for some subjects there are complex overlaps with both) but in a sociological sense. Subjects' similar experiences with dominant institutions allow them to develop shared meanings that are often counter to the official, dominant norms upheld by media, government, employers, and others; such shared understandings lead them to conduct their day-to-day lives differently from those of other Americans. Sometimes resistance leads to relatively private actions, such as refusing contact with a family of origin or manipulating official rules at a shelter. Other times resistance is more collective and can be seen as more political, such as when homeless people resist workfare requirements. Since those cut off from the benefits of society are often angry, at least some of their resistance will fail to meet the approval of middle-class observers (be they conservative politically or liberal social service workers and political activists) because it will be deemed unproductive or self-destructive. Similarly, some Marxists (see the work of Willis, 1977, and MacLeod, 1987) follow the thinking that poor or working-class subjects need to be more politically class conscious and to organize rather than individually resist controls. I try to avoid further moralizing about the poor; rather, I suggest that their patterns are rational given their social location and experience and given current U.S. conditions, including the absence of broader political and social movements.

3

The Family: No Haven

Conversation with four street people at Checkerboard Square:

Interviewer: Do you guys ever see your families?

Karl, a street person: Are you kidding? The closest my mother wants to get to me is the other side of some [prison] bars.

Interviewer: How about the rest of you? Do you agree with Karl?

Brad: Absolutely. ... You have to understand, man, we're all from dysfunctional families here. Been abused, thrown away, dumped. No, we're not family people.

Contrary to the widespread social myth that all families are loving, the street people of Checkerboard Square express a critical and cynical view of the family. Their speech, as is seen in these quotes, is peppered with psychological and quasi-psychological terms ("dysfunctional"), which subjects have heard from counselors, in self-help groups, or on the streets. It was not unusual for subjects to rattle off an array of problems originating in their families that they suggest account for current problems. Eric, for example, said, "I have trouble with relationships. It stems from my alcoholic and dysfunctional family who abused me back when I was a kid."

As I develop in this chapter, long-term experience with the streets of North City contradicts the social science image of the homeless as disaffiliated or isolated (Bahr, 1973; Bahr & Caplow, 1974; Bachrach, 1984; U.S. Drug Abuse and Mental Health Administration, cited in Fisher & Breakey, 1986; Hudson, 1988; Ropers, 1988; Rossi, 1989), not only because widespread social networks do exist among street people but because images of disaffiliation rest on the belief that the homeless are too disorganized, mentally ill, or troublesome to their families to have maintained strong social ties. Rather, an analysis of North City street people suggests they *consciously* avoided contact with families of origin and sometimes refrained from forming new families because of abuse, violence, and strife that characterized their own families. Because subjects have a critical and at times quite sophisticated view of family dynamics, which they generalize beyond their own situations to explain the situations of other street people, we understand these insights to be a type of cultural critique, or "penetration," into the dominant culture (see MacLeod, 1987; Willis, 1977).

Before I analyze the roots of street people's hostility toward the family, it is necessary to note that in our society, antagonism toward the family carries a tremendous potential cost. Whatever one's view of the family, for homeless people most families of origin have potential economic resources, such as shelter and financial assistance, that are urgently needed by subjects. In our society, families are vested with the normative roles of sustenance and support for family members in financial and emotional trouble. As noted in Chapter 1, the family is the unit upon which a variety of social welfare allocations are based in our society. Many experts on homelessness, such as Peter Rossi (1989), see the isolation of single, homeless adults from their families as symptomatic of *those adults'* personal dysfunctions and suggest that families of origin often cannot cope with the "vulnerable" homeless (e.g., the mentally ill, the substance abusers, the physically handicapped). Implicitly, then, Rossi tends to accept the viewpoint of the family of origin in perceiving homeless people as problematic in their behavior rather than locating the problem within other family members or within the entire family system.

Several family members of study subjects I interviewed generally offered frustrated and hostile perspectives of their kin. For example, Louie, the 40-year-old son of Wally—a 77-year-old homeless man who had recently died of throat cancer—told me:

We [the family] did everything we could to help him [Wally]. He just didn't want our help. [We] even got him this room once, but he didn't like it, and when he found out he lost his food stamps, he was furious. He was just no good.

As I explore, accounts by families of origin often left out many critical details, and based on the evidence gleaned from subjects' interviews as well as anecdotal information from service providers, their accuracy is suspect. Nevertheless, it is true that many homeless and formerly homeless people often rejected offers of family assistance, even when the family had some access to finances and goods. Many subjects were prepared to resist family contact and assistance, sometimes even if the cost was continued homelessness or living in less stable quarters. These seemingly irrational actions can only be explained by the struggle of these people to escape the hostility of their families of origin and by their implacable desire for independence.

In this chapter I explore the experience of subjects with their families of origin and with prior marriages or live-in relationships in order to analyze the origins of resistance to the family. I also discuss the tendency of many subjects to avoid forming new families, at least along traditional lines.

"Black Sheep": Injuries Within the Family

When interviewed about their families of origin, dozens of subjects spontaneously volunteered that they were the "black sheep of the family." In a few cases of siblings, both became homeless; however, most subjects—even those from impoverished families of origin—had siblings and other relatives who had never been homeless and who were spoken of as "doing fine."[1] As I mention in Chapter 2, such findings reinforce the viewpoint that despite the well-documented macro-level causes of homelessness (the economy, the housing market, social benefit cutbacks, deinstitutionalization, and so on), biographical and subjective data are critical to understanding the actual process of becoming homeless.

In what ways were subjects black sheep? For the majority of subjects, violence dominated their early family experiences, whereas others suffered from emotional abuse and many experienced abuse and pain in adult relationships.

Have You Seen "Carrie?" Abuse and Brutality Within the Family

Consistent with previous research on homeless people (Bassuk & Rosenberg, 1988; McChesney, 1987; Shinn, Knickman, & Weitzman, 1989; Struening, 1987; Susser, Struening, & Conover, 1987), the interviews revealed an astounding amount and degree of child abuse. Since we asked about abuse only in a general way ("Were there problems in your family when you were growing up?"), I can only assume that more subjects may have been abused than the more than half who described severe physical and sexual abuse (emotional abuse was even more prevalent, but it is not included in this figure). Subjects were abused by natural parents, siblings, mothers' boyfriends, uncles, aunts, cousins, and foster and adoptive parents (sometimes repeatedly by different family members). Judge, like many other subjects, told the interviewer horrifying stories. Judge was beaten so badly as an infant that he developed a permanent spinal and lung problem called Hylien's membrane, which nearly cost him his life. Ron was one of several subjects who was locked in a cellar and abandoned for weeks, in his case when he was 4 years old. Roy was set on fire by his father during an argument when he was 8 years old. Most of the subjects who were abused ended up in the child welfare system by their teen years, usually suffering additional abuse in foster homes.

If anything was striking beyond the nightmare of family violence, it was the casual manner in which the stories were often told. "My family? It was great if you liked sexual abuse," bantered Harry. After a few minutes, Telly, a 22-year-old street person, stated, "Well, you got used to it … he'd gesture [his foster father] and I'd pull out my pecker. … I've been abused more times and by more people than I can list for you." Of course, subjects had told their stories before, and those who did share them had steeled themselves to the trauma.

No single case was typical, but the saga of Eric, a particularly verbal and articulate 22-year-old street person, provides an especially good example of how homelessness can follow from family violence. Eric grew up in an extremely poor North City family. He described both of his parents as heavy drinkers, although his parents divorced when he was 2 and "I really never knew [dad]." Asked about his mother, Eric quips:

> My mother? Have you seen the movie *Carrie? ...* That was her. I mean, things would be OK and then, wow, if she took to the bottle, things would go flying through the air. I remember, everything that wasn't nailed down flew. I remember her trying to put me through a plate glass window. And also like [the movie] *Carrie,* she was this fundamentalist, you have to understand, with the crazy tongues. It was a crazy place.

Eric does not paint himself solely as a victim, however. He says he became a "hellcat" who constantly fought with his mother and her succession of boyfriends:

> I grew up not caring for anyone. To have no feelings. I could hate, hurt, or whatever, but I didn't feel anything. ... Supposedly I shot this bow and arrow through [one of mother's] boyfriends. I don't know, I don't remember it, but I believe I could have done it.

When Eric was 9, he was placed in his first of about eight foster homes. He still remembers the day he was brought in:

> My mom used to send me [name of department store] to wait there in the toy department until she came for me. I used to go there every day after school, and then this one day I'm in there and this guy calls my name. I said, "Yeah, I'm Eric [last name]." He pulls me into his car, and my mom is there too, and they drive me off [to name of town]. That was it ... no one ever said nothing else.

In the first foster home, Eric and his two sisters (placed along with him) were locked in a basement so they would not interact with the natural children of the foster family. "I started banging and banging on the door. I knew this was going to be worse than [mother's home]. I mean, they can't lock you up without even a bathroom!" The state department of social services finally removed Eric and his sisters from this home and then split the siblings up. At another foster home, Eric got into a fight with his foster mother, who started "kicking and kicking me. I guess I had held this inside of me," said Eric. "I just let her have it, and it took three adults to get me off her."

At 14, Eric ran away from another foster home, beginning a long cat-and-mouse game with the child welfare authorities. "They'd always catch me. I mean, I'd hide, I'd hang out with older kids. But [Department of Social Services] always got me, and I was back in these homes." At 17, Eric was placed in a group home for teenagers, and, in contrast to his other experiences, he had some positive times at the home. But at the end of a year, Eric, like many of the youths interviewed in this study, had "aged out" of the foster care–group home system. When a charge turns 18, suddenly all semblance of support (such as it is) vanishes, and he or she is felt to be self-supporting. Often the "graduate of the system," as these youngsters over 18 are called, are not given so much as a dime in public income assistance.

Eric "graduated" from the foster care system to become a homeless adult. Eric says pointedly:

Where was I going to do? There was no one I was going to stay with. Certainly not my mother. No, I said, "I'll live on the streets rather than go back there." And help? Gee, my only knowledge of social workers were these people chasing me, sending me from one home to another to be abused. I saw no one to help me, except some buddies to get booze and … later into [doing breaking and entering].

After several long bouts of living on the streets, numerous run-ins with the law, and a variety of low-paid service jobs, Eric entered the alcohol rehabilitation program at the Salvation Army, where I first met him (he still had no home). Like Harry in Chapter 2, Eric hardly sees himself as a model citizen, and after several months of sobriety, he was self-critical:

Interviewer: Was anyone in your life, in all that time, helpful to you?

Eric: Well, everything just looked the same. Everyone just seemed out to get me. How can I explain it? Sure, now I see there were a few people, like some counselors, who tried to help. Now I can see. I couldn't when I was young. They just seemed like my family, like my foster parents, the same. I would never let anyone get close to me, never.

Eric is still bitter toward his family and toward the host of surrogate families. Eric's mother has started to visit him at the rehabilitation center, but Eric resists her entreaties:

I've learned, with the help of [counselors at the center], to be a little cooler. So she comes, I say "hi," let her stay for ten minutes, sometimes she leaves me a dollar. But I can't forgive her. And she still has liquor on her breath. No, my life's not here, with her or any of my family. I'm going to get out, far away from her and all the people she hangs around with.

Survivors

Many subjects interviewed shared elements of Eric's story. First, what is most striking on examination is not just the extent of the abuse but the fact that young children actually survive it. And indeed, Eric and the many others interviewed are, first of all, survivors. Although these homeless people may be stigmatized and castigated by society, the subjects at least have *lived to tell their experiences.* They are not dead or in a hospital, and most are not behind prison walls because their implacable anger led them to commit murder or arson. This in itself is an accomplishment for children who have been burned, tortured, struck, or sexually abused.

How did they survive? Although a complete answer is beyond our scope, the amazing resourcefulness of children to find some measure of human contact away from their families is part of the answer. A number of comments made during the biographical interviews about the help given in subjects' childhoods by unrelated adults were indicative:

Dennis, who was abused by his father for 10 years: There was this neighbor across from where I lived. He took me in after I would run from home. ... I wished he was my father.

Cora, who was abused by her mother and her mother's boyfriends: I liked school a lot, yeah, because it got me out of my home. I remember, I hated to leave [school].

Rudy, abused by natural parents and a succession of foster parents: When I was in [the center for abused and neglected children], that was cool. I was away from all this stuff [abuse], and there were some nice people [there].

Second, as occurred with Eric, the experience of the child welfare system added to the bitterness felt by the young, abused children. Even under the best conditions, children taken away from their homes at early ages are likely to question the legitimacy of their new caretakers. Telly, who was taken away from his severely mentally ill mother at age 5, was typical in his negative assessment of foster care:

I was a bitter and mean kid. But, you know, I knew these people [foster mothers] weren't my mother. ... I knew the damned state had taken me away from my mother. And I couldn't forgive that, I just couldn't.

Even assuming that appropriate, nonabusive foster parents are found by social service departments, the combination of early and severe damage to the child and the lack of societal support and legitimacy for nonfamilial caretaking would seem to undermine any chance of its success. Further, subjects commented on the absence of choice and the lack of rights they had as youngsters. They described being treated like chattel, moved at will from hither to yon without appropriate procedures and with no attention to their needs. Harry described being put in a foster home at age 10 in which he was physically and sexually abused. When he was 12, the family moved to adopt him:

Now, according to [the state in which he was adopted], the kid is supposed to agree to it. I kept telling [the state] no, I didn't want these pigs to adopt me. But they [the state Department of Social Services] didn't care, didn't listen. Then we moved to [current state], the same thing [happened], they weren't going to get involved.

Alicyea, a 17-year-old homeless woman who had enough life experience for a 40-year-old, had actually contacted a lawyer to sue the state because of her continual sexual abuse in foster care:

Maybe it's just me. But I feel that if the state is responsible for me all that time [8 years in foster care] as my legal guardian, they were responsible for my getting hurt. I shouldn't have been left for 3 years in a foster home being sexually molested 7 days a week! … An 18-year-old foster brother, and you're 7 years old, come on, that's rape! And because they didn't believe anybody, I had to live in this situation. … They did no background check, believe me, because if they did, it was obvious from walking in the place, with this drunken father and naked children, that this place should never have been approved [as a foster home].

Finally, having suffered severe abuse in their natural families and usually again in foster care or adoptive families, the subjects, like Eric, often took to the streets to find freedom. Living on the streets, being curled over grates, spending time huddled on the corners with a shared drink, or living encamped in an abandoned building seems hellish to us, but to abused kids of North City, the streets sometimes represented salvation:

Sam, now 27: I came to [North City] knowing no one, nothing, just that it was away from home, from my parents. You have to understand, when you're being battered, punched, wow, when I was on the streets of [North City], this was cool. I slept where I wanted. I hung out with people, I drank. I was free as a bird.

Stanley, now 53: I left home when I was 12 [after being abused] … it was fine. I traveled, went all the way down the coast, down South. It was great, and I was never turning back, no matter what happened [to me] … nothing was worse than being [at home].

Subjects came to feel that their early instinctive actions—running away from home, sometimes countering the violence of their parents or related adults by fighting back—were a form of justified resistance. Ruth, a 23-year-old formerly homeless woman, puts it starkly:

My father was a bastard. I mean, to beat up and rape an 11-year-old … I know that now. But I spent years [at a center for the emotionally disturbed] feeling guilty, being told to go home [to her family] for visits, being made the one who was wrong. … Now I know after all the years that I'm not so crazy.

Homeless Women: Cycles of Violence

Virtually all of the women interviewed for this study were abused both as children and then again as adults (by husbands, boyfriends, and even casual acquaintances). Perhaps even more than the men interviewed, the women were matter-of-fact in describing abuse. Few women identified themselves as "battered women," and few mentioned involvement with battered women's services. Yet both the violence heaped upon them and their resistance to such violence were central to their experience of homelessness. In contrast to the dilemmas spoken of by battered women's counselors in more middle-class and working-class neighborhoods, where long-term marriages continue because some women stay in abusive relationships for many years, the women of Checkerboard Square usually just left their batterers and went to live on the streets.

In this study, patterns of abuse were repeated from childhood through adolescence to adulthood: For example, Ruth was molested by her stepfather, then later was beaten by a boyfriend; Louise was raped by her brother at age 13 and later was beaten by boyfriends; Judy was raped at age 12 by a cousin and later was battered in two abusive marriages. In general, however, marital or partnership abuse tended to be short-lived. For most of the women, getting involved with boyfriends or husbands (and often having a baby) seemed motivated primarily by the need to leave home during adolescence or young adulthood. After leaving home, the women usually existed marginally, sharing housing with their husbands or partners. The subjects then confronted the same situation of abuse they had found in their families of origin or adoptive or foster homes.

For example, Ruth finished high school at a special school for neglected and delinquent kids and moved into a dilapidated apartment with a boyfriend. They both worked as dishwashers in a hotel. After a few months, during which her boyfriend—drinking heavily—began to attack her, Ruth left. Asked about the sacrifice she made to go live on the streets, she shrugged:

> It was OK. I had loads of friends, and we all hung out. I was stoned a lot of the time. I just knew I had to get away from [her boyfriend]. I had been punched and raped my whole life, and I wasn't going to continue. But I was free, didn't have the cares I had living at home or with [her boyfriend].

In contrast to stories such as Ruth's, women with young children who were married to men who owned property or held the lease on property described far worse fates. For example, Judy married when she was 19 and had two children with her truck driver husband. After a year and a half of being abused, she left with her children one night and went to a homeless shelter. Shortly thereafter, her husband gained custody of the children.

Homeless families, particularly single mothers, are extremely vulnerable to court petitions charging them with abuse and neglect of children. While living on the streets, children will inevitably look dirty, wear tattered clothes, and go hungry. Most judges perceive street living as prima facie evidence of child abuse and neglect on the part of the adult caretaker, usually the mother. Indeed, Judy lost her children, although she was the one who was abused. Like others interviewed, this trauma led to new traumas, and Judy became one of the long-term homeless (sporadically now for 8 years) because psychiatric problems followed the loss of her children:

> I was hospitalized [then], [I] just fell apart. They said I was a manic-depressive ... but I don't know ... I just know I'll never be the same since I lost those kids, and I'm still fighting it [custody case]. I won't let him [ex-husband] get away with it, and I think it was criminal what the court allowed [to] happen.

In the interviews conducted, the age of woman and the presence of young children dramatically increased the long-term emotional, social, and financial tolls of being battered. For younger women who had "shacked up with" or married young street people with little money, the power differential was limited. Without the power of tangible resources—a house or an apartment, property, custody of children—the men did not have a strong hold on the relationship, and the women felt freer to simply leave with impunity. For example, during the study, both Cheryl, age 23, and Sara, age 24, were in the process of leaving their boyfriends because they were being threatened with physical abuse. Both had no children living with them (Cheryl had one child who had been taken from her; Sara had two children in state custody). Neither felt she would lose anything by leaving the relationship. Sara simply said:

> I'll go the city [welfare department] and say I need another place. Can't deal with [the man] beating on me. If they don't give me [a room] right away ... I'll go back to the [homeless] shelter.

Fleeing Family Pathology: Finding Independence on the Streets

Some subjects did not share horrific histories of violent abuse but nonetheless viewed their families of origin as pathological and emotionally abusive. A number of subjects lived with their families of origin well into their adult years until some kind of breaking point finally came and they left home.

Ralph, a slight, balding 31-year-old man, now marginally housed in supported housing, was a homeless person profiled in local newspapers. As a graduate of an elite college and the son of a prominent attorney, Ralph was the subject of a story that greatly embarrassed his family. Ralph became homeless after a psychiatric admission 4 years earlier. When I met Ralph, he immediately noted that he was from "a dysfunctional family." His mother was a manic-depressive who had committed suicide, and his father was a distant, critical man who "always made [me] feel miserable." Nevertheless, Ralph appears to have lived a normal life until after college, when he drifted aimlessly through a variety of occupations and became depressed after his mother's death and his father's remarriage. He became obsessed with cleaning his parents' old house and became increasingly emotionally paralyzed as he lived with his overly critical father and his new stepmother. After Ralph was briefly hospitalized and put on medication, his father and stepmother became even more hostile toward him:

> I guess the idea that I was a failure was now conclusive, and my father treated me like a leper. Then there were constant fights between him and his wife, yelling back and forth. Criticizing each other for the way I was. ... I don't understand it, but when I got into therapy, my shrink agreed [that] living there [at home] was counter-therapeutic.

Ralph came home one day, got on his bicycle, and left. Attracted to a mystical religious cult, he spent some time in a religious encampment. Disenchanted and broke after 3 weeks, he drove his bike to a city homeless shelter and began staying there:

> I just knew I couldn't go home. They [his family] controlled me in some sort of symbiotic way, and I had never grown up ... but yeah, it was weird. Who would have thought I'd be eating in soup kitchens, sleeping with the wretched of the earth? ... But I became independent, grew up.

Although mental health specialists could debate the etiology of Ralph's case (e.g., did the family dysfunction precede Ralph's psychiatric problems or vice versa?), for our purposes what is significant is Ralph's interpretation and generalization of his experience to others:

> I guess I had to live on the streets and in the shelter to be free. I think there [are] a lot of people like me and a lot of people who are called "mentally ill homeless" ... from pathological families who are probably better off being away from their parents or relatives.

The street people who most echoed Ralph's description of family pathology (without the severe physical abuse) and his flight to the streets for independence tended to have middle-class, rather than poor, family backgrounds. They were more likely to have been diagnosed as mentally ill at some point in their lives. For example, Lorraine, a 40-year-old college graduate who had been in and out of mental hospitals, came from a rich southern family that she described as "totally uninvolved. They just weren't there. I was raised by my Negro servant." Now proud of the fact that she has stayed out of the state hospital for 2 years, she says she has "finally learned to not keep going to my family for a vision of a relationship I never had."

The assessment of family pathology at which some subjects arrived finds support in some literature on young street people prior to the 1980s. For example, Blum & Smith's study (1972) of hundreds of young street people in the 1960s and 1970s noted the strong tendency of runaways to claim that they were escaping hostile and pathological families and trying to secure a "sense of competence" on the streets (p. 18). Although the countercultural alternative provided by street life at the time of Blum and Smith's study has eroded, I suggest that the economic and social pressures on families since this time have not been reduced but have escalated.

Street people like Ralph and Lorraine were under extreme pressure from their upwardly mobile families to perform well in careers and in family roles (marriage and similar roles). Psychiatric troubles can be seen as reflective in part not only of individual pathology but also of broader social conflicts, including the difficult economic terrain and conflicting cultural expectations surrounding gender roles and life-styles that characterized the 1970s and 1980s. Interestingly, both Ralph and Lorraine, as well as Arnie—a 35-year-old self-described "vagabond" from a similar family background—had involvement with religious cults. Had these subjects been 5 or 10 years older, they, like Joel in Chapter 2, might have gone to live in Haight-Ashbury or some other countercultural haven of the 1960s to escape their families. But by the later 1970s and the 1980s, few alternative routes for leaving home, other than the traditional paths of marriage or career mobility, were socially sanctioned. The cults were certainly one haven for young people fleeing their families and the pressures to conform to work and family roles, much as the counterculture served young people in the 1960s.

Marital Collapse and the Flight to the Streets

Having experienced violent or pathological families of origin, many subjects encountered further pain and upheaval in their adult relationships. Intensely stressful divorces preceded homelessness for many street people in North City. Fully two thirds of the street people over age 25 who were interviewed for the study had been through a divorce, and this figure is less dramatic than it might be because some subjects were widowed or had never been formally married. More striking than these numbers is the brutal impact separation had on the subjects, particularly the men.

The impact of divorce and separation on women is well documented, particularly the tendency of women to lose out economically when a marriage fails (see, for example, Lefkowitz & Withorn, 1986; Pearce, 1978). Only recently has any interest been focused on the problems of males (see Marin, 1991). Although not minimizing the impact of divorce on women, I call attention to the male experience because I was surprised at the extent of the trauma surrounding their divorces spoken of by male subjects. Since this study deals with those at the very bottom of the economic ladder, the usual male economic advantage in divorce is minimal. Since most of the female subjects were fleeing violence, it is not surprising that they view their separations with both positive and negative feelings, often viewing life on the streets as preferable to misery in their marriage.

Sidney, a 32-year-old formerly homeless man now earning $25 a month and free rent for managing a low-income building, broke into tears when speaking about his divorce, which had occurred 4 or 5 years earlier. The son of a rubber worker, Sidney was the product of divorced parents, and as a teenager he was shuttled back and forth between New England and New Jersey. Sidney describes his life as normal, however, before his divorce. He described his problems as emerging during a 2-year-old marriage following the birth of his son. He was working for his parents-in-law running two bakeries and working "14, 16 or more hours a day." Sidney blames himself for the marital problems:

> I don't know. Part of it was overwork and tension with her father, you know, over this business. And then I guess [my son]. Fights with her [his wife] 'cause I was working all the time, she had to do everything. I screwed up, basically. I started to drink. Drank more and more. I never hit her, though I came close.

Like many street people interviewed, emotional pain, alcohol, and flight combined in a way that led to a sharp and steady downward path of mobility. Sidney left his home, refused contact with both his family of origin and his family of procreation, and came to the streets of North City, where he knew no one and began living on the streets. Asked why he did not call upon his own family, Sidney was adamant:

> No, I would never ask them for help! The first few years [after the divorce], I never ever contacted them. They had no idea where I was. I was upset. I didn't want them to see me this way. I didn't want to rely on them, to humiliate myself.

In terms of employment opportunities, Sidney's flight from a relatively small New England town to North City made some sense. He had some skills in carpentry that he had developed as a young adult, and he felt that these combined with his bakery experience would lead to work in the city. But Sidney would no sooner get hired than he would find he did not have enough money for an apartment; then once he was settled, he was laid off because of a soft economy. From 1986 to 1989, Sidney's life was characterized by 3-month to 4-month periods of homelessness punctuated by periods of being housed, with the housing paid for by unskilled construction work. Like other people interviewed, Sidney has not seen his child, now 6, or his ex-wife since he left them.

Again and again, homeless and formerly homeless subjects—particularly men over age 35—mentioned divorce, alcohol, and flight in their stories. Older "skid row–type" homeless people such as Duke, Stanley, Barry, and Tiny were all housed and employed before their divorces. Although formerly middle-class street people such as Ralph talked of pathological families, and many subjects from low-income families were victims of child abuse, the divorce-drinking-flight families seemed to be mostly working class in origin. A direct tie between economics and emotional stress occurred in several stories, such as Tiny's description of beginning to abuse alcohol after his 25 years of employment at a venetian blind factory ended with a plant closing. Yet neither economics alone nor psychologizing alone (dismissing subjects as "dysfunctional" alcoholics) provides a sufficient analysis. The stress of working-class life—both in its economic pain and in its social and cultural conflicts in the last two decades (described so well in books such as Lillian Rubin's *Worlds of Pain*, 1976)—suggests a complex interaction of social, economic, and cultural factors as leading to alcoholism, homelessness, and downward mobility. Sidney's story, for example, contains elements of economic causation (his father hoped his son would follow him and work in the rubber plant, but the plant closed; Sidney was unable to find a skilled construction job in the declining economy of the late 1980s), of psychological causation (his own reflections on the impact of his parents' divorce; his own insight into his alcoholism), and of cultural causation (his wife's attacks on him for not caring for the child would probably not have occurred 20 years ago; his firm pride, which caused him to refuse to suffer humiliation by seeing his family and old friends once he was homeless). Neither the cavalier pop psychology of alcoholism nor overly deterministic economic arguments can explain such complex paths of downward mobility.[2]

Resistance to Family Life

It is clear that in general, the street people of North City hail from problematic and, in many cases, brutal families. For Eric and other victims of physical and sexual abuse; for Ruth, Judy, and other victims of spousal abuse; for Ralph, Lorraine, and others who came from pathological families, going to the streets was a way of escape. For Sidney and other victims of family dissolution, the streets were also a mechanism of escape and a chance, albeit against great odds, to start over. Of course, if these subjects had possessed adequate income and employment skills, their efforts to start over would most likely have more closely resembled socially sanctioned attempts to escape the family by simply finding apartments or houses of their own in distant cities or by avoiding social contact with their families.

I argue in the remainder of the chapter that contrary to the views of many social scientists and some family members of street people interviewed for this study, street people consciously resist family norms based on their conscious and semiconscious penetrations into the seamy side of family life rather than simply suffer isolation as a result of their own pathology or disaffiliation. Rather than viewing these interactions as occurring "behind the backs" of subjects, I suggest that street people are often highly self-conscious about their decisions to escape the family.

Resistance to the Family of Origin

As noted at the beginning of this chapter, the conventional wisdom on the streets of North City is that the family is dysfunctional. Most street people initially framed this analysis of family life in terms of their own families. When subjects were asked much later in the interviews to discuss the politics of homelessness in a more general fashion, however, a large number (on their own) returned to the issue of family and homelessness to develop a more global assessment:

> **Alicyea:** The kids on the street, they don't want to go home. They can't and won't deal with their families, with the drinking and the beating. You know, this is a big cause of homelessness. Family problems, screwed up families.

> **Sidney:** The families today, they don't care about the kids! Or, I don't know, maybe they have it so rough, it makes the family split up. Before you know it, kids are on the street. The stress, it's so great today that I guess everyone takes it out on one another. … I guess the family is part of the whole problem.

> **Joel:** We're concerned about families, but the real family has to be the larger, big picture, everyone, we're all family. The family, or I guess [the] nuclear family, has broken down, and it's in flux, and we need to come out of our denial about it.

Although avoidance of the family was not held as an ideological or a political precept, most street people generalized from their own experience *and* from the well-known experiences of their friends on the streets in developing a self-conscious reinforcement of each others' tendency to avoid family contact. In this sense, resistance to the family is more than merely a psychological avoidance but represents a kind of sociological insight into society.

Many street people had not seen their families of origin in a long time. Others had sporadic contact with one family member—often a sibling, sometimes an aunt, an uncle, or a grandparent, but rarely a parent or a grown son or daughter. In part the factors limiting any contact with families of origin were structural because poverty and its attendant humiliation create a lack of reciprocity in relationships. But the limited contact was also a result of resistance on the part of subjects based on their perception of hostility from their families of origin.

Randy, a 32-year-old homeless street person, was on fairly good terms with his grandparents, who lived in a nearby town, although he had no contact with his other relatives. At one point, he told me he "was lucky" because unlike other street people, he could spend the holidays with his grandparents. But at another point in the conversation, Randy suggested that he could not be in touch with them more than once or twice a year:

My grandmom, she gets very upset. First saw me on TV one time … a thing on the homeless. But what can I do? I am on the street, I smell, I don't have 20 cents for a call. And what happens if I call there? … She starts crying and crying. I borrowed some money … can't keep it up. … My cousin already has hung up on me. … Says he expected the 20 dollars he gave me. … I can't be a burden on them. I have to get out of this myself.

Randy's comments reveal that even under the best of circumstances, when families are not hostile to subjects, contact is fraught with humiliation and is limited by the impossibility of maintaining a normal, reciprocal relationship. Throughout the period of participant observation, some street people would occasionally mention the possibility of going to their family's homes. They rarely did so. For example, Mitch, who never criticized his family, told me he was going to visit his family in the Midwest with his girlfriend Katherine. A few months later, when I saw him and asked about it, he told me that he hadn't gone. "No, it would be too painful, too humiliating. What would I say to them … say about where I've been, who I am?" Further, Mitch does not want their advice and sympathy: "What's the best that would happen? They'd insist I stay there. … My dad [would] give me money. … No, I'll survive here. [I] don't want [their] charity."

Although contact with the world of parents and relatives is difficult for street people—fraught with overtones of failure and role loss—the majority of subjects also avoided their families because of prior episodes of hostility and conflict. Tina, a 32-year-old woman with cerebral palsy, had been in and out of group homes and was finally getting her own apartment several years ago when her mother arrived in town. Tina was furious in describing what happened:

She told the landlord that I couldn't live there. I'd be a lousy tenant! She ruined it for me! … She always hated me. Always has interfered with me. … I guess she just thinks I should be in an institution or something.

Our first-hand experiences with the subjects during the study confirmed the hostility that many street people blamed on their families of origin. Ron, a 38-year-old street person, gave me a telephone number of his one living relative, an uncle, so I might talk with him. I reached the uncle, only to receive a blistering attack on Ron:

He's smarter than we are … found a way not to work and to be supported. … He's lazy, oversexed, a scourge on us [name of family].

Like Tina's mother, Ron's uncle felt he should be in an institution. This was also the case in our contact with Wally's family, the 77-year-old subject who subsequently died. Wally's son Louie had tried to get his father into a nursing home and could not understand his father's resistance:

He took none of our help. Told us we were crazy, that we hated him. ... Just trying to get him off the streets, into a home where, you know, professionals would take care of him.

In the cases of Tina, Ron, Wally, and others, families saw institutionalization as the only solution to their homeless relatives' problems. Subjects' insistence on remaining on the streets and avoiding their relatives was often an exercise in self-preservation. To the relatives, of course, the loss of freedom imposed by going to a mental hospital, a group home, or a nursing home was "for the good" of the family member.

Several families were instrumental in having children removed from the custody of street people. Agnes, a 23-year-old homeless woman, had arranged to give her child to an aunt 3 years earlier. The tragic result was told tearfully to an interviewer:

I had felt good about this. I mean, instead of her [child] going into foster care, I mean, arranged with my mom and aunt that she would be kept in the family. They said, "Great, Agnes, you can visit anytime." ... Everything arranged (cries) ... then they prevented me from coming (tears) ... actually had cops remove me ... said [they] didn't want [child] to follow my footsteps.

I traveled with Dorry and Betty to visit their 22-year-old daughter Tanya, who had appeared on the cohort list of street people. Tanya now lived in a rural town in an overcrowded trailer with her husband Mark. Both Tanya and Mark had been street people in North City until 1990. During the long car ride, the parents—themselves barely surviving economically—castigated Mark at length while pledging their love and fondness for their daughter. Only after we had arrived at the trailer and I had spoken privately with Tanya and Mark did I realize that the family was in litigation over Dottie, Tanya's 3-year-old daughter.

A year earlier, Tanya's mother had reported her to the state social services department for child neglect, suggesting that Tanya was a prostitute. Dottie had been removed temporarily from the home, and Tanya tearfully told me that Dottie was due to return to the family in several months if certain conditions were met. When her parents were gone, she told me between her tears:

I've never, never been a hooker. (cries) She [her mother] made this up ... and I said so in court. ... You see, when she was a kid, she was taken from her mother, put in foster care. I think she [her mother] is jealous of me, jealous that now I have a place and a child. ... (cries) She's just a sick person.

To most street people, families of origin were abusive in nature and psychologically dysfunctional. They feared they would punish them through institutionalization or by taking away their children and disapproving of their life-style. Subjects, moreover, felt their families were hypocritical in their moralistic attitudes about work, appearance, and family life. Street people were particularly attuned to hypocrisy and to the possibility of appearances fooling people. In commenting on her family, Agnes told us:

> My family [wi]ll fool you. [They] look good. [They] make a good presentation. Tell you something … you know how my mother and father met? My aunt was screwing around on her husband with my father, and then he [her father] met my mom. Real nice, huh? They won't tell you this.

Like Agnes, street people were often scornful toward their families of origin because of deceit, infidelity, incest, violence, theft, and abuse. The stories reflected their anger and hostility but also served as an intellectual defense of their own identities. To a great degree, the street people defined themselves in opposition to their families' behavior. Randy told me, "You dress me up right, like my father, and I'd be respectable too. I'm as good as them … but I have better morals." Louise said, "I'd like to see these people, like my mother … I'd like to see them live on the streets. Not to drink or take drugs to get away from it, from the feelings. They wouldn't survive it as I did."

Although too little is known from the point of view of the families of origin to generalize, it is possible to speculate that the families' reaction to their "black sheep" is one of hurt, guilt, and anger. The families we spoke to expressed pain over the rejection by their children. This pain was closely followed by anger at the life-style and routines of their children, perhaps because they saw these as reflections of their own child-rearing abilities. It would not be surprising to find that the hostility of study subjects toward their families is reciprocated.

Resistance to Traditional Family Forms

Unlike adult relationships with families of origin, which vary greatly among the general population,[3] adult needs for companionship, social support, sex, and nurturance are normatively centered in the family. An individual's failure to re-create a nuclear family means that innovative strategies are necessary for meeting basic human needs. Although some street people in Checkerboard Square seemed lonely, few fit this stereotype. In fact, some observers in North City held the opposite belief. For example, Nina reflected some of the popular wisdom in the streets with her comments about the "goings on" among street people during the tent city protest:

> Well, let me tell you, if you came down at night [to tent city], no one was in their own tent! It was sex and more sex and more sex. Everybody knows everyone and has been with everyone. … It was disgusting … and a lot of street people are like this, always [having sex].

In our experience, the reality of life on the streets of North City seemed to conform neither to the stereotypes of isolation implied by some writers nor to a world free of social restraint in which an orgy of sex constantly occurred as conjured up by Nina and others. Although we found a strong centrifugal pull away from traditional family forms and thus certainly less committed monogamy, relatively few adult street people engaged in constant promiscuity. Although street kids and some older alcoholics (see Chapter 7) did appear at times to be free of constraints, most adult street people seemed to have two predominant orientations toward love relationships. One orientation, particularly among homeless and formerly homeless women, was to avoid any love relationships based on their horrific family experiences and poverty. A second orientation among street people was engagement in long-term, but loosely organized and permeable, heterosexual or homosexual partnerships that sometimes entailed conflict and sexual straying.

For about half of the subjects interviewed, the effects of poverty and street life, and their own critical penetrations of relationships and family, led to an avoidance of long-term love interests. Just as the roles of son or daughter, sister or brother, were often shed, there seemed to be a high premium placed on "traveling light"—not only with few possessions but also without a partner to weigh one down. Negative experiences with family and with adult relationships influenced such decisions. Such orientations appeared among street people of varying ages:

Ruth, age 23: My problem really was I always wanted to be with somebody. ... [Now] I want to be by myself. ... Look what happened to me with men. ... I don't trust anyone to be with me.

Lorraine, age 40: I got married 3 weeks after meeting my husband. Now I can give you 100 reasons not to get married ... but I see [relationships of the past] as extremely bad for me.

Tiny, age 62: Remarriage? Wow. ... No, I have a lot of other things to worry about, like just surviving and getting enough to eat. ... I'm long beyond marriage material ... this I'm sure [of].

In some instances, role shedding meant painful losses, as illustrated in the decisions of several street people to voluntarily surrender their children. Agnes discusses how she came to give up her second daughter:

I just couldn't handle it. I just didn't want her to have the same life as me. It's not responsible. I mean, this was my choice—my mom would have taken me in and then I'd be living at home, or I could give her up. Awful [choice] ... but I couldn't do it to her, let her grow up on [the] streets.

As agonizing as it is, role shedding seems understandable for street people whose daily lives are characterized by uncertainty and often hunger and danger. It is a functional, if tragic, adaptation to the harshness of street life. But it is also not an alien or an unnatural decision to disavow long-term relationships or having children, as is becoming increasingly evident in the late-twentieth-century

United States. In fact, Ruth, Lorraine, and Agnes have much in common with some of their middle-class feminist peers. Although they articulate their motivations somewhat differently, their decision to not have families resembles the same coming to terms with their own separate needs and with distancing themselves from the need for a male companion as is true for middle-class women (see Golden, 1992, for a similar normalization of the experience of homeless women). The homeless, particularly women, are caught in a no-win situation: They, like middle-class women, may be deemed unsuitable and not real women without children and husbands: but when they do have children, many service providers, as well as the public, complain about their propagating with no means of support.

Role shedding needs to be distinguished from the disaffiliation or isolation some observers have noted in studying the homeless. Ruth, Lorraine, and Tiny, for example, were not isolated people nor at all unpleasant to be with. As is explored in more depth in Chapters 6 and 7, all three had extensive social networks of friends. Their role shedding, then, is not a function of pathology or of disability but is more a conscious choice. Their failure to want the husband-wife-lover role was not forced upon them, nor did it prevent them from accepting other roles, such as friendship and membership in a group or a community.

Those street people who did form partnerships appeared to develop a range of caring relationships characterized by loose, permeable bounds. They were not established by marriage, were not usually monogamous, and were often episodic. Subjects were self-conscious that relationships were limited both by the exigencies of low-income life and by their preference for nonbinding ties, particularly among the men:

Brad, on his relationship with Cheryl: I care for her [Cheryl]: ... but if you ask me, will I be with her next month, who knows? I can't tell you if I'll be alive next month. I've never known security. Been on the streets since I've been 12 ... and, oh no, can't even talk about marriage or any of that.

Sidney, now housed for 2 years with Linda: I couldn't have stayed housed without her [Linda], we've made it together ... but marriage, oh no ... I won't go through that again. No, can't commit, not beyond tomorrow.

During the course of the study, consistent turnover and strife occurred in the partnerships I observed. Many of these quarrels and conflicts seemed similar to those that imperil many relationships in all social classes, and they sometimes turned violent. It was striking, however, that given the impermanence of the lives of street people, the pull of violence and drugs and alcohol, and the pressures of jail and poverty, so many relationships managed not only to ebb and flow but to survive. Often the couples parted for some time, evidently to allow the partners to leave the area or to change mates, but they later returned to the partnership.

For example, Jack, a 39-year-old gay man, was living with Henri when we first met him. He reported to us several weeks later that he had a screaming fight with Henri and the latter had left him and was hitchhiking to Miami. Jack was then evicted since he could not afford the rent on the SRO he had shared with Henri. After several months in which we lost touch with Jack and he was evidently homeless, he was found to be housed again and back with Henri. "We made up," Jack reported. "He had to get his anger out of his system. [I] think he went back to some [other] guy for awhile."

Karl and Lois, both in their twenties, have been a couple sporadically since the tent city protest and have a child named Ian. They can frequently be seen crossing the plaza of Checkerboard Square hand in hand. Yet Lois and Ian live in an apartment recently arranged by social services, and Karl is still on the streets. Karl, despite new AFDC rules allowing married males to be covered, is not included in Lois and Ian's welfare check. Karl and Lois frequently squabble, separate, and avow that they will never go back to each other. Neither considers marriage or even living together at this point, a decision that is supported by various counselors involved with the three.

The raising of children also provides some contrasts with dominant middle-class or working-class patterns. A majority of these subjects, generally classified as single homeless, were parents. In many cases, as noted, their children had been removed by the state protective services. Others had left children with former spouses whom they had not seen for years. A surprising number, however, had also arranged for their young children to be cared for by housed members of the community. Ian stayed with his mother, Lois, who was housed, and a number of Nina's homeless friends brought their children to stay with her. Beth, Sara, and Amanda were all friends with young children who at various times had lived at Nina's home rather than on the streets. They grew up calling Nina, rather than their biological mothers, their mother.

The loose partnerships and innovative strategies of both partnering and child care create havoc for census takers and researchers attempting to categorize street people. A researcher arriving in North City would find Karl describing himself as single, as would Lois. Sara, Beth, and Amanda would all probably appear to be childless. Such underestimates of the degree of affiliation and family ties of the homeless is not simply a result of carelessness but stems from the fact that on any given day, Karl might tell a census taker that he has no girlfriend, Lois would say she has no boyfriend, and Beth, Sara, and Amanda might not mention their children. (Mothers who are on the street do not volunteer this information often for fear of reprisal by welfare officials, who can charge them with neglect and find their temporary caretakers to be poor parents; others are so distraught about their situation that they prefer to not discuss their feelings of pain and loss surrounding their children's fate with any strangers.) Because love relationships and parental ties are not obvious or immediately observable, only a longitudinal approach to research can document these patterns of relationships.

Street people also do not always conform with middle-class notions of morality. For example, a student researcher was surprised that after she had interviewed Amanda, a 29-year-old homeless person, Amanda left for a rendezvous with Zack, her friend Sara's husband. When Sara found out, she was furious and even blamed the student researcher for driving Amanda to meet Zack. The scene was complicated somewhat by the fact that Sara was planning to leave Zack because of his threats of abuse. We were often unable (and unwilling, for privacy reasons) to verify many reported liaisons between the street people, although we did hear many stories.

In sum, in the Checkerboard Square community we found both conformity and much resistance to dominant social norms, in terms of romantic and family ties. To the extent that most street people did seek to have one partner for companionship, sex, and sustenance, the language and expectations of the mating game between the sexes (and among the gay men[4]) resembled the culture of other classes. The language and symbols of partnership (although we must keep in mind the fact that the people were addressing middle-class interviewers) were similar to those with which we are all familiar. Yet in many ways, street people were resistant to traditional family forms. Most street people were contemptuous of marriage ("Never get me to city hall," "I'm not going to no ceremonies" "Ain't getting me into that again"), tolerant of promiscuity and changing partners ("Yeah, it doesn't bother me, it's natural," "That's the way of the streets"), and innovative rather than relying on traditional nuclear families to raise children.

The interpretation of researchers depends on which norms are seen as natural. Many researchers admit the decline of marriage in the low-income community but stress its temporary nature; for example, Wilson (1987) documents the "low marriageability pool" in the ghettos as preventing more marriages. It is true that innovative and nonfamily forms are adaptations to poverty and that many homeless people, particularly men, mentioned their failure to make a living as preventing any commitment (a point similar to Wilson's). Yet as we have seen, the nonfamily consciousness of the street people also suggests that such adaptations were also based on their desire to avoid further experiences with divorce, domestic violence, and other hostile and bitter experiences in marriage or in long-term partnerships. So rather than saying that poverty prevents the natural desire for marriage and stable relationships from occurring, we might cite the fact that once people—particularly men—are freed from the bonds of property, inheritance, and conventional norms of respectability grounded in middle-class or working-class life, they find no particular gain or reward in marriage or other trappings. The self-conscious resistance to marriage among these street people, then, may or may not be deviant but rather simply reflect the absence of the societal pressure and social control over relationships that exist in other social classes.

As noted in Chapter 1, the different patterns of "family" life that do emerge in Checkerboard Square often result in the poor being severely punished by the social welfare system. For example, if a woman places her children with others (as

Agnes and Nina's friends did), she sacrifices all her welfare benefits since she is no longer eligible for AFDC. The decision by Karl not to live with his girlfriend Lois prevented him from receiving AFDC benefits. Because most partnerships formed by those on the streets were informal, North City's better-financed system of family shelters did not serve these homeless people who were judged to be "nonfamilies." At the time of the tent city protest, for example, Mark and Tanya were denied a bed at a family shelter in North City because they were unmarried. In this sense, alternative forms of family—from unmarried heterosexual partnerships to gay partnerships to children being cared for by nonrelatives—are subverted and repressed by the social welfare system, making deviants and pariahs out of some of the homeless and the very poor.

Notes

1. It must be noted that since the subjects interviewed occupied, by any assessment, the lowest social status in the United States, their frequent attribution that a sibling was "doing fine" is very relative. Interviewers probed the status of parents, siblings, and other family members, attempting to secure accounts of their occupations and current living situations that were as complete as possible. In some cases, subjects were too out of touch with their families to answer questions adequately. In almost all cases in which data were obtained, however, some siblings (as well as parents, aunts, uncles, cousins, and others) were "doing well" in the sense of having housing, or work. Of course, "doing well" varied between families of origin that were middle class and those that were quite poor. But even among families that were quite poor, no widespread homelessness was usually found throughout the entire family system.

2. It has become fashionable, even among otherwise progressive social service workers and consumers of self-help groups, to cite alcoholism or alcoholic family members ("adult children of alcoholics") as an explanatory concept, as if having labeled this social problem they have explained it. The zest with which some people apply this analysis reminds me of William Ryan's (1971) "the savage art of discovery," in which a label is used to essentially dismiss something and to "blame the victim." Some analysts, however, would seek to reduce all homelessness to having resulted from economic causes, but, of course, even groups of unemployed workers from the same plants have different degrees of access to resources and far different social outcomes to economic distress based on a host of variables.

3. Rosenthal (1989), in comparing family contacts among homeless people with those of the general population, takes the position that the difference between their contact is significant but not remarkable. He cites Klatzky's (1972) finding that 21 percent of all the sons surveyed had contact with their fathers one or fewer times a year and Davis and Smith's (1988) finding that 41 percent of the public surveyed had contact with their parents less than once a month.

4. We were not aware of lesbian relationships within this particular sample. It is unclear whether the gay relationships were simply more public than lesbian relationships or if the latter were absent from the streets of North City at the time.

4

"Get a Job": The Limits of the Work Ethic

A discussion with several street people about job openings at a large North City restaurant known as a tourist trap:

Interviewer: Are any of you going to apply for these jobs?

Harry: Not me, I can survive without that guy.

Sidney: Let me tell you about [the owner]. ... What a phony he is. ... I worked there, so did Roland, so did Rudy [other street people] ... never even paid us what he owed us. ... Screw him.

Agnes: [We] may be poor, but we have some pride. ... I can do a lot of things rather than work there.

To those who constantly berate the homeless or the very poor to "get a job," responses such as these in which jobs are rejected are considered the source of the poor's problems and are immoral. Christopher Awalt, a columnist who was once presumably sympathetic to the homeless but is now hostile, writes sardonically in *Newsweek* (Sept. 30, 1991) that most homeless people will not work, and he challenges the reader:

> Please don't take my word for it. The next time you see someone advertising that he'll work for food, take him up on it. Offer him a hard day's work for an honest wage, and see if he accepts. ... My guess is you won't find many takers. The truly homeless won't stay around. (p. 13)

In sharp contrast to Awalt and other critics of the poor, advocates and most social scientists have suggested that lack of work, a deindustrialized economy that provides too little income from work, and structural barriers to work are the basic causes of poverty (see, for example, Blau, 1992; Hopper & Hamburg, 1984; Kozol, 1988; Marcuse, 1988; Ropers, 1988). Normally, the liberal defense of the poor—including comments by social workers, service providers, and social scientists—is to deny that poor people typically reject work and to suggest that all poor people want to work. As with the debate about "choice" and the homeless discussed in Chapter 2, my experience in North City suggests the complexity underlying the normative discourse about the very poor in U.S. society. Indeed, unemployment, structural barriers to work, and deindustrialization shape the context of poverty in North City. But although the liberal and social scientific approach to poverty is a vast improvement over the purely moralistic view of much of the public and of observers such as Awalt, on examination this vision of lower-class life is as utopian as the conservative view is punitive. Asking the poor if they want work, like asking almost anyone if they want to be a doctor or a lawyer when they grow up, is sure to get a positive answer. The desire to work for decent wages begs the question of what actual structural choices exist for the poor, not only in the 1980s and 1990s but more generally in U.S. history. The poor want to work at good wages, but they do not usually *expect* to do so any time soon (or within their entire lives); hence, their actions differ from the psychology of the blue-collar worker or the middle-class professional. Rather than being immoral, I suggest that people like the homeless in Awalt's example often consciously resist the demands made on them by employers, city welfare officials, and the public that their income-generating strategies follow a clear path to McDonalds, Burger King, or other low-wage jobs. Since poor people suffer severe penalties for refusing certain types of work, they usually do so in a hidden way and often do not advertise such actions. Contrary to conservative and liberal rhetoric, poor people are often quite realistic about the limits of work in bringing about upward mobility.

Myths About Work and the Poor

Awalt's (1991) article provides a good example of the ideological context of work and poverty in the United States. It is worth examining because the actions of street people only come to be defined as deviant within a rigid, highly stereotypical context that tends to be applied exclusively to poor people in America. Awalt (1991) asserts:

> For every person temporarily homeless, though there are many who are chronically so ... these homeless are content to remain as they are. They enjoy the freedom and consider begging a minor inconvenience. They know they can always get a job for a day or two for food, cigarettes and alcohol. The sophisticated among them have learned to use the system for what it's worth and figure that a trip to the welfare line is less trouble than a steady job. (p. 13)

Awalt's harsh description is consistent with views that go back 300 years in its characterizations of the "undeserving poor." First, Awalt acknowledges no barriers to regular, steady employment for the homeless or the very poor. Presumably, the unwashed, smelly, tattered individual is to show up at some place of employment and ask for work. Having not eaten or slept sufficiently, and very possibly suffering from some physical ailment or psychological stress, these people will nonetheless find a warm welcome from employers, who will place them on an assembly line or behind a cash register. As I describe, most of North City's subjects have tried to do just this, usually to be hastily shown the door (if not a paddy wagon) by those doing the hiring.

In this stereotypical view of the undeserving poor, barriers that would be taken into account for middle-class or working-class people are forgotten when applied to the poor. That is, if told that a middle-class person was physically or mentally ill, had been burned out of his or her house or apartment, or had been a victim of a flood or an earthquake, most Americans—liberal or conservative—would think of disaster relief or health care rather than asking about the person's current employment status. If, however, the person is poor and visible, work status seems to become the primary public concern rather than hunger, illness, disease, or frostbite.

Second, and also consistent with the past 300 years of mainstream Western thought, Awalt is contemptuous of the fact that some of his homeless "get a job for a day or two." One would think that an author so committed to the work ethic and responsibility might applaud such a pattern as opposed to having the impoverished show no work initiative. Yet credit is withheld since presumably, such work is not "a steady job" and is entered into and left *at will* by the street person.

Here, then, is a historic theme that middle-class observers agree on: Consistent, regularized work for a low-wage employer is required of poor people, although self-employment, casual work, or "off-the-books" income is ignored or accepted if performed by those in higher social classes. As we will see, the homeless and formerly homeless of North City engage in a wide variety of free-lance work, casual work, day labor, and off-the-books work ranging painting pictures and performing music to cutting fish and washing dishes (not to mention some illegal pursuits such as selling drugs or being a prostitute). Perhaps the only explanation for this dualism (e.g., a typist working her way through college can sell her services off the books with a minimum of disapprobation, whereas a poor person cleaning houses or babysitting off the books is more suspect) can be gleaned from the purposes of the "deterrent doctrine of relief," best described by Piven and Cloward (1971:33–35). Relief and consequent social control over the poor in Western society were entered into with the purpose of "spurring men to contrive ways of supporting themselves by their own industry, *to offer themselves to any employer on any terms*" [italics in original] Piven & Cloward, 1971:34). If capitalist society is dependent upon recruiting a supply of workers for low-wage industries, as Piven and Cloward argue, then the ability of many low-income people to resist workplace discipline by surviving through nonmarket transactions (as well as through social benefits) historically came to be conceived of as criminal. The success of poor people in avoiding the marketplace was a mark of viciousness and indolence.

The stigmatization of the poor who work as transitory workers or casual workers appears to be as old as U.S. history. Citizenship in the colonies and in early U.S. history was based on ownership of property, usually from full-time farming. In their original Poor Laws (see Trattner, 1989), the colonies reserved the harshest treatment for those poor people who were not locals but who were migrating from town to town. Katz (1986, Chapter 1) has shown how the victims of poor relief policies in the nineteenth century were often seasonal or migratory workers who were out of work. Although no doubt part of the thrust of the U.S. regulation of the poor through the Poor Laws and the harsh U.S. settlement laws was fiscal (to limit the poor tax each town had to collect) and to a degree was also xenophobic (the stranger in town was a subject of religious and, later, ethnic fear), over time this became a class prejudice. All those without "settlement" (a home, a farm) were judged as deviants, and their poverty was associated with a wide variety of maladies, ranging from religious dissent to political trouble. One often forgets that the "liberty" touted by the American Revolution applied only to white men with property who were, in Jeffersonian terms, the "yeomanry"—that is, those who owned property. Those people who wandered to get occasional construction or canal work were excluded from all such rights.

With the rise of industrial capitalism and the need for a cheap labor pool, these attitudes hardened. The nation was developed and expanded through the creation, first, of a large native labor pool and then through a large, cheap immigrant force. Employers and government officials fought any efforts to regulate working conditions or to potentially raise the wages of this cheap labor force by developing adequate poor relief. The large, cheap "reserve army of labor" created by U.S. capitalism reinforced already existing prejudices of Americans toward the poor who worked.

Importantly, as Piven and Cloward (1971) note about the doctrine of "less eligibility," which had begun by at least the nineteenth century, government joined a growing private sector in forcing the poor to work at low-paying jobs. The policy's intent was never for the able-bodied poor to collect relief, but it was also not for the poor to work sporadically. Implicitly, the poor could gain respectability only through formal labor as farm hands, factory workers, and so forth. Henry Miller's (1991) social history of the poor reminds us that the American "hobos"—the migratory workers who served the needs of Western expansion in the 1865–1917 period—were highly stigmatized, and the group was felt to attract men who were already deviant and restless. After the closing of the West, the creation of skid rows led to a class of "bums" who were closely linked to the need for day labor in the central cities of Chicago, Seattle, New York, and elsewhere. These poor people always worked but often on *their own terms* (as is the case with North City's street people). For at least 300 years, then, the poor person who works but who does not do so in a regular, steady, and settled way has been associated with vagrancy and deviancy.

Finally, Awalt's (1991) description contains a third myth—that "use of the system" (going on welfare) is easier than working. Such a thought would be laughable to our subjects, who bitterly resent welfare requirements, the surveillance imposed upon them as a result of collecting benefits, and the stigma of the modern poorhouse, including the treatment they receive in homeless shelters (see Chapter 5). The reality in North City, as elsewhere, is that most people enter the relief system only with great trepidation, and once they do, they become engaged in a constant struggle to retain benefits. Most people receive benefits only temporarily or periodically (Levitan, 1990:7, 55).[1] Until recent years, many people had been able to combine benefits with work; only because of the reductions in the possibilities for supplementing assistance with work due to government policy (Levitan, 1990:54) is there now an incentive either not to work or to work off the books if one is receiving social benefits.

In actuality, the subjects of North City moved and off social benefits depending on a variety of factors, including availability of work, the wages offered, working conditions, travel time, fringe benefits, and so forth. It is interesting that whereas such decisions (to work or not, and where and when) arouse moral fervor when they involve the poor, these are the very same elements other classes weigh in making economic decisions. For example, many members of middle-class society leave their jobs—particularly jobs that pay poorly or that are disappointing—to care for their children, and surveys indicate that an increasing number of men as well as women either opt out of the marketplace for a period of time or reduce their hours or earning potential to be with their families (*Boston Globe*, November 24, 1991:1, 26). A large number of middle-class people, particularly the young, quit their jobs to go to school. They often consciously plan such studies to coincide with the receipt of unemployment insurance, social security survivors insurance, or veterans' assistance—all of which are social benefits. Middle-class workers quit their jobs regularly, often without having another or to go to work for themselves (the "burnout" literature in the social services and in nursing contains many accounts sympathetic to these professionals; see, for example, Kramer, 1974, and Cherniss, 1980). A middle-class person, such as a social worker or a nurse, can quit a job because of poor working conditions or lack of satisfaction or because of a desire to fulfill other needs (child care, work closer to home, and the like) and not be castigated. But low-income people who act in an identical fashion are immediately subject to disapproval by the public, as well as to suspicion and repression by the welfare system.

Deindustrialization as the Economic Context

As noted in Chapter 1, deindustrialization is the primary social structural change involved in the current increase in poverty. The lack of employment and the decline in the number of blue-collar jobs that once provided decent wages for many Americans with relatively low levels of education provide our context. Such framing, however, does not mean a one-to-one relationship exists between homelessness and deindustrialization: Whereas some authors (see especially Ropers, 1988) imply that the homeless are recently laid-off workers (the "deserving" poor), this study, as well as others on the homeless, does not find this (Rossi, 1989; Shinn & Weitzman, 1990; Snow & Anderson, 1992). Some former blue-collar workers do become homeless, but this usually follows a number of intervening events. Other subjects who are too young to have experienced the prospects of having blue-collar jobs, are affected as dramatically by the crisis; and other older poor people, who never held jobs as steelworkers, autoworkers, or textile workers find their prospects to be totally closed off.

Many younger subjects in our study have *never* held good jobs and never expect to find them. They are not the victims of layoffs or plant closings: Deindustrialization is the unseen context that has closed off areas of opportunity that structured the U.S. economy between 1945 and 1973. Hence, the impact of deindustrialization transcends the millions of immediate victims and more permanently limits the structural alternatives of millions of others.

As with other samples of homeless people, subjects in the North City cohort have a low level of education, with most never having finished high school.[2] Many grew up in small urban or rural New England communities that depended historically on mill work or farm labor. In decades past, our subjects would have followed their parents into shoe mills, textile mills, paper mills, light manufacturing factories, and farming. The largest percentage of homeless interviewed for this study, in fact, grew up in working-class or farming homes as sons or daughters of operatives, skilled or semiskilled workers, or farmers. In discussing their biographies, the young men in particular (ages 18–35) in this study noted with disappointment that they were unable to follow their parents' or neighbors' footsteps into industrial jobs:

Sidney: My father worked 20 years in a rubber plant, my [older] brothers went there too, but when I grew up this plant had closed. … [I had to] start working in a gas station.

Mark: Let's face it, I saw no opportunity where I grew up [rural area of New England]. … [My] father was a meat cutter, [but] there weren't any jobs like that any more. … In fact, he was [forcibly retired]. … What was I gonna prepare to be in school? A toilet scrubber?

Our subjects grew up with little hope of achieving the kind of steady employment their families had enjoyed. Some reacted to this fact (obviously in conjunction with other factors) by developing a rebellious attitude as early as junior high or senior high school, leaving school and entering the underground economy, where they engaged in illegal activities. Others went to work in fast-food restaurants, hotels and motels, or convenience stores. A few—primarily those from more middle-class backgrounds and with more education, such as Joel, Ralph, and Mitch—held some low-level white-collar jobs. Many of the women were even more cut off from the job market than were the men, often because they dropped out of school at a very young age and became pregnant early. Female subjects' work prior to becoming homeless was overwhelmingly in low-skill or casual employment such as babysitting, hair styling, housecleaning, or waitressing.

Of course, these low-paid workers received no fringe benefits, had no union protection when they had grievances, and had no employee assistance programs to help when they had personal or job-related problems. Many subjects had been repeatedly fired from or quit a variety of jobs following personal crises or economic disasters, which are common in the low-income community (a car breaking down means being unable to get to work; an illness without sick time may mean being fired or forced to quit; marital conflicts or problems with children occur and no personal days are available; a fire or broken furnace in the apartment means missing work). It is this combination—of low-wage work combined with the wide variety of problems that have always plagued low-income people—that led to increased levels of homelessness in the 1970s and 1980s (in conjunction with the decline in the amount of low-income housing and cuts in social welfare benefits).

The difference between my focus and that of other authors who discuss deindustrialization (Blau, 1992; Harrington, 1984; Katz, 1989; Kozol, 1988; Wilson, 1987) relates to the degree to which I argue the context of deindustrialization has changed the aspirations of the poor, particularly the young, and how anger and resistance mark their daily lives. Since our subjects do understand in an insightful—if nonacademic—way that options are closed, they frequently confront employers, resist work demands, and choose other survival strategies that are independent of the primary labor force. To the extent that this norm of resistance dominates a subculture of poor people, it is not clear whether the creation of more jobs alone or possibly even of good jobs will immediately change the world of the Checkerboard Square subjects.

Is "Get a Job" a Realistic Response?

No matter what work experience subjects had prior to becoming homeless (since the Checkerboard community includes subjects ranging in age from 16 to 77, the length of work experience varied from a very few years to several decades), the possibility of working while homeless is fraught with such significant barriers that subjects had considerable bitterness toward those who nonchalantly demand that they work in that situation. Most subjects stated that they had tried to work while homeless, only to have employers reject them (or in some cases to hire them, then fire them after a short time). Virtually all subjects cited a lack of adequate clothing and an inability to keep clean due to a lack of public shower facilities as major problems in getting and keeping jobs. Many pointed out that it is hard to be disciplined about work when one has no alarm clock or transportation and must comply with shelter requirements such as curfews, which often do not fit work shifts. Many employers categorically refused to hire people with no address, presumably because they are unavailable for overtime or cannot be contacted if they are absent. Cora and Darryl were typical in citing the many problems of homeless people regarding work:

Cora: I had a couple of jobs [while homeless], but they didn't last too long because I didn't sleep good at night. I mean, you don't know what it's like to be sleeping under a bridge and being scared all the time, getting maybe 2 or 3 hours of sleep. Sure, I was late [to her job at a pizza place], and I fell asleep there a few times. That's why they fired me.

Darryl: I got a job at [name of restaurant]. I figured, "Ok, I'll save a few dollars and get a place [to live]." Well, 3 days later, the manager, he says I'm violating [the] restaurant code because I was cleaning myself in the kitchen. … I mean, where else was I going to clean myself?

Problems with health, with the police, and with travel are just a few of the many other barriers cited by subjects that interfered with their working. Bert, for example, was a street person who was diagnosed with cancer while working as a waiter in a restaurant. Bert said he liked his job and thought the people there liked him, but when he asked for 3 days off to go to the hospital for an operation, he was told, "Sorry, Bert, we can't hold jobs for anyone, 3 days, whatever. It's not personal, Bert, it's just business." Randy was working as janitor in an auditorium when one day he was picked up by police and held after a minor scuffle:

I kept trying to call them [people at the auditorium] to tell them I wasn't coming in, and [I] would get no answer. It's pretty hard from the jail to make calls, and by the time I did reach them, they said, "Sorry, Randy, you've been fired."

Roy, one of the relatively few subjects who had held a number of skilled jobs—some when he was living out of his car in the mid-1980s—lost a job doing dry wall construction in the suburbs after he lost his car:

The city towed my car! I mean, this is something maybe, yeah, happens to other people, but they [the city] wanted $200 in fees. I couldn't pay it, I was just surviving, and then when they wouldn't give me my car, after I pleaded, I couldn't get to the job and I had no home! [I] ended up back on city [welfare] and in [a] shelter.

During the tent city protest in 1987, jobs became a public issue for North City's homeless when a group of employers came to the encampment and made a highly public offer of jobs. "If they want to work, they certainly can," claimed local employers at a press conference. A day later, Rudy, a young homeless man who had recently been fired by a restaurant owner who had just offered jobs to the homeless, spoke at a counter–press conference organized by the protesters. Rudy had gone back to his employer but was not given his job back despite the employer's public offer:

This was totally hypocritical [on the part of the employer]. Just a public relations thing! When I went up to him, he said, "No, you need an address to work here, I won't hire you." Yeah, so I participated in the TV conference. I was pissed.

Almost all of the subjects interviewed remembered, and commented with hostility toward, the actions of the employers in July 1987 and the reaction of the public (many people wrote letters to the local newspapers during the tent city occupation urging the protesters to get jobs!). Unquestionably, as can be ascertained from press reports and subjects' memories, most of the "jobs" offered never materialized. Some resistance to authority characterized the Checkerboard community, however, as can be seen in Eric's claims that he told off the group of employers even before he looked into any of the jobs:

So these people [employers] come down [to tent city] and offer us these jobs. … They say, "You know, you don't have work, we'll hire you for $4 an hour." Some of us said to them, "Come on, you guys, we sleep on benches, we have no homes, we have no clothes, come on." I said, "I'm getting angry … look, how about offering us room in your nice homes for awhile, and then [sure], I'll take a job with you."

Eric's anger is indicative of the close tie that exists between the subjects' bitterness and their resistance to employers and others' entreaties to "get a job."

The Hidden "Culture of Resistance"

As is the case with the homeless families interviewed by Kozol (1988) and those discussed in the thousands of human interest stories about the homeless, in interviews North City subjects stated that they wanted to work. But although a number of subjects worked consistently in the service sector and two or three subjects had escaped poverty through work,[3] for most subjects followed over a period of years, it was not only the limited availability of work and the barriers to working while homeless that limited work but also their resistance to low pay, employer control, and poor working conditions. Some subjects even fit Awalt's (1991) stereotypes of rarely seeking formal market work.

Many subjects would take certain jobs and not others based on pay:

> **Sidney:** They offered me $4 or $5 an hour [to work as an agency "temporary"], I wouldn't take it! You can't live on that. I have my tools [carpentry], and I won't work below a certain figure.

Other subjects doubted whether any of the types of work available locally would meet their needs. Ron, a 38-year-old street musician, who earns a rather small amount from his performing, when asked if he wanted work:

> No. I like music, and that's what I do best. No, [I'm] … not into getting some job flipping burgers or stuff like that. I'd rather do my music.

Ralph, a 31-year-old college graduate on disability but facing possible termination of benefits as his psychiatric condition improves:

> There is all this pressure to work. Financial, my brother, he pushes me, but my therapist [also], everyone [says], "It's healthy to work." But [the question about work] is an interesting one. No, I don't have an overwhelming desire to work. Not for myself.

In further examining the life histories of the many subjects interviewed in North City, we found that although subjects had held hundreds of jobs, both prior to becoming homeless and while on the streets, many left employment after a short period of time. A number of subjects blamed themselves for their frequent unemployment:

Roland, a 27-year-old formerly homeless man who hangs out at Checkerboard Square:

> Work? I've had seven jobs in the last 2 years. [My] jobs last maybe a few weeks. I guess I just get too pissed off [at bosses] too easily. I have a temper, and when I see them treating people bad, well, I guess I don't hold it in.

Many others expressed the view that employers were at fault for mistreating them and reneging on agreements made at the time employment was entered into:

> **Dennis:** So he [owner of cleaning company that cleans factories and power plants] had told me [that] after 3 months, I'd get a $1 [an hour] raise. What happens? The time passes and [I get] zilch. I went to him and he said "Oh no, I didn't say that." I told him, "Take your goddam job and shove it."

Brad: So this guy [employer at a fish processing company] says we didn't do enough work, and [we] had to stay until so and so amount of fish were done. … I said [to him], "Are we supposed to work for nothing?" Well, one thing led to another, I was out the door.

Just as in Chapter 3 subjects sometimes stated that they would go back to their families of origin but then they did not, we observed that Checkerboard Square subjects often did not follow up on professed intentions to secure jobs. For example, Mark was supposed to leave North City in the summer to pick blueberries in Maine. Several weeks later, Mark told us that he had gone and started to work but had returned after a week because the pay rate on bushels of blueberries had fallen to an extremely low rate and he had a fight with the employer, who Mark said was exploiting his migrant workers. Nina declared a number of times that she was going out to get work. She usually seemed to come back without accepting employment (in the early period of this study, a large number of low-paying jobs were still available; by the 1990s these had been eliminated because of the major recession) or after working only a few days. Nina reported that the wages for institutional housekeeping in the area were so low that she was better off on social benefits and doing cleaning off the books, as she did sporadically. Nina also complained about the working conditions at local motels.

Resistance Versus the Myth of Laziness

If, however, middle-class and official stereotypes about what constitutes work are ignored for the moment, the reality in Checkerboard Square was that most subjects *did* work. The popular ascription (Awalt, 1991, for example) of "laziness" among the poor can only be upheld by ignoring the dominant underground economy of nonwage labor, as well as other productive activities such as parenting, participating in social service activities, and scavenging in order to survive.

At any given time, it appeared that only about a sixth of our subjects were working full time at wage labor. However, at least another half of the subjects had significant earnings off the books in a wide variety of pursuits. At least 50 legitimate types of work can be identified.[4] A few of these were relatively lucrative: Louise, a hairdresser, had developed a considerable clientele; she is now housed. Herb, also now housed, ran a major crafts business out of his home that included producing and selling deerskin coats and wind chimes made of seashells; he also did landscaping. Tiny made a modest income producing picture frames and selling them to galleries.

A large number of subjects were attached to areas of employment that were casual and sporadic, marked by surges of heavy labor alternating with periods of unemployment. The fish piers and the carnival industry were the most popular sources of jobs because in warm weather, when work was busy, one could report to work without concern for dress or demeanor, without the need to make a long-term time commitment, and without the necessity for lengthy job applications or references. More than a dozen people known to researchers would leave Checkerboard Square in the summer to work long hours at the fishing piers or in the amusement industry.

Other Checkerboard Square subjects became associated with local landlords and repaired and rehabilitated their buildings. Such work was popular because it was relatively high paying (and untaxed) when it was available, was highly autonomous, and drew on the blue-collar and construction skills that subjects like Sidney felt required greater skill than did service work (the preference for industrial and construction work is discussed in the section "Holding Out for Skilled Jobs"). Work with social agencies, although much less lucrative than industrial and construction work, was also popular. Mitch, for example, worked on the computers at Friendly Center; Theodore had a job for awhile doing janitorial work at a homeless shelter; and Greg worked for a time as a dishwasher at a program for the mentally ill.

Many income-generating strategies fit the term "shadow work" (Snow & Anderson, 1992)—work traditionally done by homeless or low-income people, such as scavenging, selling junk, performing in public, or selling illegal goods. Jonathan and his girlfriend Nora were profiled in a local newsweekly as part of the number of "bottle people" who combed the streets of North City daily looking for deposit bottles; according to the article, the couple made $20 on a good day. Arnie combined selling his surrealist paintings with doing various types of yard work and hauling junk to landfills when he could borrow a vehicle. Both Judy and May had done work in massage parlors, for escort services, and on telephone sex lines. A large number of the men admitted to having sold drugs, and some admitted to theft. Although our ability to gain subjects' confidence was based in part on our not pursuing details of illegal activities, I was frequently told that "so-and-so" was "laying low" because of criminal activity or a current court warrant. Two subjects interviewed in prison casually named a number of other subjects as having been involved in theft. Such pursuits were often just alluded to, as when Judge told me, "I don't have money problems. I can always get some dough. ... Don't ask me how, please, or I won't talk [to you]." Other times illegal activities were obvious, as when Harry and three friends were unloading video cassette recorders not far from Checkerboard Square.

Questions about the morality of these activities aside, none of these people could be characterized as lazy. Some, like Herb and Louise, were so busy with work that they rarely appeared on the streets. Quite a few subjects disappeared during peak work times in good weather. Subjects like Sidney or Seth working for landlords, and Alicyea working as a live-in babysitter in exchange for room and board, put in twelve-hour days.

Nor does the label "lazy" fit the group at Checkerboard Square, who rarely worked either in the regular or the off-the-books economy. As noted in Chapter 2, many people like Amy and Cora spent a great deal of their time going to AA meetings, attending committee meetings, going to counseling sessions, and so forth. Ralph—while on disability benefits—sat on the executive board of North City's Coalition for the Psychiatrically Labeled, volunteered at the Drop-In center, and worked on a congressional campaign. This hardly fits the usual image of laziness!

Those who rarely performed work of any kind were primarily the mothers of small children and some of the literally homeless who were ill and exhausted. The latter were so bogged down with the struggle for survival that they spent their days in a constant search for shelter; in long lines at the welfare office, soup kitchens, homeless shelters, and clothes closets; and at appointments (often futile) with landlords. This group also spent many hours scavenging for food, panhandling for money, building makeshift shelters, and carting personal belongings long distances.

Just as we separated the issue of "choice" from the limited debate about the homeless in Chapter 2, the issue of work and nonwork must be separated from that of laziness. The visibility of groups of street people spending time in Checkerboard Square obscures the fact that almost all the subjects had hard lives in which they struggled to survive. With the exception of those few who were too battered to care any longer, most subjects also struggled to maximize their incomes within the limited opportunities available to them. Within the framework of their own culture, maximizing income while retaining some autonomy, as well as some hope for the future, involved a subcultural norm of resistance to low-paid wage labor, particularly in the service economy.

Penetrations into the Work World

Brad: There aren't enough laboring jobs around, and we [the poor] don't have the skills for desk jobs … that's about it.

Joel: I'm confronted with the conventional, more mainstream idea of work and a more alternative one in which I think about making a meaningful contribution.

Agnes: They have all these discrimination laws, but they don't talk about discrimination by class—people who can do all the things for a job but just don't have the education, the looks, whatever.

As these quotes attest, some street people of Checkerboard Square had quite sophisticated understandings of work and the economy, including, in a rudimentary way, the gist of deindustrialization (Brad) and the human capital theory of economics (Agnes). Although not all subjects were as sophisticated, they shared a common recognition that they faced a hostile economy, that their futures were bleak, that employment met the needs of low-wage employers rather than of workers, and that they occupied an exploited position within the workplace and society.

The sources of such penetrations into the reality of life at the workplace were varied. Many theorists of education such as Giroux (1983) and Willis (1977) argue that social class relations are reproduced through the educational system and that working-class and low-income students often develop both clear insights and resistant subcultures in school. The biographies of many subjects from lower-class families of origin revealed a strong propensity to resistance long before the subjects became homeless. For example, Eric, Mark, Alicyea, and others noted that they began to skip school and cause problems for teachers as early as grade school. All had given up any real hope of "making it" at an early age (see MacLeod, 1987, for a discussion of aspirations). In contrast, a number of subjects were from middle-class families and were not necessarily down on their luck during childhood. These subjects developed a more conscious and politically oriented resistance later in life. Subjects such as Joel and Arnie, who had extensive counterculture experience, and those like Mitch, who were disgruntled veterans, gained political insight through a social movement orientation. The interaction over time among ex-hippies, radicalized veterans, and the majority of homeless who are children of the poor and the working class in places like Checkerboard Square may help to account for an instinctive form of critical consciousness that exists among many street people.

In contrast to groups of organized radicals or militants, however, subjects' insights remained at the level of a gut feeling or of shared insights. Moreover, they lacked any strategy for effecting change. Most often the antagonism street people felt toward employers took a form that would be considered self-destructive from a middle-class perspective or from a labor or political organizer's vantage point.

Subjects expressed resistance toward and anger at low rates of pay and benefits, at employers' failures to meet commitments and contract stipulations and even to observe laws, at the low levels of skill and the poor working conditions at workplaces, and often at the very structure of work and the priorities of employers.

As in the accounts of Dennis and Brad, many subjects clashed repeatedly with employers over issues such as wages, hours, job security, and working conditions. Like Dennis's experience with the owner of the cleaning company and Brad's experience with the owner of the fish processing company, most subjects quit their positions after arguments with employers. Sidney was hired to do some construction work on a new city shelter. At first he accepted the hourly wage, even though he felt it was low for the framing and finishing work he was hired to do. He began to demand higher pay and also to protest the assignment of nonskilled work, such as dumping trash, to the carpenters. When the contractor refused to make any changes, Sidney quit. Sidney drew upon this and other examples to stress the inequality of the social system:

> They [the rich] expect you to live on nothing. But when you ask for a decent going wage, they think you're crazy. I mean, it's OK for these banks to keep going up [in the city], and these guys make what, $75,000 or $100,000, but if [you] ask for more than

$7 or $8 dollars [an hour] to put up the bank, you're the one that's crazy. It's a greedy world.

Agnes was typical of subjects in describing how she quit her job at Burger King after clashing with the manager about the rule against talking while working:

> I guess I get mad too easily. I can't do this meaningless type of work [that] you could do in your sleep. ... And so you're having a little conversation with someone next to you, and this broad comes out and says, "No talking!" I looked right back at her [the manager] and said, "Is this America, or have I been taken to Russia?" She says, "No" [it's not Russia], and I say, "Well then, I have a right to talk to whoever I want to. ... I came here to work but not for you to tell me what to do. Well, she got real mad, and it was basically quit or I'd be fired.

At times, subjects did petty, antisocial things to get back at employers they disliked:

Del, after getting fish poisoning from cutting shrimp and being denied workers' compensation by the employer:

> So we went back there, a few of us, we were pissed because of what he [the employer] did to us. ... We made a big scene throughout the piers until everybody believed this guy sold diseased shrimp. ... [He] couldn't do business [sell his fish] for weeks after we got through.

Rudy, angered after a girlfriend was fired by a fast-food restaurant for being late:

> So I went and filled out an application and got hired. I called in sick the first day, I called in sick the second day, and the third ... kept doing [it] for a week before they said, "Don't bother." So at least I kept them hanging, holding them up for a week.

Many of the interviews with street people revealed that a high degree of idealism had caused subjects to get in trouble at various points in their work lives both before and after they became homeless. Randy had a job as a mechanic trainee at a tire shop in the 1970s. He felt he needed to spend a certain minimum amount of time checking tires, but the shop he worked in was "more into speed than accuracy. ... [They] just wanted to get them [customers] out [fast], really, they became just salesmen, not mechanics." Randy reported that one day he was fired because his boss learned that had referred a customer to a competitor across the street. "I told him once, I was going to give people the choice of having some service," complained Randy, seeming to still have difficulty comprehending why he was fired more than a decade after the incident.

Subjects from middle-class backgrounds told numerous stories about how their visions of work frequently clashed with those of employers or of job training officials:

Arnie: My first job when I was out of school was in this schlock place to make certain painting designs by the thousands. You know, a stencil of a cow and barn or something. ... Well, of course, you know, I'm into art, and I sabotaged it as much as I could ... always putting little signature-type different things on. I was fired.

Joel: So when I go into voc[ational] rehab[ilitation], they had in mind I could do a clerk job or something. (laughs) I told them I wanted to do massage or holistic healing. The guy looks at me like I have three heads. "No, not practical," he says.

Even some relatively successful ex-street people we met had retained their idealism and sense of self-worth by refusing to do certain types of work or refusing to make certain compromises. Herb, the 48-year-old American Indian Vietnam veteran with the off-the-books craft shop, told us he was approached by a major, nationally known wholesaler. He refused to work with them:

I don't trust them [wholesalers]. I don't trust the price they'd give me, I don't trust that they [would] distribute them [his crafts]. I don't trust that I wouldn't get ripped off. Besides, I'm loyal, my roots [are] as a Navajo, not to some big corporate-like thing.

Louise and Agnes, in separate conversations, both described how they were asked to remove homeless people when they were employed at fast-food restaurants. Both refused on principle, and Louise barely managed to keep her job:

I was furious. Can you imagine, me, I had been there and they wanted me to throw this [homeless] guy out? I got my cool and said to [her co-workers], "The guy is not doing anything, he's having a coffee, and where can he go? There is no place for him. Not until the shelters open." Well, this went round and round, and the manager comes out, but I wouldn't let them throw him out. I told him that if he threw him out, I'd leave, and he [the manager] didn't do anything.

Most subjects recognized that low-paying service jobs would never allow them to escape poverty. Some, like Eric, were optimistic that they would eventually escape the low-wage sector through education:

So these jobs [I've had] flipping burgers, dishwashing, there's no real skills. Any idiot can do these things. [That's why I'm] trying for job training and need to finish school [get a general equivalency diploma]. I'll be down here [on the streets] as long as I don't have degrees or real skill.

Others, such as Telly, were pessimistic about ever escaping the indignities of low pay, lack of security, lack of benefits, and poor working conditions. When he returned to his job as a security guard after a several-month layoff, Telly told me:

I went back. I don't know why except it's better than welfare. But [name of company] it's "bend over and we'll screw you some more." They just take my dignity away every time I take their check. To be standing all night in the cold for less money than it takes to do my laundry! All I ask is to be making $12,000 or $14,000 a year. … You wouldn't think in this country that this is asking too much, is it?

Some Resistant Strategies for Survival

The subjects' insight into the work world—that it is exploitative and that they occupied the very lowest rung of the social ladder—informed many of their strategies to survive. However, their subjective analysis was forced to confront the social reality that they would die of hunger or frostbite on the streets of North City without income. The choices most subjects made about how to generate income were often a compromise between avoiding employer control and exploitation at work and gaining enough income to survive temporarily.

These strategies of survival were hardly random but were structured by the exigencies of the job market and the complex rules of social benefits, as well as subjects' subjective understandings. For most subjects, long-term acceptance of low-paying service work—as waiters or waitresses, cashiers, security guards, or housekeepers—was avoided through three alternative strategies: (1) holding out for blue-collar, industrial, or other skilled work, (2) preferring casual work or day labor, or (3) gaining some relatively regular[5] social benefit income, such as SSI or Social Security disability,[6] and potentially supplementing it with off-the-books work.

Holding Out for Skilled Jobs

I have my tools, and when a good construction job comes, I'm ready.
—Sidney

Particularly among the men of Checkerboard Square, a strong norm existed that blue-collar, industrial, construction, and other skilled work was superior to service work. It made sense to reject low-paying work and to hold out for a "decent job" rather than lose one's dignity (and time and money) working as a cashier or flipping burgers.

The orientation of subjects was influenced by their hostility toward service work and other low-paid labor, which caused them to employ some rational and some not so rational strategies. Peter Marcuse (1988:76) argues that nothing is inherent in service work that dictates that its wage rates should be so low or that this "type of work … facilitate[s] an aggrandizement of power by an employer." Rather, the failure of unions to organize the service sector has meant that wages in that sector have remained artificially depressed; that the industry has avoided paying fringe benefits; and that authority relations in fast-food restaurants, small stores, hotels and motels, and other parts of this employment sector are one sided, with arbitrary production requirements imposed by employers and arbitrary discipline and dismissals.

The low pay, limited benefits, and one-sided authority relations strongly influenced the subjects to avoid such jobs. Seth, who, like Sidney, had construction skills and worked intermittently for landlords, was typical: "Look, I can make $200 in a couple of days [if there is work], so why should I go down to McDonalds and not make that in a week?" Although unions were seldom discussed, implicit in many subjects' conversations was their powerlessness in relation to that of their employers. Kirk remarked:

> Look, my father was a paperworker. They wouldn't stand for this crap we have to put up with. You go to work like in [local security company] and they own ya'. You can't do anything, you can't say a peep or they fire you on the spot. My father wouldn't [have] put up with this.

There are good, pragmatic reasons for some subjects to refuse low-paying work, just as many middle-class people who hope to be professionals or businesspeople do not take low-paying jobs when they are in school or awaiting better jobs. Money can be made much faster in more skilled employment, where adequate benefits also exist to pay for health care and retirement and working conditions are more pleasant, but the vagaries of the economy often make it difficult to predict when skilled employment might become available. This is certainly the case in construction work. Sidney, for example, bemoaned the fact that when the building boom was on, he was "too down under" from homelessness, drink, and lack of skills to compete. He has now finished an apprenticeship and feels he must be available for work: "So if there's a building going up, even in New Hampshire, I've [got to] be ready. What's the point of committing to some other job?"

Yet there are also indications that blue-collar or industrial jobs were often preferred by subjects for reasons that were not economic. Just as Paul Willis (1977) found that part of the "culture of resistance" of young British "lads" he studied included an association between manliness and good, hard blue-collar manual labor, I often felt that service or white-collar work was not perceived as "real" work by many subjects but was indicative of softness and a failure to be strong and manly. This was a consistent undertone in interviews with subjects from working-class families of origin:

> **Del:** I want to be a mechanic. Do something real, not push a pile of papers. That's not real work.

> **Telly, making gestures:** All this crap, "Can I help you, sir," "What can I get you, madam," this type of work is for faggots. It's not for me.

The attributes service employers often seek in workers contrast with those for other types of work and in turn affect potential workers' desire to apply. Blue-collar or casual labor usually requires only physical prowess, skill, and willingness. In contrast, restaurants, hotels, or boutiques seek young, attractive people who are well dressed and who will present themselves to customers with a pleasant and subservient demeanor. The servile aspect of service employment was distasteful to some women as well as the men, as Cora stated clearly: "I hate this kind of work where you have to act like a servant and you see all the highfalutin types who think you're scum."[7]

The combination of low wages, minimal job control, and images of service work as being feminine and subservient or, alternatively, of forcing workers to affect the demeanor of the "highfalutin" led many subjects to avoid the low-income jobs that had the greatest availability in North City. This stance may or may not be judged to be rational by a middle-class observer. For Sidney and Seth, who were now housed and making a small income, their construction skills seemed sufficient to allow them to avail themselves of better opportunities, should they arise. But a number of unskilled men—like Del, Kirk, Harry, Greg, and Roland—had the same orientation with no clear job skills. For Harry and Del, who wanted to be mechanics, and Greg, who wanted to be a welder, the resistance to other types of labor may seem less rational because they tended to be unrealistic about what it took to enter their preferred fields. Both Harry and Dennis told me, in separate interviews, when I asked about their enrolling in a training program, "Job training! No, it takes too fuckin' long … need money now." Some Checkerboard Square subjects had absorbed the dream of good-paying, "decent" blue-collar jobs from their families and neighbors when growing up in New England, but in the present economy, which no longer provides many such jobs, their desire for good work seemed unlikely ever to become a reality.

Preference for Casual Work

When you work at the docks, there's no b.s. As long as you want to work, they don't care what you do. You could stand there with no clothes on as long as it [the work] gets done. Literally, they don't care. [You] come to work whenever you want, leave whenever you want, take three days off, nobody says, "Why aren't you here?" … [They] don't give you shit.

—Agnes

As Agnes's words suggests, there are many good reasons why the street people of North City preferred to do piecework at the piers or to join the carnival-amusement industry in the summer rather than work at a fast-food restaurant. Such work requires no "b.s." such as interviews and references, no special attire or appropriate demeanor, no long-term commitment, and no standard of evaluation other than the work being completed.

Agnes, who claimed to be "the best woman dogfish cutter in town," has made as much as $800 or $900 a week cutting fish (paid by the pound). The possibility of good piecework wages apparently compensates for serious workplace hazards, such as fish poisoning, as well as for the high rate of workplace injuries at the piers. Agnes cannot work with shellfish because she says she is so allergic to them that she breaks out in large hives; last summer she could not work at all after the dogfish supply ended.

But it is not primarily the money that makes the piers and the amusement industry popular. Subjects are comfortable in these environments; their friends are working there, and they maintain a camaraderie and solidarity that are unknown at Burger King or Dunkin' Donuts. The employers in the area of casual labor need numbers of workers quickly when work is available, so they hire in groups and look for people who are immediately available. Work is off the books, so social benefit eligibility can be maintained. Eric, who left for 12 weeks last summer to work for an amusement vendor, spoke with excitement about the experience:

> I had a great time. Wow, a whole bunch of us who knew each other traveling around, so it was always fun. And then you pitch in, help make sure there's enough food, switch off working with the rides. Nobody hassles you as long as things are moving OK.

These types of jobs were different from jobs in the service economy because of the combination of low barriers to entry, high levels of camaraderie, some job control among employees, and fairly easy acceptance for the sometimes disheveled—if not unkempt—workers. When I attended a summer festival in North City, a number of subjects were at work. Unlike workers in many restaurants, bars, or stores in the area, the men conducting rides for children were often in their undershirts, and their long, knotted hair was uncombed. Although the ride attendants were courteous to the public, they engaged in a minimum of conversation (much less subservience), usually simply counting the riders on line and smoking a cigarette with one hand while nonchalantly operating the ride with the other hand.

There were also less tangible reasons for the street people's preference for casual work. Most street people enjoyed carnival work because it required a fairly short commitment and because it allowed them to travel throughout the region:

> **Brian:** I'm a travelin' man, that's kinda who I am, so I love the work in the fairgrounds [carnival]. Love the feel of going out of town, keeping on the move, always, never in a place for more than a day or two.

Some street people told stories of quitting during the carnival tours, getting off at particular towns they liked or hopping on a bus or train to go elsewhere.

The allure of relatively quick money, traveling, and camaraderie could probably be seen by some middle-class observers as just being part of a dysfunctional personality in that casual work rarely gave the poor much long-term opportunity to save money or to develop job security or a career. Many subjects made money (particularly from the carnival business), then spent it on drinking or other pursuits in the towns they visited.

Brad, who, like Agnes, preferred the casual work of the fish piers, typifies the resistant strain of the Checkerboard Community by rejecting middle-class notions of security and respectability:

> I've been on the streets since I was 12. … Security doesn't mean much to me. I can survive and cope whatever comes along … so get a few dollars here [at the fish pier] and get me a music box. … Hope I can stay in [housing] and then, well, [I'll] deal with what comes next when it comes.

Surviving on Social Benefits

> What little I have, I feel I have earned it, and that includes my SSI [Supplemental Security Income].
>
> —Nina

Prior to the tent city protest of 1987, almost all of the subjects had been rejected by local welfare officials or been denied—often illegally—eligibility for Social Security benefits; this was, indirectly, a major reason for the month-long protest that drew homeless advocate Mitch Snyder to North City. As documented elsewhere (Wagner & Cohen, 1991), the major factor that led to the large increase in the number of people housed among the sample during the first phase of the research between July 1987 and the summer of 1990[8] was the acceptance of subjects into social benefit programs. The increase in the number of homeless people approved for General Assistance (GA) welfare, Aid to Families with Dependent Children (AFDC), Social Security or Supplemental Security Income (SSI), or veterans' assistance made the difference between having money to pay rent—even if on a tiny SRO room—and being out on the street or being able afford meals, clothes, and laundry or literally starving.

Contrary to public conceptions and some conservative sentiment, no one lived luxuriously on any of these benefits. In fact, as we see in Chapter 5, city welfare officials played a major role in keeping people poor by continually denying them stable benefits and often making them wait all day at the city welfare offices for a $3 or $5 food voucher.[9] Because city welfare was so niggardly, subjects fought to get on AFDC (if they were single parents with children) or SSI, Social Security, and veterans' assistance. These benefits, although more consistent than city welfare, at best offer amounts that are far below the federally defined poverty level (such income rarely exceeds $400 a month for SSI or about $475 for a family of three on AFDC).[10]

Rather than fitting the image of living "high on the hog" on benefits, many subjects lived in mortal terror of having benefits terminated. This response was understandable because the system made it hard for subjects to enter and reenter the benefit rolls and, during the 1980s, the federal government had cut 500,000 people from Social Security and SSI benefits. Moreover, if a subject lost AFDC or SSI benefits, he or she would likely lose housing and eligibility for Medicaid and food stamps. Ron, a formerly institutionalized mental patient who had been cut off from disability benefits once in the 1980s, and Ely, a mild-mannered unemployed man with an apparent psychiatric disability who received only local welfare assistance rather than Social Security or SSI, were typical:

> **Ron:** No way I'm gonna risk my SSI! I'll do whatever they [social workers, doctors] tell me. ... I don't want to be homeless again.

> **Ely:** I won't go to city [welfare] without having Katherine there [a leader of North City's homeless]. ... They intimidate me, make me cry, and I can't even talk with them unless she's there so I can fill out the forms.

In this study, we found the use of social benefits to be far more complex than described in most conservative or liberal dialogues. Contrary to Awalt's (1991) view, no one liked being on social benefits. Subjects derided welfare benefits as "paltry" and "peanuts" and hated the control of welfare workers over their lives, which was a condition of receiving aid. Yet some subjects had also learned, at least since the tent city protest, to make use of government regulations to eke out an existence on benefits, sometimes illegally in combination with off-the-books work—a fact that, if not denied, is hardly emphasized in most liberal or advocacy literature on the poor.

Most subjects who received social benefits saw this as a temporary method of survival. Even if they were on disability (SSI or Social Security), which is expected to be a more permanent benefit, subjects talked about getting off benefits. Yet subjects faced a dilemma that shapes the lives of all low-income people: If a legitimate job became available, how could one guarantee that it would last beyond 3, 5, or 10 days? How could one survive if it paid $5 an hour without medical benefits? Would one lose housing before getting paid? (Sidney, for example, described three rounds of homelessness he experienced while awaiting checks from construction jobs for which he was only paid biweekly). Importantly, taking a job carried a dramatic risk—of losing housing if housed, of losing health insurance (Medicaid), of losing child care—with no guarantee of long-term security.

Moreover, in this context it is not surprising that subjects came to see welfare benefits as a minimum income "floor" that they would then accept. The fear expressed by conservatives that a person will not work for, say, $60 a week (on the books) if he or she receives $400 a month in benefits is accurate in North City. As

Rudy remarked, "Why should I be blamed for not working for nothing? I'd rather have a roof over my head and be on welfare, as much as I hate it, as work and [be] homeless."

Some subjects were highly functional, from a middle-class perspective, in using their time on social benefits to prepare themselves for work or to increase their level of education. Since 1987, about 15 subjects from Checkerboard Square had received general equivalency diplomas (GEDs), and a few others were taking advantage of being housed to take courses at college or in Job Corps training. As we have seen, subjects like Harry, Roland, and Seth still looked for blue-collar work and continued to work off the books or to engage in underground work while on benefits. Mitch, who was on SSI, continued college. Randy, who had gotten on SSI, was working off the books and was taking a travel agency course he hoped would someday bring enough income to eliminate his need for benefits. Theodore, who was on city welfare, was working for the homeless shelter as a janitor. Cora, on AFDC, hoped that after giving birth to her child, she would someday go into human service work and get off welfare; she had completed a 10-week theatre course over the summer.

However, a growing number of subjects also talked openly about "using the system." In fact, over the course of the study, by "playing the head games" mentioned in Chapter 2, Harry and his friends Roland and Brian had all gotten onto SSI pretending to have psychiatric disabilities. A North City social worker, who usually spoke fondly of many of our subjects, expressed anger: "These guys, a number of them, have figured out how to get SSI, and they're [using] the system. … It's very shocking to me."

Getting on disability seemed to be a new trend late in the participant observation. In North City, single men or women or couples without children face the prospect of receiving almost no benefits from city welfare except being placed in a shelter and given some food stamps. They are usually ineligible for AFDC, unemployment insurance, and other federal benefits, so the Social Security system is the only system that—if they are accepted—can provide enough money for minimal housing and automatic eligibility for Medicaid (if SSI). Moreover, if they are successful at getting Social Security, subjects enter a bureaucracy that is geared toward the deserving poor, that—at least on a daily basis—is more hospitable to the elderly and disabled than is the local welfare system. Subjects were normally informed of the system by legal aid attorneys, sympathetic social workers, or ministers or priests.

Evidently, the subjects mentioned—some with no psychiatric history—learned to present their family backgrounds (the dysfunctional families of Chapter 3), their struggles to live on the streets (including experience with substance abuse), and their difficulty in keeping employment in such a way as to receive a psychiatric diagnosis that made them eligible for SSI. This is not easy since it requires numerous trips to Social Security offices and to doctors and psychiatrists, acceptance of a stigmatized label, and agreement to be rehabilitated.

Without having access to case files or having done a psychological examination, it is hard for me to evaluate the actual mental conditions of these subjects. I can agree with the North City social worker that some of these subjects did not seem particularly impaired. Yet it is ironic that social workers and other mental health professionals should complain about the use of such benefits when it can be argued that they invented not only the labels but also the ideological paradigm upon which the benefits are based.

In the normative world view of the psychiatric community, subjects who move from job to job, have bad tempers, and clash with employers are strong candidates for a psychiatric disability since these symptoms (possibly combined with poor impulse control in other areas of their lives) often lead to a psychiatric diagnosis of "personality disorder," particularly "antisocial personality." In fact, the American Psychiatric Association's (APA) diagnostic manual (APA, 1987) defines an "antisocial personality" in part as a person who fails to sustain consistent work, who does not fit social norms, and who "travels from place to place."[11] By the APA's standards, perhaps all homeless people should be given SSI or Social Security disability automatically. Moreover, social workers and other mental health professionals are often relieved when a client is placed on SSI because otherwise, they must find employment or training programs for such people. And indeed, the government is happy to not count such people as unemployed or in need of work (which would make them potentially eligible for local welfare). Given that Harry, Roland, Brian, and others live in a society that denies that their personal responses to the work world (showing a temper, quitting jobs, fighting with employers) have any political or sociological significance, it is not surprising that having learned that a variety of their behaviors (poor impulse control, antisocial behavior, failure to form appropriate relationships or to accept responsibilities) are "symptoms," they go to Social Security offices and are examined to see whether they qualify for SSI benefits.

Observers like Awalt (1991) and some liberals also find it objectionable that some subjects were able to use the approximately $400 from SSI (which could barely provide one with a tiny closet of an apartment or scarcely enough to eat) as a base for their income-generating strategies while working off the books or waiting for other types of work. Indeed, Nina could serve as a volunteer at the AIDS agency and help house other homeless people at her apartment while on SSI and still reject some housekeeping jobs; subjects like Harry could wait for blue-collar work while aided by SSI; subjects like Joel could aspire to work with alternative organizations or, like Ralph, could work on political campaigns while on SSI. These subjects were violating not just the work ethic but also the principle that the poor should work for the lowest wage available rather than receive social benefits (the principle of "less eligibility," Piven & Cloward, 1971:33–35).

Subjects often defended social benefits as entitlements. Arguing that their families, and often they themselves, had paid taxes to support schools, roads, and the military, they saw benefits as a right and saw the entire welfare debate as an ideological smoke screen:

Eric: If they [the public] is so concerned about where their money goes, let them look at the billions in defense, the billions going to the bankers, what is it? the S&Ls, the tax writeoffs, foreign aid ... this whole thing is just "blame the poor."

Nina: The taxpayers, they say, "Why don't you assholes get a job?" It makes me furious. I'd like to say, "Why don't you shut up until you live it!" Some of this fancy people [would be] the first to want money or benefits if they fall from grace, [get] a divorce, [have] a fire, whatever.

The more educated and previously middle-class denizens of Checkerboard Square tended to the most critical of the work ethic and the most resistant to the argument that they were sponges on the system. They argued that it was ironic that the public put down the homeless and the poor as being helpless and pathetic but then saw them as being so clever that they could live on the system. Perhaps, then, the poor deserve admiration, not consternation:

Arnie: I don't know what's so great about working 40 hours a week. People are always saying, "These people [the poor] can't help themselves." As soon as they do, by working under the table, by figuring out how to get welfare, they [the poor] are condemned. It's just a class thing. They [the rich] just want the poor to starve.

Joel: It is disturbing to people, how [the homeless] fulfill what they need to, what they are ingenious about, the way they put their lives together, panhandling here, borrowing there, exchanging food stamps. It's just totally unacceptable [to the public]. We don't look at this form of living as acceptable, but the truth is, [the ways the street people survive], it's ingenious and it works.

An Alternative View

In this chapter I have described the street culture of Checkerboard Square as one in which there is a high level of awareness of economic inequality and exploitation of the poor by the "system." Such insights cause subjects to support each other in developing innovative forms of informal and casual work and in relying on social benefits, as well as engaging in formal work. At times, street people will refuse types of work they feel are exploitative or humiliating, despite their poverty.

Our data cannot disprove either conservative or liberal positions because they relate essentially to a moral-religious level of meaning. For conservatives such as Awalt (1991; see also Murray, 1984; Mead, 1986), any failure to work at anytime is immoral. I cannot counter this argument since it is tantamount to a religious precept. Liberals counter that all people want to work, and this is also a philosophical-ontological level of argument rather than being factually provable.

Moreover, the emphasis of advocates on only structural variables and generally only on the impact of Reaganomics as constituting the total cause of recent poverty (see Blau, 1992; Kozol, 1988; Ropers, 1988, for example) is very limited in understanding both the culture of low-income life and the historical consistency of poverty.

There is nothing strange or idiosyncratic about Checkerboard Square. It is as rational for poor people to weigh economic options for survival among formal work, social benefits, and underground earnings as it is for middle-income and upper-income people to weigh tax advantages in making business decisions or for working-class people to strategize ways to raise their earnings near pension time or to achieve a little extra money "off the books" as well. The patterns of the poor, then, are not deviant per se but only become resistant based on a nexus of government regulations that enforce formal work through eligibility rules and workfare requirements, by expectations of employers for a low-wage workforce, and by the public's incessant demands that the poor work. Just as the culture of resistance was seen as being suspicious of family forms, subjects expressed little belief that formal work-force participation would improve their lives and were rebellious about authority relations.

Some noted social scientists have recently begun to look at the impact of culture, particularly among black men, in resisting low-wage employment.[12] This study supports such endeavors because it reminds us that not just the presence of jobs and job readiness is of issue in low-income communities, but the very different meanings low-wage work may have to different cultures within low-income communities must also be considered. Where I differ from social scientists such as W. J. Wilson is in the judgment that all such rejection of low-wage work is regrettable. Rather, I suggest that the poor well realize the limitations of mobility and respectability low-wage work can provide and that it is an ideological construct of both conservatives and liberals that the poor should be morally obligated to accept any and all work, whatever the terms.

Finally, I suggest that the actions of our subjects and the general state of the poor in the nation differ far less dramatically from trends extant throughout U.S. history than many advocates suggest. If what is today labeled an underclass is viewed historically, there is nothing new about millions of people being marginal to the work force. For at least 200 years, a "reserve army of labor" has existed that at times has been drawn on by employers for labor and at times discarded when the economy is depressed (see Piven & Cloward, 1971). Ironically, even at the height of Pax-Americana in 1959, nearly one person in five was officially poor (Levitan, 1990:6), a higher percentage than existed throughout the 1980s— although, of course, there was far less homelessness and little or no debate about poverty.

The relevance of the historical perspective is not meant to breed apathy toward poverty but rather to suggest that the actions of those who are the most poor— cut off from an industrial work force—are best understood not by comparing them to blue-collar workers but through comparisons to the long history of vagrants, paupers, and hobos (see Miller, 1991). Although organized workers have a long, well-documented history, the resistance of those cut off from long-term work-force participation is rarely written about, except for the occasional riots. I suggest that cut off from organized collective forms of resistance at the workplace (strikes, unionization), lower-class people *do* exercise some compensatory forms of control over their lives by refusing certain jobs and authority arrangements, by developing alternative forms of income that have a degree of control (from collecting bottles to doing casual day labor), and by eking out relief.

To the public, such phenomena are shocking, and they lead to calls for benefit cutbacks and tightened eligibility rules. Yet there are alternative visions. A guaranteed annual income, a proposal once actually embraced by both political parties 20 years ago, is rarely supported today even by liberals (Katz, 1989:232–33), who also do not entertain any strategy to raise wages and reduce complete employer control. In Chapter 8, I return to such alternative approaches.

Notes

1. Ironically, in terms of our discussion of the undeserving poor, the major reasons cited for there being a new class of people who are "welfare dependent" are the mothers and children on AFDC. Even if a single man or woman or a childless couple wanted to linger on social benefits, they could not according to the laws of our welfare system. As has been true since the nineteenth-century poorhouse (Katz, 1986), the negative rhetoric about the unemployed male has obscured the fact that women and children have almost always constituted the majority of the recipients accepted onto relief.

2. Of the 76 people for whom enough data were available, 34 (44.7 percent had a high school degree in 1990, but this includes at least 15 subjects who obtained general equivalency diplomas (GEDs) after the tent city protest in 1987, so at the point at which the subjects all were homeless (in 1987), no more than a quarter had high school degrees.

3. As noted in the text, about 10 of the 65 subjects followed most closely were usually regularly employed. A few subjects enjoyed service work. Darryl, who made $76 a week delivering newspapers, bragged that he "had always been a worker" from age 18 onward, including through many periods of homelessness. JoJo, who was on SSI because of psychiatric disability, spoke to me with enthusiasm about getting a job at a local restaurant ("I really like being a waiter"), although it was unclear how long he worked there.

Although there are too few subjects to make a very meaningful comparison between those who were enthusiastic about such work and the bulk of the subjects described above, the small group of enthusiastic workers included a number of mentally ill subjects like JoJo, who seemed to see being able to work as a badge of ability and normalcy. Also, a number of subjects from extremely impoverished families of origin (as opposed to middle-class or working-class families of origin) appeared to work with little expectation of having livable wages or good working conditions.

Additionally, at least two subjects, both of whom had long left North City by the study's end, and possibly a third, who remained in the area, could be counted among the success stories news editors often look for to give readers hope of "bouncing back" from poverty.

Lester had been a welder who fell on hard times in the late 1980s; after being homeless for about 6 months, he had "dried out" through alcohol rehabilitation, worked for a social agency, and then had returned to a fairly high-paying job as a welder. Ruth, who was a young, runaway homeless 18-year-old when the tent city protest started, was taken in by a local minister. With the minister's help, Ruth got an abortion, got help with her alcohol problem, received counseling, and eventually—after the two moved to Pennsylvania—went through job training. When I last had telephone contact with her, she had secured a computer operator job at $11 an hour in Pennsylvania.

Roy, who, as noted earlier, had already had a history of craft jobs before becoming homeless and part of the tent city protest, still lived in the area and attended breakfast at the Drop-In center, as well as still occasionally spending time at Checkerboard Square. Although his story is less dramatic than those of Lester and Ruth in terms of his current income, Roy proudly described how he had completed 2 years of work as a full-time loader at a city-run agency on the piers (not to be confused with the piecework fish cutters). Roy made a "decent wage" with full fringe benefits and civil service rights. He seemed to enjoy his work.

To some, the success of these few subjects will "prove" that those who try hard enough can "make it." It should be noted, however, that two of the three success stories already had long work histories, with some marketable skills and strong résumés, before becoming homeless—something most street people do not have and probably will never have. Ruth was the beneficiary of very unusual and generous attention from a middle-class professional who still lives with her and helped shape a major change in her life.

4. I am distinguishing here between work pursuits such as cutting hair, creating art, or cutting fish, which would not be illegal if taxes were withheld, and activities that by their nature are illegal in the United States, such as selling drugs or prostituting.

5. As the massive Reagan-era cutbacks in all benefits, including Social Security disability and SSI, suggest, no social benefit is really "secure" in the United States. Nevertheless, SSI, Social Security, and even AFDC (the "categorical programs") should be distinguished from local welfare or general assistance in that once accepted to a categorical program, one maintains a consistent check until he or she becomes ineligible and usually has the right to hearings before being terminated. For subjects who were nondisabled, single, or childless couples, the only social benefit available in the state North City is in—general assistance—is highly variable, it may give $5 in vouchers one week and nothing the next, so that any modicum of security concerning shelter and food cannot be sustained. Many states have no general assistance welfare.

6. Social Security disability and SSI are both benefits for the physically or psychiatrically impaired that are administered by the Social Security Administration. Social Security disability, like retirement benefits under Old Age, Survivors, and Disability Insurance (OASDI), requires years of work credit, which only a very few of our subjects had. SSI—created by Congress in 1972 to absorb the old welfare programs for the disabled, elderly, and blind—applies to far more members of the North City sample (and many more poor people nationally) because it is "means-tested" (income-based) relief for those disabled or elderly who lack sufficient work credits to qualify for Social Security.

7. My 1991 study of 453 textile workers in Maine who were laid off (see Wagner, 1991) suggests that more stably employed blue-collar workers also engaged in resistance to service work. The predominantly female textile workers felt that low wages, few benefits, low levels of unionization, and job control, as well as discrimination against middle-aged and

older women, made work in the service industry a last choice for work. Many even preferred to take retirement or to remain unemployed over the prospect of accepting such jobs.

8. Depending on the definition of homelessness one chooses and the use of the population base of 65 or 98 for our sample, between 71.4 percent and 89.2 percent of the homeless cohort from July 1987 was housed in the summer of 1990, although many later became homeless again (see table 3A in Wagner & Cohen, 1991:550). We argue that such a change was the direct result of increases in participation in social benefit programs.

9. The state's general assistance program provides no cash benefits but only gives vouchers for shelter and food and occasionally for travel or cleaning supplies.

10. See Levitan, 1990:48–58. The state in which North City is located did supplement federal SSI, making its amounts slightly higher than those in some other states. The state ranked about 20th in AFDC payments—much lower than high benefit states such as California, New York, and Massachusetts but well above states in the South and in most of the West—in 1987–1990.

11. The "antisocial personality disorder" is characterized by indications of the following (APA, 1987:345): lack of "consistent work behavior," including "significant unemployment," "repeated absences from work," or "abandonment of several jobs." Criterion number two is that the "person does not comply with social norms." The fifth criterion is that the "person fails to plan ahead" and includes descriptions such as "travels from place to place" and "lacks a fixed address for a month or more." Not surprisingly, the APA itself (p. 343) admits that this "disorder is common in lower class populations because it is associated with impaired earning capacity."

In addition to the antisocial personality disorder, other personality disorder diagnoses were common for North City's homeless, such as "borderline personality disorder" (APA, 1987:347–349), which appears to be a popular catchall diagnosis for people who seem strange and who are often inexplicably unable to develop stable work lives and family attachments.

12. Jencks (1992) argues that "cultural conflict" between black men and employers needs to be taken into account, as well as the economy, in studies of the ghetto. According to a recent article (DeParle, 1992), Wilson and associates are studying the impact of cultural resistance to low-wage jobs among black men (in particular contrast to immigrant groups) as a factor in urban poverty.

5

Institutions of Control: Social Welfare as Contested Terrain

The Altruistic Purpose of Social Services

As with the recent discourse about family and work, the public debate about social services and social welfare institutions has been conducted along very narrow lines. Classically, the conservative position on social welfare has echoed the clichés of laissez-faire economics, defining "big government" as the problem and social benefits and social services as forces that create moral degeneracy. In contrast, the liberal response to criticism of the welfare state has remained fairly consistent with the comments of Jeffry Galper (1975):

> The liberal position has tended to rest on the assumption that the social services are basically a "good thing" and thus sees the major problem with the services as the absence of enough of them ... "more is better" summarizes a good part of conventional analysis. (p. 2)

Interestingly, both the conservative and the liberal perspectives rest on a degree of denial about the actual history and social functions of social welfare. When generalizing about the "character-weakening" effects of the welfare state, conservatives conveniently forget that much of the history of social welfare, dating as far back as the English Poor Laws, has been a product of their own creation. It was political conservatives who generally insisted on the need for social control over the behavior of the poor and other groups that produced much of the bureaucracy they now often bemoan. From the institution of the workhouse in the eighteenth and nineteenth centuries to the "man-in-the-house" rules of AFDC and workfare requirements in recent decades, the social welfare bureaucracy exists largely to enforce social control demanded by conservatives in the name of the public. In this light, the large staffs, numerous rules, and considerable paperwork that characterize the welfare state are arguably at least in part a conservative contribution. Further, large expenditures to control criminals, drug users, and other deviants have almost always been supported by conservatives. Large payments to private parties, which constitute a major part of social welfare spending, have never been opposed by conservatives; these include Medicaid and Medicare payments to physicians or nursing homes, welfare payments to support landlords, and housing subsidies to reward developers. In fact, as the Housing and Urban Development (HUD) scandal during the Reagan administration demonstrated, these types of payments are arguably more frequently abused under conservative administrations.

A complete defense of the entire social welfare system, as sometimes voiced by liberals and even radicals, must either ignore or downplay the social control purposes of social welfare policy, including behavioral control and surveillance, enforcing of low-wage work, and intentional stigmatization and repression of certain populations. Such a defense cannot begin to explain why many poor people (and also working-class people) avoid many social services, particularly child welfare, public welfare, and mental health services. The call for more services fails to note the historical opposition of labor and the poor to "charity snoopers" and "lady bountifuls" from the late nineteenth century on.[1] In the 1960s and 1970s, a wide variety of attacks on social welfare institutions and programs was developed by the Left, yet over the past decade or more such criticism has been muted. One reason is, of course, that the widespread attack on social services by the Right has placed all supporters of social services on the defensive, and there is great fear that criticizing certain aspects of social benefits or service programs will provide fodder for those who seek budget cuts on state, local, and national levels. Although understandable, such a stance as Wineman (1984) points out, has narrowed and limited the debate about social welfare, seeming to place progressives on the side of all big government programs while paradoxically sometimes placing the right wing on the side of decentralization and social change (witness efforts by Republican officials such as Jack Kemp, the secretary of HUD under George Bush, to seize the mantle of "empowerment" for conservative causes).

Second, since the major expansion of social welfare in the 1930s and 1960s, middle-class citizens have increasingly become consumers of the welfare state. Whether as recipients of Social Security pensions or veterans' benefits through the GI Bill or more recent participation in mental health services (particularly psychotherapy), day care, and child development; drug, alcohol, and employee assistance programs; and a host of family and educational services, the middle-class experience of social welfare is completely different from the experience of the poor. In demanding more day care or more health care or better pensions, the middle class and its political spokespeople have every reason to believe that these benefits and services will be helpful and supportive.

Social welfare programs, however, frequently do not operate in an altruistic fashion toward the poor. Whereas middle-class people are often voluntary consumers of child and family counseling or other mental health services, the poor are more often "involuntary" users. Their families are primarily the ones investigated for child abuse and neglect, and their children are those most frequently removed from the home. They are the group most often ordered to undergo counseling or drug treatment or are those incarcerated in prisons and mental hospitals. Nor can the poor's involvement with public assistance or shelter programs be adequately described as voluntary, although technically they have the right to freeze or starve rather than apply for benefits. The power differential between a client and a social worker who can make life-and-death decisions as to whether that client will be granted a welfare check cannot be compared with problems middle-class consumers have in their relationships with physicians, therapists, or teachers.

In simplistic terms, it can be argued that whereas the carrot of social welfare usually goes to the more affluent, the stick is most often applied to the poor. Social welfare advocates and middle-class people usually visualize social welfare as providing support and rehabilitation. They are either unaware of or support services that strip-search homeless people who enter a shelter or, more metaphorically, strip poor people of their rights and dignity in return for a few dollars in food stamps. Few of the subjects interviewed in North City regarded the purposes of social welfare as altruistic, at least not those of the dominant bureaucratic institutions such as welfare departments, homeless shelters, or child welfare agencies. These institutions were viewed as hostile and controlling components of society's police functions. Arnie's comments, although extreme, certainly suggest that the poor do not often share the conservative-liberal consensus about the comforts of the welfare state:

> Some of the social worker–welfare people I have dealt with [in North City] seem to have the belief that the only homes we [homeless] deserved were gas chambers and crematoria.

This is not intended to argue the extreme position that the function of social services is only to serve as an instrument of social control. As we see in Chapter 6, subjects were strongly attracted to certain social agencies in North City, particularly voluntary agencies that provided social advocacy, some forms of community, and various counseling programs and self-help groups that were not conditioned on behavioral controls. Nor did subjects who faced the specters of starvation and frostbite categorically reject the use of public social services. Subjects responded, however, to the invasion of privacy, the "degradation ceremonies" (Garfinkel, 1956), of welfare and other institutions, and to the paltry levels of aid provided, with a variety of strategies, alternating between resistance and manipulation, accommodation and avoidance. In this sense, the social service system with which the poor of North City have contact cannot be described as consisting of either helping institutions or institutions of control but rather as an arena of "contested terrain" in which the degree of client pressure, protest, and manipulation sometimes succeeds in achieving and sometimes fails to achieve a modicum of humane or altruistic treatment.

The "System" and Homelessness

Just as the Checkerboard Square subjects struggled constantly to eke out incomes in a work world that was hostile to them, they were also involved in a constant struggle to survive under the pressures and rules of bureaucratic institutions. But unlike the situations that existed in their generally individualized relationships with workplaces and families, subjects were at times able to alter their relationship with service institutions through collective protest. The predominant impact of bureaucratic institutions on subjects prior to the tent city protest in 1987 was negative and coercive. In this respect, the institutions functioned more to foster homelessness and poverty rather than to alleviate these problems. Since the 1987 protest and the increased organization of the very poor in North City, some positive changes have occurred. The situation for poor people in North City, however, remains essentially hostile, although some subjects have gained increased sophistication in securing social benefits and some have reached accommodations with certain social institutions.

The major bureaucratic institutions with which poor people interact—the shelter system, the public welfare system, the child welfare system, the mental health system, and the criminal justice–correctional system—play a significant role in exacerbating the crises of homelessness and poverty. They do so not only by the well-documented sin of omission—providing inadequate income, benefits, and services for people to survive—but also by sins of commission: They so oppress and control poor people that many self-respecting individuals choose to retain their dignity and live on the streets rather than submit to a "degradation ceremony" in which the cost is their freedom and personal control.

The Shelter System

One of the key issues of the 1987 tent city protest in North City was the lack of adequate shelter space and the humiliating, degrading conditions that were imposed on shelter users. The majority of the homeless participants who were surveyed by the Coalition for the Dignity of the Homeless and Poor in July 1987 had been rejected for shelter and used city streets, bridges, and parks as their "homes." The shelter system that was in place in North City prior to the settlement of the protest was hardly unusual but in fact typified the most common approach to sheltering the homeless nationally (see Blau, 1992:223); namely, reliance on private not-for-profit agencies to operate shelters supported in part by public funds.

In order to be "cleared" for shelter, a client had to obtain an approval slip from city welfare workers. This voucher would then be turned over to one of the private shelters. This system was harsh to begin with since it required that clients engage in daily supplications to welfare workers rather than have the city make the assumption that the homeless person was likely to need shelter for longer periods of time. After a long wait in line at a city welfare office, homeless people were often told that they would not be cleared for shelter because (1) they made too much money (Wally: "They said since I got SSI, I didn't qualify"), (2) they refused to conform to requirements that would prove that they had looked for a job or performed workfare for the city (Lois: "I was refused shelter. Worker said I didn't follow job search requirements"), (3) they did not conform to appropriate behavior (Jamie: "So because I made a stink at [name] shelter one time, the city said I could never be taken in again"), or (4) they were substance abusers or mentally ill or were *not* substance abusers or mentally ill (since before mid-1987 most beds for the homeless were "categorical," the subject would have to be "lucky" enough to have [and admit to] the right personal diagnosis to obtain shelter). This last situation would be laughable if it were not for its deadly results in the number of people who were forced to live outdoors in New England winters:

Harry: So I get thrown out of [shelter] for drinking but then went to the other one [a shelter for alcoholics], and [they] say, "No, you're not drunk now," so I was turned away.

Ron: So they [city workers] ask me if I'm mentally ill. ... I don't know what to say, you know, but I finally say "Yeah, I'm mentally ill, if that's the answer you're looking for." I just wanted to get a bed to sleep on. So they say, "Sorry, there's no room at that shelter tonight. You'll have to go to [the] streets."

Second, not only was getting into a shelter as difficult as getting accepted to an exclusive college, but like all social benefits—such as acceptance onto welfare—the subject risked exposure to a variety of controls, including having children taken away, being institutionalized, or being imprisoned. Agnes remarks:

You're in an extreme catch-22 situation. I mean, if you talk to them [city welfare workers, shelter attendants] and they find you're living on the streets under a bridge and you have children, you'll end up at [department of child welfare] and have your kids taken away. If you say you're distraught, well, you may end up in [a mental institution]. ... I learned the hard way, don't say anything! And then, of course, they think I am a weirdo because when I go to the shelter I say nothing.

Agnes's comments were not idiosyncratic or paranoid. Many subjects did fear losing their freedom, their children, or their social benefits by presenting themselves for assistance and being identified by workers as irresponsible, as substance abusers, as mentally ill, as criminal, or as unfit mothers (ironically, in order to get shelter, homeless clients often had to feign psychiatric illness, yet such feigning could have disastrous future consequences).

Those "lucky" enough to be granted shelter faced extensive social control over their behavior. A major complaint, historically consistent since the nineteenth century ("Long-haired preachers come out every night, try to tell you what's wrong and what's right," from Joe Hill's song, quoted in Miller, 1991:45), was that prior to 1987, most shelters were religiously affiliated and mandated prayer and religious study:

Tiny: The [name] shelter? They just want to brainwash you into their religion.

Darryl: I got thrown out of [church shelter]. I didn't go to [church] services because I had to work on Sundays. They said, "No, it's required."

Jonathan: [The] captain [at Salvation Army] and me didn't get along. All these rules, all this god stuff … he tried to control my life.

Whereas almost all homeless protesters criticized the religious requirements of the shelters, most also objected to mandatory curfews—sometimes as early as 6 or 7 P.M.—to segregation of the sexes, to discrimination based on behavior, to body searches, and to deplorable physical conditions:

Herb: This isn't Russia! They have this curfew of 7 o'clock, come on! You should be able to come and go as you please.

Theodore: They have orders to keep me out. … They know I'm an advocate, and when they see me coming, they have a ban on me … tried to stop me even from talking with other [homeless] clients.

Teddy: The shelters? They try to run your life. I've been submitted to strip searches. I've been thrown out for smoking and eating. I've been told that I can't come back unless I do [city] workfare. … In a nutshell, they want to run your life, like a prison.

Tobi: So they give me this bed, it's filthy, with blood-stained sheets. I complain and [the attendant] says, "Don't worry about [it]. I slept there last night with a virgin." And that's how it is there. Appalling conditions, and if you complain, you get banned.

Protest and the Shelter System

As a result of the 1987 demonstrations, including Mitch Snyder's appearance in North City, the city recognized the legal right to shelter and developed a municipal shelter system. In a number of ways, conditions have improved: The homeless need not report to the welfare department daily for a voucher but, space permitting, are accepted directly into a shelter; religious shelters still exist but need not be used when space is available at public shelters; since most shelter beds are no longer categorical, one need not declare oneself to be a substance abuser or mentally ill in order to gain a bed; and, importantly, from 1987 to 1990, active advocacy groups have continually lodged grievances and complaints with city officials about discrimination by staff, poor physical conditions, and behavioral controls, which had led to some improvement in physical conditions and staff treatment of clients.

Nevertheless, reports from advocates, city personnel, and a majority of the street people at Checkerboard Square confirm that the North City shelter system, although somewhat improved over years ago, still represents a hostile and punitive system designed to humiliate and control the homeless population. Larry, a former shelter attendant, quotes a city official as stating at a staff meeting, "We can't make things comfortable for the clients. Otherwise they'll flock here and enjoy staying here." Another attendant, Annie, was fired after she was simply seen talking with a homeless advocate. Since North City still follows the basic doctrine of deterrence (Kozol, 1988; Piven & Cloward, 1971), it intentionally permits both poor physical conditions and a variety of forms of social control and discrimination over clients in order to make shelter life onerous.

As is the case in many shelters, the physical space in the North City shelters is set up to minimize privacy and dignity. Larry reports that uncomfortable, rickety cots are placed one foot apart, although far more space is available, and that both of the bathrooms have no doors, which is a major source of complaints— particularly from women. He contrasts this with the spacious, carpeted bedrooms with real beds, a kitchen, a shower room, and full bathrooms that have been set up for homeless families on the third floor of a municipal shelter, where families can come and go at will and are given a key to the building. Families are apparently considered "deserving" poor; hence, physical conditions are better for them, and fewer social controls are imposed. Moreover, many of the shelter staff who service the homeless are untrained and are punitive toward clients; they hardly exemplify a "service" ethic. Judge reports, for example, that when he stayed at a city shelter, several employees took a television set donated for the homeless from the shelter area and chained it to the wall in a staff room. When he protested (including conducting an interview with the press), the staff replied that "you're not here for fun. You don't need a tv. You're not supposed to be living high on [the] hog, now, are you?" The staff, meanwhile, continued to enjoy watching television frequently while on duty.

Avoidance, Accommodation, and Resistance in Shelter Use

The intention to deter use of the shelters succeeds to a great extent, causing continued homelessness even when shelter beds are available. Theodore and other political activists are banned from the shelter. So are a fairly large number of people we spoke to at Checkerboard Square who had been charged with "misbehavior," such as Duke: "I'm on a permanent ban. So, of course, I live down by Hobo

Jungle" [an encampment by the railroad tracks]. The shelters now also ban those who exhibit signs of drug or alcohol use, but since the categorical shelters have extremely limited space, if one is thrown out of a municipal shelter for having alcohol on one's breath, he or she is likely to end up on the streets. In recent years, the city decided to ban subjects who are on Social Security and SSI from using the shelter for the first 14 days of each month. The justification for this policy is apparently that these disabled clients must be forced to budget their money properly and not to occupy space that can go to others. As before, many subjects are afraid to enter the shelters because their children may be taken from them; they might face enforced institutionalization, arrest, or detoxification; or they may be forced into mandatory workfare. As a result of these deterrent conditions and policies, a number of Checkerboard Square subjects never use shelters and remain literally on the streets:

Duke: To me the shelters are the express [track] to [the state mental hospital]. I'd rather sleep outside than take my chances in there!

Lois: I'm too afraid to go into shelters. It's terrifying … people who attack you … and no protection, no, don't trust staff.

Sam: It's a prison, basically, that's all it is. I mean, there's one or two nice workers there, but you really take your life in your hands, not only crime, but whether you have your freedom the next morning.

North City's shelters are smaller, less crowded, cleaner, and less crime ridden than many shelters in large urban areas. Nevertheless, in reviewing the opinions of approximately 100 homeless and ex-homeless subjects,[2] I found that going to a shelter was their next-to-last choice; it was preferred only slightly to staying outside in the elements without protection in extremely cold New England winters. In order of preference, homeless subjects favored (1) staying with friends or others in houses; (2) living in cars, vans or other vehicles; (3) sleeping in protected conditions, such as abandoned buildings or makeshift quarters; or (4) if it is warm enough, staying—even unprotected from the elements—on the street rather than in a shelter.

Of course, on any given night and in any given situation, subjects (except those banned from shelters) determined their shelter usage based on the physical conditions they faced, the whereabouts of friends, and their perception of social control, including which shelter staff members were working that night. Brian explained this as follows:

It's [shelters] my last resort, you know. I can't sleep the night there, looking around, checking people out. I can't stand their rules, the searches, the shit they put you through … but sometimes you need 'em. I mean, I check out where my buddies are, if we have a warm spot, who is where, and naturally in depths of winter, if nothing else comes along, yeah, I'll go there. I'm proud, yeah, but I don't want to freeze to death.

Brian's quote and the comments of others suggest that subjects consciously weigh the loss of freedom and control imposed by services against the physical dangers they face and also weigh the relative strength of their social networks on the street and in the shelter. Importantly, as I have argued, for most subjects the paucity of services (not enough shelter beds, not enough workers, poor conditions) was a grievance, but equally important was the *nature* of the "service"— that receipt of a bed for the night came at the expense of a surrender of freedom and dignity and sometimes a more permanent loss of autonomy. For some subjects, though hardly all, the nature of such social control reinforced their tendency to resist the control of authorities and to choose literal homelessness over submission (avoidance). This outcome, which is then used to assign blame to the homeless ("they won't come in from the cold"), is rather the clear result of the deterrent doctrine embedded in U.S. social welfare policy, which emphasizes harsh social control and punitive conditions as part of providing "assistance" to the poor.

However, also consistent with my argument, the homeless were not simply passive victims whose only choices were accommodation or avoidance (e.g., not using shelters at all), although subjects did both. Subjects developed many methods of resistance—from subtle ones, like Agnes's refusal to talk when in the shelter, to more active manipulations, such as using aliases to protect themselves, making false declarations about their diagnoses or histories, and faking job search and other requirements. Advocates and others banned from shelters were often sneaked into shelters by friends. At times, more politicized resistance occurred. For example, on a particularly bitter January night, when a woman and a small child arrived at a city shelter from out of state 2 minutes after the curfew and were denied admission, peer advocates and many other homeless people were outraged, although they did not know the woman. Although the woman and child evidently left the area, the issue did not die for weeks; every detail was reported to the press, to attorneys, and to angry street people, who lodged vocal protests.

The Welfare System

Contrary to the public image of a benign welfare state, North City's local relief system tends to contribute to the problem of poverty. It is structurally dedicated, despite employing some committed workers, to deterring the poor from asking for assistance.

Prior to the tent city protest, almost all of the participants in the month-long protest had been rejected for city welfare, and most—for a variety of reasons— had also been denied AFDC or SSI. Although many of these denials were based on repressive federal policies—the cutting of many mentally and physically disabled people from SSI rolls and the complex catch-22 provisions of AFDC—the limitations of city relief reflected state and local decisions to deter assistance. City or local relief, the direct descendant of the English Poor Laws, is totally discretionary and in this state provides only noncash aid—limited vouchers for rent, food, and occasionally for travel or toiletries. Since in North City most assistance was for rent, the homeless were almost a categorically cut off from the program because without an address, the city could not provide rent assistance or supplementation. Moreover, the able-bodied poor—if they were assisted at all—were subject to enforced work (workfare), in which the recipient owes the locality free labor in return for the aid given.

Even the most cynical of the street people interviewed expressed astonishment at the byzantine operation of welfare programs that provided a minimum of aid coupled with a maximum of intrusive questions and humiliation. Subjects repeatedly stated that they could not believe that after spending 5, 6, or 7 hours waiting at a welfare office and answering a series of personal questions—including queries about their sex lives—the worker would either issue a denial form or approve a $3 or $5 voucher for food:

Eric: I'll be honest. I just flipped out. I had filled out every goddam application in the world, and then [the] worker says, "I'm sorry." I just couldn't control myself.

Lester: So I go and wait and wait. I tell them right away I'm unemployed. … So what do they say after all these hours? I should get a job, I'm not eligible! You think at least they could tell me this in 5 minutes.

Sidney: I decided I'd never go back [to city welfare] and be humiliated. Spilled out my guts, and then I get a $2 voucher. Never went back … and [I] never will.

Nina: You go on your hands and knees [to welfare], and what do they give you? All I ever got was $7 or $8 a week, and you tell them everything, if you shit, shower, shave, ask you about your sex life, get real personal with you … they [workers] act is if you're taking the money from them personally.

The motives of control and deterrence are embedded in all aspects of the welfare process. First, the all-day waits can only be ascribed to a latent function of deterrence, often resulting in the client leaving or possibly breaking down (as Eric did). There are simply not that many clients in the midsized city studied to account for such delays, particularly in the mid-1980s when the local economy was booming (and hence there were relatively few welfare recipients). Moreover, as Lester notes, long delays and lines could be reduced by clear information and guidelines provided to clients so they do not waste entire days (or in some cases weeks) only to learn that they are simply not considered eligible.

Second, in the expensive New England economy of the 1980s, such abysmal "grants" as $2 or $5 or even $8 vouchers can only be described as a cruel joke. At best providing a meal or a bus ticket to a shelter, the assistance program fails even to approach the limited claims of rehabilitation and temporary help to "get one on one's feet."

Third, the combined restrictions of AFDC, SSI, and city assistance provide a program for intrusion and harassment that is mandated by strict regulations. Since AFDC eligibility is based on single-mother status,[3] the presence of any male in the house is suspect and is policed by both state and city workers, leading to close questioning of the woman's dating and sexual habits. As noted in Chapter 3, the care of children is also closely examined. Perceived mistreatment of a child can be grounds for charges of abuse and neglect. Judy, for example, says she got along on AFDC until her caseworker was changed:

> I liked my first [social] worker, but then I get this witch. She just hated me, I don't know why. And she said my kids were dirty and not fed well. She got them taken away from me, and I've never been the same.

However, the lack of rationality and responsiveness of the system prevents other mothers from caring for their own children. The catch-22s embedded in welfare and other programs prevented Cheryl from obtaining custody of her child. After her husband ran off with their daughter, Cheryl, who was homeless, was told by the courts that she could have the child back if she obtained housing and earned enough money to care for her. Yet when she applied for AFDC and city assistance, she was told that since the child was not living with her, she could not be approved for benefits. "I broke down in tears," remembers Cheryl. "I said, 'Ok, you've worn me down to nothing. I'll do anything to get my child back,' but nothing worked."

Men are by no means spared the personal intrusion of welfare workers and the byzantine complexities of the system. Rudy was released from prison with $2 in his pocket. His probation officer helped him get a welfare grant, but when he was subsequently evicted, the officer became angry: "I can have you sent back to jail. You need to be housed as a condition of [your] probation." When the welfare worker learned that Rudy was living at the tent city in the summer of 1987, he reported him to probation. Rudy claims the worker told him, "I'll see you back behind bars." Telly reports that homeless people sometimes use words that can get them into trouble.

> You have to hide your feelings, disguise them. I was saying to this social worker something like, "I feel so angry I could skin someone alive," or words like that, or "crack someone up." These social workers don't understand my language, just an expression. This [social worker] thinks I'm going [to] go out and kill someone, and I get reported to this cops by this stupid [worker].

Fourth, the conflicting regulations of social programs and the lack of coordination of benefits could cause anyone the become so disgusted as to decide to never again apply. Wally, an ill 74-year-old, was given housing by the city in 1986, only to find that the combination of his rent supplementation and his Social Security check made him ineligible for food stamps. His family controlled his Social Security check, so Wally had no money for food. He eventually became homeless again. Randy was ordered by a welfare worker to perform city workfare after being told "he wasn't looking hard enough for work." But Randy had physicians' notes confirming that he was disabled and was applying for Social Security disability. The worker refused to continue Randy's relief, saying, "Well, when you get on disability, I'll remove the workfare order. Until then you're fine and healthy," Randy became homeless between the time of this denial of relief and his eventual acceptance onto disability a year later.

Fifth, the enforced work requirements, although actually enjoyed by a few subjects, were rejected as "make work" and a "sham" by most. Both the principle of workfare—the obligation to work for free in exchange for public assistance—and the actual work and its conditions rankled most subjects. Dennis spoke for many in saying:

> I can't believe that in return for giving me a shelter bed for a few nights and a couple of dollars in food stamps, they say I owe them work! This is like a chain gang mentality. ... I'm not in jail, I didn't do anything. Why should I be a slave laborer? Why not help us get real jobs?

Just as the old workhouse used treadmills and tasks such as digging holes and filling them to keep inmates busy for political and disciplinary reasons (see Katz, 1986), the kind of work provided on workfare often resembled "make work." Subjects raked leaves back and forth at a park, unfolded laundry at a nursing home, and placed bottles into recycling bins. Roy suggests, "It doesn't take a person with half a brain to figure out [that] rather than recycle bottles for nothing, you could make more redeeming them yourself. This work is for chumps!" Like Roy, many subjects left workfare to make money in the casual or underground economy.

Protest and the Welfare System

Along with the restrictive shelter system, the welfare system topped the list of grievances in the tent city protest. The protest and its mobilization of people, allies, and the media led to a dramatic short-term change in North City. Fearful that the protest would escalate, the city welfare department issued orders in July 1987 to approve *all* protesters for immediate relief. In the context of social unrest, a large number of subjects obtained benefits for the first time:

> **Cheryl:** So we went down to city hall as a group. ... City hall didn't deny us then ... any of us. We were all eligible for assistance all of a sudden.

> **Sam:** So here was this guy [Wally] weak, living in the park, [he] couldn't talk [from cancer], and the city, the state, no one would help him. ... We confronted [the head

of social services] and said, "OK, you want this guy on the 6 o'clock news tonight, or are you going to help him?" Next thing you know, he got food stamps, welfare, Medicaid.

In addition to approving protesters for relief, the city made a variety of administrative changes that favored the poor, including changes in formulas for relief and the suspension of the workfare requirement. But the most critical gain from the protest was certainly unintended by the city: The intervention of legal aid attorneys and advocates to explore the cases of the subjects led to suits and to new hearings for subjects with the Social Security Administration, the state social service department for AFDC benefits, and other agencies. As explored in Wagner and Cohen (1991:550), six times as many individuals were receiving social benefits in the aftermath of the protest as had been prior to it in July 1987. Consistent with broader trends historically (see Piven & Cloward, 1971, 1977), the protest movement led to the loosening of restrictions on relief, partly because political leaders were unable or unwilling to alter the structural causes of poverty and also because offering relief provided a quick, tangible response to disorder.

As important as the protest was locally, it was much too weak and isolated to have a long-term impact on most of the arcane requirements and inadequate levels of social benefits. At best, it eliminated some areas of discretion that local officials and social workers had previously had. This, along with the ever-present fear of protest, which lasted for several years in local memory, made those in the system more cautious and sometimes allowed some benefits of the doubt to go to clients. However, the main criteria for both federal and local programs remained the same (if they were not made worse by continued federal and state cutbacks), and most subjects living on benefits continued to complain of inadequate benefit levels and behavioral controls.

Accommodation, Avoidance, and Resistance to the Welfare System

As with the shelter system, subjects self-consciously weighed the combination of physical necessity (to avoid starvation or freezing), the loss of independence and freedom, alternative options for survival, and the actions of comrades in considering their behavior. Some subjects accommodated to the system, particularly if they were able to secure a relatively regularized benefit, such as Social Security disability or SSI. As Ron, the formerly institutionalized patient, stated in Chapter 4, there was no point in "rocking the boat" and possibly losing his SSI and ending up homeless. Bert, a rather genial, formerly homeless man who now combines Social Security with income from his job as a security guard, was almost "mellow." Although he lives in a tiny basement apartment with almost no furniture and hardly even has spare change, Bert said, "You should have seen me a couple of years ago. Life is a hell of a lot better [now]." He ascribed the improvement in his life to the tent city protest, to getting on Social Security disability, to receiving medical care and psychological counseling, but also to the passage of time:

You know, I've lived here all my life. By this time everyone knows me. It's funny … in the old days, the cops would hassle me. The city workers. But now they know me. They actually give me money. I ran into this cop the other day, and it's "Hi, Bert, go buy yourself a meal." So its funny, I have no hard feelings. They're all just doing their job.

Yet for every Ron or Bert,[4] there were other subjects—particularly those who were still literally homeless—whose strategy for survival was basically one of avoidance. Often they were subjects who were found to be ineligible for benefits, even in the immediate aftermath of the tent city protest, or those who were unwilling to accept any behavioral controls as a condition of benefits. Most prominent among these was a group of older male alcoholics who accepted the label "the drunks" and spent more time at "Hobo Jungle" than at Checkerboard Square. Many of these subjects, who resembled the skid row bum stereotype, had been thrown out of shelters or halfway houses for drinking, and some were banned from city facilities. Most had little consistent source of income.

Not surprisingly, subjects who engaged in intermittent criminal activity also avoided the benefit system. Dennis, a homeless subject interviewed during a stint at the county jail, forcefully stated that he had never received social benefits and avoided even soup kitchens, saying, "I just don't do the charity thing!"

Others had quite justifiable fears of involvement. Tanya and Mark, as noted in Chapter 3, had seen their child removed by the state child protective office when Tanya's mother complained about her. When I visited them, they were eligible for—but not receiving—AFDC, food stamps, Medicaid, and possibly other benefits. Tanya and Mark realized this, but despite the fact that the income maintenance division of welfare is technically separate from child protective service, Tanya stated sharply:

We're having no contact with these agencies. The more they see you, the more they look at you and your family. No, I'd rather starve than [call] welfare. … All we want is [name of child] back, that's all.

Perhaps ironically, in view of the stereotypes about welfare, it is those driven out of the social service system due to its barriers and the principle of deterrence who tend to become the long-term homeless and those most feared by society (criminals, drunks, and the like). In this sense, the system is accountable for creating, rather than alleviating, homelessness and poverty. Those subjects who receive even a small AFDC or SSI check have, by anyone's measure, fared far better since 1987 than those with no social benefits (Wagner & Cohen, 1991).

As with the shelter system, other subjects found ways to quietly resist or manipulate the system, and some also resisted through continued political or legal action. I have noted the considerable underground work done by subjects while on social benefits (in violation of the rules), as well as the number of subjects who bent the truth to secure benefits. Many subjects had gained considerable sophistication in understanding their legal rights, in knowing how to talk with officials, and in telling workers what they wanted to hear. They were often aided in the process by supportive workers:

> **Del:** The [social] worker I have now is real cool. And I can even tell him some stuff that … you know, is not on the up and up … kinds of work I do [illegally].

> **Cora:** You have to be kind of sophisticated and know who you're dealing with. There are [a] lot of social workers, therapists, who've helped me, and I know now who I can go to if I need advice … and without the [advocacy groups] I would be lost altogether.

A number of subjects were engaged in ongoing struggles with bureaucratic agencies, often at a risk of personal retaliation. Theodore, a self-styled peer advocate who led his own small advocacy group, was a dynamo who ran around North City arguing with welfare workers, shelter attendants, city officials and anyone else who would listen. Theodore had reached a political understanding of homelessness and the "system" and was almost unconcerned about his own fate:

> Yeah, everything has happened to me. [Been] banned from shelters, thrown out of [the] welfare [center]. [Last] landlord evicted me. But I don't care. I'm fighting not for myself but for every poor, mentally ill person who can't help himself or anyone who doesn't know the rules, and I know they [reference unclear] hate me for it.

Alicyea, a highly intelligent and sophisticated 17-year-old who has been in the system since she was 5, was another dynamo of litigation and protest, but not from a political perspective. She had enlisted a local legal aid service to defend her after she and her child were evicted by a landlord for having a dog. She enlisted the service again when she was homeless and the state threatened to take her child. As noted in Chapter 3, Alicyea was apparently considering filing a suit against the state for treatment she received when she was a foster care child. Unlike Theodore, Alicyea did not think of her efforts as political but just as a method of personal survival:

> *Alicyea:* [It's been] an ongoing battle from day one [with the system]. I was fighting every day to survive. And I figured it out a long time ago, and ever since that day I decided there is no way [it's] gonna run me down.

> *Interviewer:* Do you ever get discouraged? Just think the heck with it … these fights with the state?

> *Alicyea:* (laughs) You know, I lived on the streets for a year and a half. Eating nothing but a doughnut a day or something. So this ain't so hard, I can survive this … that's only reason I'm doing it, for myself, no one else.

Other Social Service Systems

Child Welfare, Mental Health, and Criminal Justice Systems

Although subjects interacted with a large number of service systems, the child welfare, mental health, and criminal justice systems all deserve mention as major contributors to homelessness and targets of avoidance and resistance by subjects. As noted in Chapter 3, a large number of subjects were abused children whose first contact with any government system was with child protective agencies, state agencies that investigate child abuse and neglect. To put it mildly, child welfare employees are in a veritable "hot seat" since workers are caught between society's mandate to keep the family together and the reality of frequent scandals and public reproach. No matter how professional the staff is, child welfare agencies in most states are limited by the lack of acceptable alternative placements for children (good foster homes or group homes), the hostility of family members when a child is removed from their home, and U.S. society's harsh legal repression of children and adolescents.

Subjects' memories of their childhoods suggested that the child protective agencies either supported abusive natural and foster parents or simply acted irrationally. Harry, for example, remembers that after the first time he ran away from his adoptive home, a child welfare worker and the police made each child in the home say he or she loved the parents. Harry refused to say he loved his abusive adoptive father, and as soon as the police and the social worker left, he was beaten up. In a very different example, Cheryl remarks that she spent a few years with a wonderful foster family ("some say it's the best in the state"), yet she was removed when the parents experienced some financial and personal problems. "There must have been a way to save this home. I loved them," Cheryl said tearfully. Of course, it is impossible to second-guess all of the actions of child welfare workers, and in some cases what subjects regarded as punitive or irrational actions were perhaps necessary or unavoidable. As is the case with many poor people, however, the key point is that subjects' first contacts with the "system" were negative ones that served to structure and influence the development of a culture of resistance later in life. For example, Harry's comments made it clear that he saw the police and child welfare officials as powerful allies of his abusive father.

Clearly abused and neglected children in the United States who refuse to submit to parental discipline are subject to repression and hostility by public and voluntary agencies. Even teens at age 16 or 17 are not considered adults and, if found by police or child welfare officials, are returned to their homes regardless of their preferences. When the teenager is able to forcefully assert the claim of being a victim of abuse, he or she is generally denied the right to live on his or her own or with friends but is typically placed in a shelter and eventually into the foster care or group home system. In most cities and towns in the state studied, older adolescents are denied all relief since they are not considered needy individuals but are viewed as wards of either their parents or the social service departments.[5]

The denial of adult rights to adolescents combined with the lack of social benefit assistance leads to battered and neglected youngsters "voting with their feet," fleeing abusive natural or foster parents for the streets, highways, and abandoned buildings. Cora explains the dilemma she confronted:

> I'm 16, I'm being clobbered. I run from this foster home and then [social service department] puts me in another. And then another. It's a shuffle, back and forth. I go to the city [welfare], but they won't help me [because] I'm underage. They say, "Go back to your home." So that's how I ended up running away and living with my sister [in North City].

As noted in Chapter 3, teens placed in foster homes and group homes through child welfare officials are "aged out" of the system when they turn 18. They are generally not provided with social benefits or assistance at that time. Magically, somehow abused and neglected children who have been in a foster home, group home, or an institution—sometimes for years—are supposed to have enough money to live on their own and possess the skills necessary to successfully adjust to the adult world.

As with the child welfare system, the mental health system has received mounting public criticism for its role in generating homelessness. Despite the effort to blame homelessness on deinstitutionalization, however, institutionalization also remains part of the problem. The problem, succinctly stated, is that few, if any nonrepressive sources of psychological aid to the poor remain. Most subjects had experienced a refusal on the part of local private practitioners or mental health centers to serve the poor.[6] Confronted with a poor or homeless person with no insurance who is potentially severely mentally ill (or a substance abuser), most mental health agencies and practitioners either deny services or place the prospective client on a long waiting list. In response to the lack of services, compounded by their homelessness, a number of subjects began to use the state mental hospitals for both psychiatric services and a place for shelter:

> **Ben:** I went to this place and that and then the other. I wasn't eligible, they said, not for this [mental health agency] or that. And I'm losing it. Need med[ication]s. Nowhere to stay. I just kept going up to [state hospital], using [it] as a place to stay, rest, and, yeah, the meds.

> **Lorraine:** I'd get so frustrated, so alone, and so little care [from psychiatric services she was enrolled in] that it sounds funny, but I'd just call [state hospital] and say, "I'm coming," and it was a relief, if [they] let me in.

Despite the paradox of homeless people using the state hospitals for shelter, the critique of psychiatric hospitalization over the past 40 years remains valid. Even when admission is voluntary, the treatment at such institutions is at best cursory and impersonal and at worst repressive. The hospitals also (at least for most years that the subjects recalled) failed to adequately plan for patients' reentry into the community:

> **Mitch:** Oh, don't get me started on [the institution he was in]. I was so over-medicated, I think at one point they had me on 20 drugs. I couldn't stand up straight. ... I was talking suicide, and a psychiatrist, he said something like, "Don't discount the idea."... No, [I] got the heck out [of] there. Just walked out onto the streets.

> **Greg:** I was discharged [from the state hospital] with a bus ticket [back to North City] and $2.

> **Interviewer:** Nothing else? Were you referred to housing or a group home or anything?

> **Greg:** Nothing. They said I was OK now.

Both Mitch and Greg ended up homeless.

The state in which North City is located, like many other states, is under a court-supervised consent decree to reduce its in-patient psychiatric facilities and to provide comprehensive community care of the severely mentally ill. Despite fits of progress, state budget cuts, along with practitioner reluctance to serve the chronically ill and the "not-in-my-backyard" movement among citizens opposed to group homes or halfway houses, have seriously impeded a solution to the institutionalization-deinstitutionalization problem.

May's experiences provide an example of a recent scandalous situation in the state in which the mentally ill are being forced to rely on prisons and jails because of the lack of appropriate psychiatric care. Clearly suffering from serious psychiatric problems, May was serving a nine-month jail term for making harassing telephone calls. May's circumstances were nearly identical to those in the widely reported scandal involving the former president of American University, who is now quietly receiving private therapy. May, however, was imprisoned for her activity. She receives few services and is terrified of the jail situation. Police admit she is inappropriately imprisoned but say there is no place for her except in prison or in the state mental hospital. May outlined the problem of the mentally ill in a manner consistent with recent local newspaper editorials:

> Deinstitutionalization has been a joke in this state, We need alternative care. But there isn't [any]. [Name of agency], they take only the cream of [the] crop. [Agency] is always full. And that's it. Otherwise, the person is homeless, wandering the streets or in and out [of institutions]. It's a scandal. And the blame is with the state [government].

As with the child welfare system and the mental health system, the criminal justice system has become a repository for homeless people that denies any real role or responsibility for the results of its actions. First, the system fails by sins of omission. Concerned only with their mandate to "get the crooks off the street," neither courts nor prisons take any responsibility for exploring the fact that homeless people sometimes intentionally commit crimes in order to secure a warm bed. They fail to offer services for the many street people whose life on the streets causes them to fall into the criminal justice system. Few prisons in the state provide treatment or adequate social services. One homeless person I visited in prison was terrified by being incarcerated and spoke of suicide. He was receiving no counseling, and no protective measures were in place.[7]

Rudy, a North City street person sent to a prison 300 miles away, has begun a personal campaign on the issue of homelessness and prison. He claims, although his figures may not be accurate, that between 15 percent and 30 percent of the state's prisoners have been homeless and that after their release, most of them will return to the streets. He was released from jail in 1986 with only $1 from prison officials:

> They're [prison] supposed to give you $50 and a bus ticket, and, of course, [they're] supposed to make some effort to see you get housing. They did nothing for me. ... I've told them already I'm contacting [a local television anchor], and I'll blow the whistle on the department of corrections.

Of course, societal attitudes and other factors also vastly complicate inmates' reentry into society (as well as that of the discharged psychiatric patient). Both Rudy and Jamie claimed to have lost housing when their respective landlords found out that they had been in prison, precipitating their bouts of homelessness in the 1986–1987 period.

Although the focus of much comment and social criticism has been the sins of omission of these systems—lack of adequate services for children, the mentally ill, prisoners—these critical issues still assume that the systems involved are basically benevolent. Certainly, all of the systems noted in this chapter do employ some committed and idealistic workers. But the structures of the child welfare system, mental hospitals, and prisons (as well as of the shelter system and the welfare system) were historically founded for the purpose of social control. They were not set up as a "service" but as a means for controlling the "dangerous classes," even when nineteenth-century reformers couched the reforms in the language of rehabilitation.[8]

Homeless subjects were not convinced that these systems were going to serve them, even when on occasion a street person entered the state hospital voluntarily or got himself or herself arrested. Rather, as noted in Chapter 2, it was simply a case of the choice between certain harm and protected shelter being decided in these instances in favor of protection from the elements. Although subjects sometimes found staff members they liked and struck up friendships, on the whole they were far more realistic about the efforts of child welfare, mental health, or criminal justice systems to actually administer treatment or rehabilitation than is much of the public.

Resistance to Service Institutions

Obviously, the easiest method for resisting child welfare officers, psychiatric hospitalization, or prison is avoidance. As typified by Cora's running away, many of the young subjects ran to the streets to avoid foster homes, institutionalization, or other societal controls. Similarly, like Tanya and Mark, a large number of subjects refused services to avoid the possibility of having their children taken from them. And, of course, as was noted by Mitch earlier in the chapter, many subjects fled mental hospitals or avoided mental health clinics for fear of losing their freedom. Naturally, subjects were also engaged in a daily cat-and-mouse game with police since many actions, including committing victimless crimes, could land them in jail.

In contrast to shelters and welfare centers, the institutions above are far less amenable to organized protest due to the low legitimacy given inmates of prisons and those in mental facilities or residential homes for children and to the obvious police power that would be brought to bear in such cases (e.g., prison riots). Thus, subjects' resistance to these systems tended to consist of manipulation and efforts to control the situation through deception or through gaining subtle power. Many young subjects learned to lie to and manipulate child welfare workers and the staffs of residential facilities. "Working the system," they covered up their activities with their peer group and their absences from school or flights from their parents or guardians while on scheduled visits or releases. Interestingly, the group home or residential setting appeared to give much more power to adolescents than did the more atomized family or foster care setting. A number of subjects described group homes or transitional residences for street kids as "cool." Eric describes how he was able to manipulate the staff of his residence:

> They [staff] thought I was a "good boy," smart. And they were only there from Sunday to Friday. So all week, we're straight, we're cool. But then on the weekend, wow, you name it, we had everything, booze, drugs. ... Now I think of it and I wonder whether [it was] so cool, really. I mean, I was screwing up, really, and yet the staff kept telling me I'm doing great.

Del told a similar story about an adolescent shelter in North City. Describing the staff as "cool" and telling of activities ranging from pool to video games, he also describes how a gang of street kids was able to dominate the shelter:

> We were tough, and nobody pushed us around. The staff, everyone knew it ... so we got what we wanted a lot, and after awhile I didn't mind being there at all ... sort of miss it now.

In a similar vein, the staffs of mental health facilities are also subject to manipulation and passive resistance. Subjects who possessed some intelligence and became familiar with the system were able to maintain some independence and autonomy by carefully gauging what workers wanted to hear and avoiding workers they distrusted. Lorraine had spent a great deal of time in transitional residences as well as in psychiatric hospitals:

> So you sit down with these caseworkers, and [they want] you to set goals. They give [you] this goal and that goal crap. ... You have to fit into their progress reports, so you give them a little news. You comply because it's easier to [do so]. But then, other workers I avoided like a plague. It becomes a game, really, because you're just trying to survive, never mind all this stuff about meeting your potential.

Resistance becomes more collective at times when patients violate rules that are imposed upon them by facilities, rules they regard as foreign to their nature. Randy was thrown out of a supported residence for the mentally ill because he went out with a group of friends at night in violation of curfew and other rules. Teddy was kicked out of a transitional residence when he and a few friends started arguing with an administrator.

Whether one believes subjects acted in the most appropriate fashion, the key point centers on these subjects' perception that the bureaucracies of the welfare state were essentially a control device arrayed against them. At best, these institutions were tolerated for awhile in exchange for a bed and some other services; at worst, these facilities felt like concentration camps. As we will see, however, rather than condemn all social services, most subjects wanted certain services. The types of services they wanted, however, were those with no behavioral controls and those in which services were provided as an entitlement. Finally, as we see in Part Two, subjects most appreciated settings that were small communities in which they and their friends were able to maintain a strong amount of control and have social interaction. The approval and even enjoyment shown by subjects for these alternative service agencies suggest that as a society, we certainly have the technology to help the homeless and the very poor if we so choose.

Notes

1. The social control embedded in early social welfare and social work was a key complaint of labor unions and working-class groups in the 1890–1930 period. Two quotes that could well have come from our subjects serve as examples: "Social workers are people peeking through your window, seeing how you live and what you are; called to see what your wife was doing and knew her business maybe better than you did" (quote on worker's perception in Dubofsky, 1968:26); and "Let social busybodies and 'professional morals experts' reflect upon the perils they rashly invite under the pretense of social welfare" (Sam Gompers of the American Federation of Labor, quoted in Withorn, 1984:13).

2. Much of the information about homeless people's opinion of North City shelters and the local welfare system was gleaned from 63 completed fact-finding questionnaires collected by the Coalition for the Dignity of the Homeless and Poor in July 1987, as well as from the 65 in-depth interviews done for this study (since 27 questionnaires were from subjects not interviewed in 1990, this makes a total of 92 people). Moreover, in addition, as noted in Chapter 2, my research assistants and I talked to dozens of other street people as well so that far more than a total of 100 people were surveyed.

3. The Family Support Act of 1988 has, for the first time, mandated that all states must have an unemployed parent provision under the AFDC program, which could include a 2-parent family. Its conditions are extremely restrictive, however. As of this date, probably 98 percent of AFDC recipients remain single mothers and their children.

4. Of course, accommodation with the benefit system is clearly more likely when subjects obtain a consistent benefit, such as Social Security. However, other factors that relate to accommodation, resistance, or avoidance are political activism, psychological state, and social network membership among subjects. For example, Mitch, though on SSI benefits, continued to be a thorn in the side of all systems through his militant advocacy efforts. The social network consisting of the self-declared "drunks," however, did not engage in active resistance even when they were treated quite harshly by welfare officials and received few social benefits.

5. Local newspapers revealed in 1990 that some towns were in fact aiding some teens on general relief, which caused consternation among taxpayers and in the newspapers. Generally, however, even when local relief funds are given to teenagers, the funds are for payment to shelters or group homes, transportation to these facilities, and similar provisions rather than to support youths who wish to live on their own.

6. A local newspaper ran a series of exposés in 1989 on the failure of local mental health agencies to serve the poor and the chronic psychiatric population despite state mandates and funding to do so. Agencies found this group less profitable than private patients or other third-party reimbursement and also preferred the more middle-class neurotic patients, who were considered more "amenable to psychotherapy."

7. In one recent highly publicized case in the state, a mentally troubled prisoner was tortured to death by other prisoners. Newspaper editorials expressed shock that this particularly gruesome incident could occur virtually under the watch of prison guards, and a state investigation is underway of both the case and the broader issue of the protection of mentally ill, unstable, and unpopular prisoners from fellow inmates.

8. Important historical treatments of social control in the development of institutions include Foucault (1965, 1977), Rothman (1971), and Katz (1986). For a critique of the movement to deinstitutionalize as a new method of social control, see Scull (1977).

Part Two

The Social Organization of the Streets

"To the rest of the city [Cornerville] is a mysterious, dangerous and depressing area, ... Respectable people have access to a limited body of information [about] Cornerville ... people appear as social work clients, as defendants in criminal cases, or as undifferentiated members of the 'masses.' There is one thing wrong with such a picture: no human beings are in it."
—*William Foote Whyte, introduction to* STREET CORNER SOCIETY *(1966 ED.:XV).*

"As part of ... [a] team [to count the homeless] I ... took a ground-eye view of the homeless habitat. ... Somewhat unexpectedly, we found that even here, order and routine prevailed ... if sleeping rough isn't anarchy, neither is it madness. Like 'the heath' in Shakespeare's time, the 'street' in our own has come to signify a kind of repository of things evil and alien, and that is a badly damaging misrepresentation."
—*Kim Hopper, president, National Coalition for the Homeless,* SAFETY NETWORK *(April 1991:4)*

Beyond the Pathological View

As William Foote Whyte noted in 1943 and Kim Hopper suggested more recently, the public equates the streets, the slums, and the poor with social pathology and social disorganization. Whether the slum areas are occupied by lower-class Italian men, as in Whyte's famous study, by black street-corner men (as in Liebow, 1967; and Anderson, 1978), or by predominantly white New Englanders in North City, the public tends to avoid these areas and often looks upon them with disgust.

We do not completely understand why people so fear the slum. Whyte (1966) brought out one important factor when he described the misleading nature of media reports:

The newspaper presents a very specialized picture [of Cornerville]. If a racketeer commits murder, this is news. If he proceeds quietly with the daily routines of his business, this is not news. ... The newspaper concentrates upon the crisis—the spectacular event. ... It is not a good way to understand [the people of Cornerville]. For that purpose, the individual must be placed into his social setting and observed in his daily activities. (p. xvi)

Indeed, a similar scenario exists in North City. Press reports cover extensively the rare murder in the poor parts of North City but provide virtually no coverage of normal routines and events among the poor. Occasionally, during the severe winters, human interest stories about the homeless appear. When violence does not dominate the rare news about street people in North City, stories that evoke pathos do. Generally, the local media portray the downtown areas occupied by street people as, at best, worthy of charity but to be avoided and, at worst, as centers of social disorganization and crime.

Fear of violent crime, overdetermined by the media, affects the general public view of the slum. Much of the public may also fear aggressive panhandling or soliciting on the streets; and for some the sight of the poor and the homeless give rise to feelings of guilt and depression. The motorist or pedestrian passing through a rundown section of the city wants to avoid danger and get through the area as quickly as possible. With little or no opportunity for or interest in face-to-face interaction with the very poor, the passerby takes a protective stance. The context of the exchange, as Anderson (1990) so well describes about the social construction of the black male and white passersby in the inner city, is one of protective maneuvers between potentially hostile forces. The middle-class person takes no chance of misinterpreting either the verbal or the nonverbal cues of the people on the street and often moves to the other side of the street when he or she spots a perceived member of the "underclass."

The ethnographer (and perhaps to some degree the cop on the beat, the settlement worker, and the local priest) sees the slum differently than it is viewed by the general public. Trained to look at the local social structure and wanting entry into the social groups of the poor, the ethnographer tries to understand the culture of different groups. Ethnographers report that "what the middle class person looks upon ... as a mass of social confusion, a social chaos, the insider finds ... [to be] a highly organized and integrated social system" (Whyte, 1966 ed:xvi); they are usually accepted and trusted by slum dwellers and are often treated warmly by them. In North City, street people always knew that the researchers were not *of* their own culture but were pleased that some people from the dominant culture offered them even a modicum of acceptance and interest. Once street people understood that we were not police, "narcs," or city welfare workers, they showed warmth toward us along with expressing surprise that anybody wanted to learn their opinions or was interested in their lives.

The nonpathological view of North City's streets does not deny that a wide variety of behaviors are found there that a majority of the public (and most mental health and social service professionals) might regard as pathological. There is plenty of drinking and drug use on the streets and in the abandoned buildings of North City. There is property crime, particularly petty larceny, and a small segment of the homeless population engages in breaking and entering. Some street people have been prostitutes. Those who see such behaviors as opposed to their moral code would probably not want to spend time on the streets. Nevertheless, a nonpathological view reflects the fact that a majority of the street people are not criminals or sociopaths; some admit to having had times in their lives when desperation forced them into these behaviors, whereas others have never engaged in more than minor deviancy (panhandling, loitering, petty stealing of cigarettes).[1] Most important, in contrast to the stereotypes held by the public, deviant or dysfunctional behavior on the part of some (or even all) members of a social group hardly contradicts the finding that street people have their own norms, culture, and community—a finding that is usually ignored by those intent on avoiding close contact with them.

Community

Despite the tremendous obstacles to existence that grinding poverty, lack of shelter, and exposure to the elements present, the street people of North City can be described as inhabiting a community with its own set of institutions, norms, social networks, and subcultures. This view was often expressed by street people themselves, particularly those who have been physically or geographically cut off from the community:

Arnie, now living in Florida: I'll always remember the friends I made on the streets in [North City]. We stuck together; there was a real community up there.

May, interviewed in jail: We were like a family, [particularly] at tent city. People took care of one another. And around this time, I felt needed, wanted, and connected to them [street people] ... [the] only time I felt this way [in my life].

In fact, street people are so strongly associated with the social networks they develop on the street that as Katherine comments and I return to in Chapter 8, the worst thing that can happen to some street people is to be isolated from their peers:

When you're homeless, you have no privacy, no corner of your own. You're often with people 24 hours a day. And this seems weird, maybe [to the public], but you get used to it ... and then it's not good when you get placed [by social workers] in some small room far away and you're isolated [when] you're used to being with people. That's why people, they keep going to places like soup kitchens. A lot of them [formerly homeless] don't eat, they'll have maybe a coffee, they're there to socialize, see their friends.

As Wellman and Leighton (1979:387) note, it may well be that the very paucity of resources and the unfavorable circumstances the poor and some ethnic minorities face lead them to form stronger social ties and greater solidarity than do middle-class people. In other words, given the possibility of danger and starvation on the streets, street people cannot ignore their neighbors or be hostile toward many people. Moreover, since they lack the resources available to the middle class, they cannot rely on exchanges through the marketplace and the workplace to meet their needs but must engage in mutual aid in order to survive.

A caveat is in order, however, lest I give the impression that all homeless or formerly homeless people of North City are part of a community. For a variety of reasons, the number of homeless people in North City is always larger than that in the active street community. Some people become homeless for a short period of time after a fire, flood, or unemployment, and, particularly if they are in traditional families, they may secure relatively quick relief from the "system." If their period of homelessness lasts for a week or two or even a month, and if they are fearful of the streets, they may avoid as much contact as possible with the longer-term homeless. At the opposite extreme, some longer-term homeless people are completely isolated, including the relatively few (in North City) who are actively psychotic. It is possible to be homeless in North City and avoid or isolate oneself from the street community.

In Chapters 6 and 7, I focus on two aspects of the Checkerboard community that contrast most strikingly to the public view that life on the streets is pathological or disorganized.

Alternative Institutions

In Chapter 6, I discuss the presence of a number of formal organizations and institutions in North City that play a key role in the lives of many street people. In contrast to the institutions of social control discussed in Chapter 5, street people eagerly became affiliated with some organizations they regarded either as "their own" or as supportive of their community and culture. In contrast to some earlier classic ethnographies (see Whyte, 1966; Gans, 1962, for example) in which the community rejected outside intrusion, the Checkerboard Square community was not hostile to outside influences. In fact, many members of the community embraced political, religious, and therapeutic causes that were promulgated by some social workers, ministers and priests, and professional advocates. However, despite the importance of formal organizations and social movements in understanding the street community (and its informal organization, discussed in Chapter 7), street people—like many Americans—are profoundly ambivalent about organizations and movements and sometimes abandon them when suspicions, or the reality, of personal dominance or outside control were present.

Social Organization

In Chapter 7, based on participant observation and data from key informants, I outline the structure of the street community of North City by dividing the overall community into a number of subcultures. I examine the different norms, patterns of affiliation, and cultural values of each subgroup and the linkages among the different groups that form the whole. I argue, along with Susser (1982:ix), that the social organization of street people reflects not only common life-styles or values among these primary groups but broader socioeconomic and historical trends as well. Different degrees of societal hostility toward subgroups of homeless and poor people, and different access to resources among subgroups at once unite primary groups and sometimes divide and limit overall social cohesion within the street community.

Notes

1. It should be noted that North City is located in a region with a relatively low violent crime rate. In 1991, North City had 276 violent crimes per 100,000 people, compared with 758 nationally and 832 in Boston for a regional comparison (Uniform Crime Statistics, FBI). I suggest, however, that the overall thrust of my comments is not unique to North City or to New England. As Katherine Newman (1989) noted, in no community in the United States are a majority of citizens criminals or even unemployed. Using data from central Harlem (New York City), Newman suggests that the pathological view of the black inner city is also skewed based on exaggerated media reports.

6

Alternative Institutions and Movements Among Street People

It is interesting for several reasons to describe and analyze the formal organizations and social movements in which street people participate. First, not only does homeless and poor people's interest in, curiosity about, and involvement with a variety of institutions in North City contradict the public stereotypes of the homeless and the very poor, but, as I discuss in the "Discussion" section of this chapter, it also contradicts some ethnographic research that has viewed primary groups of poor and working-class people as aloof from formal organizations and hostile toward the intrusions of "alien forces," such as middle-class-dominated settlement houses (Whyte, 1966:98–108). Second, the description of several elements of alternative institutions in North City will help us to understand the overall social organization of the streets presented in Chapter 7. Some subgroups among North City's street people had a relatively shallow attachment to organizations and movements, whereas other subgroups were actually formed around their participation in organizations and movements. The presence or absence of organizational ties, as well as belief systems (political, religious, and similar systems), among different parts of the homeless community either linked them with others or differentiated them from others and often translated into different amounts of material and social resources.

The Drop-In Center and Other Service Agencies as "Free Spaces"

Interviewer: So what brings you to [Drop-In Center] every day?

Murray: Well, it's really not the breakfast, not the social workers. It's to meet [my] friends. You see, this place is a common meeting area, it's our space.

On the edge of the downtown slum district about 5 blocks from Checkerboard Square, in the morning hours a passerby observes a large cluster of poor people smoking cigarettes and talking in small groups behind a wire fence in front of the rather dilapidated exterior of the Drop-In Center, housed in the basement of an old church. The crowd could be waiting at a welfare office, but it is too diverse (including elderly people, women with young children, large groups of adolescents) for the Department of Social Services, and there is too much kidding around and relaxed conversation for it to be a waiting line at a bureaucratic office.

In 1974, long before the crisis of homelessness struck North City, the Drop-In Center was founded by a local university professor who had participated in New York City's Mobilization for Youth (the controversial program that was the model for the national "war on poverty" in the 1960s). The center's founder self-consciously followed the settlement house and community action traditions in social work, which suggested "low barriers" to service and an advocacy-oriented model of social service. The Drop-In Center serves breakfast to about 200 poor people daily; provides housing assistance and other counseling and advocacy services upon request; and, in recent years, has added group and community services such as men's and women's groups, art groups, and a consumer-run community meeting. In the past few years, the large crowd at the Drop-In Center has attracted a growing number of outreach workers from a host of other agencies (alcoholism and drug, vocational services, and public health agencies), as well as ancillary services ranging from haircutting to free dentistry. A majority of North City's homeless use the Drop-In Center as their mailing address, and many use the lockers there to store personal belongings.

The Drop-In Center received strong praise from almost all of the street people. This was true of only a few other service agencies in North City: some soup kitchens, several innovative settlement-like programs for adolescent street kids and the mentally ill, and the adolescent shelter that opened after tent city. The center demands nothing of people who come there. One can simply go for breakfast and leave or have breakfast and spend time inside or in front of the building (there is no smoking in the building, hence there will be a crowd outside even in cold weather). Quite often, however, the street people we spoke to had requested and received a social worker from the Drop-In Center to assist with housing, city welfare, employment, or personal problems. These people strongly differentiated the Drop-In Center from the institutions of control in North City:

Agnes: This [Drop-In Center] is a good place to come ... so many places, it's so much red tape you have to go through. I mean, they [social workers] want your whole life history before they even give you 50 cents. ... [It's] not like that here. They care.

Jonathan: They [Drop-In Center staff] treat you with respect and dignity. It's the only place [where] I feel this way ... it's a category by itself, like family.

Another way in which the Drop-In Center differs from most social service agencies, comments Jonathan, is that "everybody knows everyone down here, there's no distinction." Indeed, at the center one is hard-pressed to identify the staff. Everyone from the executive director to student interns is dressed very casually and can be seen mingling with the crowd. Indeed, over the course of the study, we found that as many as a dozen formerly homeless denizens of the street had volunteered as breakfast workers at the Drop-In Center, further complicating an easy division between staff and clients. When a problem broke out at the center, it was common to see staff and more long-term clients work together to help. For example, when a man had an epileptic attack and fell to the floor, clients advised a young student intern on how he should be treated, and other clients rushed out to summon an ambulance.

Indeed, staff-client roles are blended in more important ways. The center serves a majority of North City's homeless and has always had some focus on community action; thus, its directors have frequently been involved in the political and advocacy efforts of the street community. Jimmy, a former director, helped with tent city and was considered a personal friend by many street people. As described by Arnie, "Jimmy was a cool guy, please say 'hello' to him. I mean, he was so helpful, but also he's nobody's fool. He understood what was happening with every one of us, but he knew also when to watch his back." At times, the center's telephones, mimeo machine, and space were used by indigenous homeless activists for planning demonstrations, for strategy sessions, or for fundraising.

Staff, particularly the large number of interns who were pursuing social work degrees, struggle to learn and maintain a professional role and, consistent with their professional training, try to maintain some social distance. Most street people are men, and most of the social workers are women. It was not unusual, when we were conducting interviews at the Drop-In Center, to see a street person run up to a worker, put his arm around her, and proudly proclaim, "This is [so-and-so], she's my worker. Have you met her?" Close relationships occasionally caused problems. A street person chatting with a member of the research team complained that his worker came up to him and said, "You're the client and I'm the worker, and that's as far as it goes." Complaining that a "wall" still existed between client and worker, the middle-aged man stated, "Look, if I go to the dentist, he works on my teeth. But if I see him on the street and [we] talk about baseball or something, I consider him a friend. It's not a contradiction." Of course, we were not privy to what behavior preceded the incident between the worker and the man; it may well have included sexual innuendo.

Quite a few subjects met spouses or partners at the Drop-In Center or at soup kitchens, and a number of reunions took place here. An informant, Larry—who now works as an outreach worker—told a story of Lonnie, a middle-aged alcoholic, meeting his ex-wife for the first time in 8 years at the Drop-In Center.

It was an emotional scene right in front of me. They were really happy to see each other! She was now in the family shelter, he at [the alcoholic shelter], and she gave him pictures of [their] two kids, and all day he kept showing everyone [staff and clients] those pictures.

Although the center's workers and student interns seek to develop their skills involving social casework, engagement strategies, and ways to intervene with clients, it was clear from the interviews that street people appreciated the center most for its concrete material services (breakfast, housing referrals, haircuts, dental and medical checkups, mail service, lockers, help with city welfare), for the fellowship with workers, and—most of all—for its "free space" to spend time for a number of hours protected from the elements, to mingle and catch up with old friends, to gossip, and to see old friends who had just returned to town (the Drop-In Center was almost invariably the first place street people came to when returning to North City).

Some irony is evident in the occasional complaints of staff, particularly student social workers, that homeless clients are "not changing" or "are using" them or the center services without "getting their lives together." It seems almost endemic for service staff who work with poor people to go through a period of frustration, or burnout. For many social workers, the concrete assistance and fellowship offered are often conceptualized as a means to engage the client in a meaningful counseling relationship that has goals, such as stopping drinking, obtaining housing, finding employment, and so forth. Many street people did successfully use the center's counseling or case management services, and some did show improvement that can be evidenced in case files. But interestingly, social work and mental health ends are seen differently by the clients. To street people, what makes the Drop-In Center special is not its proficiency in counseling but its acceptance of all sorts of differences and behaviors:

> This place is great for my mental health. It's home away from home. And I don't have to conform to anything here.

> To me, [Drop-In Center] is like a social club. Yeah, a good place to come by. Always accepting.

> This place [Drop-In Center] is my family ... the family I didn't have. 'Cause they accept you back here whatever you did, whatever your color, belief, however dumb or smart you are ... no matter what you done.

The Friendly Center: A Mental Health Club

> Mental illness is not a stigma [at Friendly Center]. ... It's worn as a badge of honor.
> —informant Larry, a former staff member at the center

About 2 blocks from the Drop-In Center is a rundown triple-decker building with old cars crowded in the driveway that could easily be mistaken for one of the many apartments housing the destitute of North City except for the ubiquitous crowds of cigarette smokers out front and the constant movement in and out of the house. The center looks better inside than out. One walks into a nicely furnished living room that leads to several smaller lounges with television sets and stereo equipment. The main room contains a large message center for "members" of the Friendly Club, as well as a sign-in sheet for tasks such as shopping, cleaning, and staffing the telephones, with names written next to the tasks. The club's newsletters are prominently displayed, as are newsletters from the North City Coalition for the Psychiatrically Labeled, with which the center maintains ties. On the second floor is a member-run restaurant called the Do Drop In Restaurant, and offices for staff and vocational training are on the third floor.

Founded in 1982 by the Alliance for the Mentally Ill, the Friendly Center represents a consumer-run alternative to the medical model of a treatment center for mental illness. Just as in many subtle ways the Drop-In Center represents the fruits of 1960s activism and experimentation among social workers who work with the poor, the Friendly Center represents the impact of the self-help mental health movement of the 1970s and 1980s (see, for example, Chamberlin, 1978). Modeled after Fountain House in New York City (a world-renowned center that provides a normalized environment for the mentally ill, including consumer control and an emphasis on work and vocational training), the center's literature and comments by staff reflect hostility toward the dominant treatment model for mental illness and state and national policies concerning the mentally ill, as well as anger at the stigma and mistreatment of the psychiatrically labeled.

The center serves large numbers of people, and 20 of the subjects we interviewed or spent time with at Checkerboard Square were Friendly Club members. Sine the Friendly Center did not open until 1 P.M., it was common to find subjects using the Drop-In Center in the morning, staying at Checkerboard Square for awhile, and then going to the Friendly Center for lunch. Some would stay into the evening.

Friendly Center is technically "higher barrier" to clients than the Drop-In Center since the "member" must admit to having a psychiatric diagnosis and agree to participate in activities, including some vocational plans. Obviously, a number of mentally ill street people in North City did not want to do this or did not want to spend time with those labeled *mentally ill*. As Larry—a former worker—comments, a number of subgroups of the mentally ill do not use the Friendly Center: These include the affluent and the middle class (although Friendly Center is formally open to all, the dominance of the center by the very poor has created an ambience that is evidently not pleasing to the more affluent), some actively psychotic or extremely low-functioning mentally ill who refuse the label, and some people who may be high functioning but who do not fit into the informal social group that controls the activities at the center.

Despite the formal barriers and rules, Friendly Club members tend either to avoid or to manage the formal demands made upon them, particularly those that are vocational. An average day at the center for the subjects we spent time with tended to involve playing cards, telling stories and sexually oriented jokes, and gossiping; battles also raged between couples who were going out or breaking up or somewhere in between. Social life was a key focus of discussion. Reports Larry:

> Wow, you'd see whole lives led right in front of you. Holly and Paul, they started their relationship, fought and bickered, ran and called the cops on each other, broke up, got back together, and, you know, everything, all the stages [of the relationship] were played out in front of everyone's eyes. And the [other members], they all took a side in the couple's squabbles.

Many subjects who had secured disability (SSI or Social Security disability) were not very interested in the work program and spent their days spending time at the center and going on the many outings the Friendly Social Club sponsored (to the beach in the summer, to movies and plays year-round, to softball and volleyball games). Others, men more than women, did enjoy serving in the "prevocational" program in which they staffed telephones and did kitchen work or janitorial work for the center. Although the idea of prevocational training was to prepare members for real jobs outside the center, it was unclear how often that occurred. As was the case at the Drop-In Center, Friendly Club members stressed social relationships, caring exchanges with staff, and fellowship as the key benefits of membership:

> **Karl:** I met [staff member's name] a couple of years ago, and I've been crashing at his place since then. … I don't know what I'd do without his help.

> **Nina:** [The staff] cared, they understood, helped me a lot when I felt suicidal and when I was drinking and drugging a lot. … I'll always be involved with them for this reason, not [because of] the programs.

> **Herb:** I worked out of the kitchen [at Friendly Center] for 3 years. No, not much training, really, but hey, I met my wife there, I made friends I'll have my whole life. You can't beat that.

Staff-consumer lines were even less clear at the Friendly Center than at the Drop-In Center. The widespread use of consumers for prevocational work and the commitment to hire the psychiatrically labeled meant that at times, there was little distinction between members and staff. Katherine, a leader of the tent city protest and of other political and religious movements in North City, was employed here, as at times was Nina, the mother of the street profiled in Chapter 2. As we see in Chapter 7, the cross-fertilization that occurs between staff and consumers and the highly organized informal social structure that exists makes the social club one of the "tighter" subcommunities among North City's street people.

The center's formal member-controlled organization was illustrated at a "Centerboard" meeting attended by a research assistant. The Centerboard is an elected board of members that meets twice a month. An hour-long meeting was held using Robert's Rules of Order. A staff person chaired this particular meeting, but discussion was not dominated by staff members—they simply participated as members of the community. The key issue of the meeting was the disciplining of a member who had allegedly threatened another member. Testimony was taken from all sides, with Telly—the 22-year-old sporadically homeless street person we already knew—denying his culpability in the incident, stating that the aggrieved party had evidently misunderstood him. Telly was not popular at the Friendly Center, and the group was vehement in wanting to suspend him (Nina and Amanda led the attack against him). Telly countered that they were prejudiced against him because of his outspoken fundamentalist beliefs and antigay views. Over staff members' mild protests, the group did opt for a suspension. However, after Telly protested that he would not be able to get his mail and telephone calls from his employer, both of which he received at the Friendly Center, the staff assured him that they would meet him at the door with his mail and telephone messages during the 2 weeks he would not be able to come into the center.

Although the Friendly Center was clearly not for everyone—even among the homeless mentally ill of North City—its community was greatly appreciated by the members we met, as was the large number of concrete benefits: meals, shower and cleanup space, social outings, and assistance with benefits, housing, and other needs. A few street people were ex-members and had some bitter feelings. Complaints did not usually involve the staff or the center's services but were directed toward as ex-staff member Larry called it, "the controlling clique" at Friendly Center, which was led by Nina and others. For those who were part of the Social Club at Friendly Center, a strong feeling of social solidarity existed, as well as a deep belief in the abilities of the mentally ill and in the right of homeless and poor people to receive benefits and proper treatment from society.

Religious Movements and Organizations

Henry Miller's review of the history of homelessness (1991) reminds us of a long religious association with begging, wandering, and leading a life of poverty. In medieval times, the vagabond or beggar was not stigmatized but was seen as reflecting Christ's image. The Franciscan ideal led to diverse groups of poor people wandering for alms throughout the realms of Europe. Sometimes these groups included students, mendicant priests, troubadours, and minstrels as well. In post-medieval times, a variety of antinomian and millennial religious movements arose periodically that led followers to live a life of simple poverty in the streets and to proselytize abandoning materialism and preparing for the Second Coming.

A surprising number of street people in North City claimed to have had religious callings to their experiences on the street, and they framed these experiences in ways similar to the Franciscan ideal: that poverty allowed one to see that there is more to life than mere material goods, that many of the rich and middle class were sinners, and that equal justice and equality would come only when Christ's way was accepted.

> **Paula, a street person who is also a self-declared advocate for the homeless:** I was moved by the Lord's voice to help. God is using me to help others. There is more to life than just the material ways of this world. Simple charity and compassion must replace the godless world.

> **Arnie:** Having had my religious experience, how can I explain? ... It sets you free. I'm in a different realm. [I] know that there's more to life than just surviving. You are in touch with the Lord. And the poor, they are the ones who know life, and if they are mistreated, well, its scriptural. The judgment you give is the judgment you get. It's cosmic. The society will get back some day what it gave, only that much.

Religious visions and millenarian ideals in North City often tended to mesh with political social movements and self-help ideologies. Katherine, a key leader of the tent city protest and for years a prominent leader of indigenous political groups, told me: "How did I get involved [in tent city]? I had a vision. A religious experience. The Lord said, use his churches and take his body together and feed the hungry." Many street people cited the example of Mitch Snyder (who several knew personally from the tent city protest) as exemplifying active faith harnessed to social action. Such a dual religious–social change mission was quite common among the leaders of the homeless movement. For others such as Eric, who had become involved in Alcoholics Anonymous through the Salvation Army, religion and self-help were intertwined:

> It was my growing belief in the higher power that led me to stop drinking and accept AA. To accept the Lord and his power and to accept the help of his voice.

It is difficult to estimate the impact of organized religion on North City's street people because some were religious without being churchgoers (like Arnie), some were churchgoers without having much faith or strong religious conviction, and many were not religious or were even hostile toward religion. Based on interviews conducted and observations made over a 2-year period, I would estimate that at least half of the street people studied participated in religious organizations.

Formal religious involvement included several Roman Catholic churches, the Church of the Living Presence—an urban ministry founded by a social worker–minister prior to tent city—a number of Pentecostal and other evangelical Protestant churches, the Salvation Army, a local Baptist church, and an Episcopal church. Religious philosophies differed dramatically among street people and among the ministers and priests who sought out the homeless.

Carla Reets founded the Church of the Living Presence and used the basement of an ornate nineteenth-century Victorian Lutheran church to develop, along with several tent city activists, a clothes closet there 2 nights a week, as well as holding religious services. Reets, a very liberal minister and social activist, insisted that the church be nondenominational and essentially ecumenical in its approach to fighting poverty, with empowerment through community and faith. Reets had left North City for Pennsylvania before I began the study, but she allowed me to review her membership records, where I found the names of 10 active tent city homeless people. When I visited the church, I found half a dozen street people involved in services and a much larger crowd entering and milling about the basement, waiting to receive free clothes.

After services, I met Fredrick, a tall, graying man, who turned out to be a local anesthesiologist. Fredrick was one of the lay leaders of the church who replaced Carla. As we talked, Amy—the mentally ill street person described in Chapter 2—came and sat down next to Fredrick and placed her head on his shoulder. She had been crying. She told Fredrick that she did not know why she was so different from normal women, why God had made her ugly, and why her life was so stressful. Fredrick gave her a little hug and comforted her, telling her she was one of his favorite people in the world. Fredrick told me later:

> Our mission is to care for people—we don't push religion on them. A lot of people come here [be]cause it's a place of caring, a good place to chat, to have coffee and see friends. The [Lutheran] church [the owner of the building] doesn't trust us and makes sure one of their people is here each night to watch us.

In contrast to the nondenominational, almost secular religion of the Living Presence, a variety of fundamentalist groups had developed a significant following among street people. Theodore, Paula, and Dickie—three indigenous homeless advocates—became involved in a Bible study group inspired by their participation in a fundamentalist tent meeting held in a North City park. Their leader was a widowed school teacher, and they met weekly to review scriptures. They tended to have very conservative and rigid ideas about sex roles, homosexuality, and other social issue. Telly, a particularly active fundamentalist, frequently angered the more liberal street people with his rantings about satanism. communism, and widespread homosexuality. The rigid fundamentalism of some street people caused hostility among others:

> **Harry:** Get me away from those bible thumpers! I can't stand these Holy Rollers. I'll chase them out of my sight.

Tobi (criticizing Katherine's and Mitch's religious calling): They keep saying they're doing God's bidding. Give me a break, keep religion out of this! I want to believe what I believe, and if they want to help the rest of us [homeless], don't mess with my mind.

In general, however, it was our experience that church involvement among the homeless was not aimed at proselytizing and that street people's involvement with churches was at least as much for social, recreational, and affiliational reasons as for religious reasons (if not more so). The Salvation Army's Thursday night women's league was popular among the homeless, explains Katherine, not for religious reasons but because of its fresh baked goods, its clothing bazaar, its camping trips and theatre trips, and the feeling of community. Katherine brought as many as 15 people, many from the Friendly Center, to a Christian dinner club about once a month. "No, nothing religious, really. It's a five-course meal, then there's drama or dance or music … it's just good, clean entertainment. No sex or violence or drugs." Cora and Cheryl became involved several years ago with a nondenominational church about 10 miles from North City. They liked the youth leader who ran activities there and enjoyed the camping trips. The church became interested in the homeless and to this day picks up as many as 10 street people in North City by van to bring them to the church.

Quite often the personal relationships that formed between a priest, a minister, or a lay leader and street people determined the church's popularity. A change in leadership could cause street people to leave a church. "Mrs. B" was apparently a very popular lay Salvation Army leader who commanded a following several years ago; when she retired, however, street people had difficulty trusting other leaders who did not display her compassion and her nondenominational approach to charity. Carla, the Living Presence minister, also had a following among many who were not religious. Sam, who was listed as a member in the Living Presence records in 1987 and 1988, told me he had never been religious before this and that since Carla left North City, he had not gone to church: "She was influential on me very much, but basically I'm not that into church."

Katherine, who as a religious activist might have been expected to claim great religious conviction among the homeless, did not believe street people who were actively involved in religious organizations were any different from other street people. Rather, she suggests that since tent city, the churches of North City (not the homeless) had changed:

Interviewer: Do you think people are changed by their involvement in churches? I mean, I'm sure some would hope they'd be less into drugs or alcohol or crime or get themselves off the streets, whatever.

Katherine: No, to tell you the truth, no. I don't see any pronounced changes. Sure, the churches would like that, but it's not their main motivation, either. Before tent city, you would never find a street person at some of these churches, and they didn't join us in marches or in fundraising. They now are more sensitive to the poor and to homelessness. They've made it their issue, and they've accepted them [the homeless]. Sure, they're happy to gain members, if they do, but it's much more of a spiritual, social, community thing now to serve the homeless. … You ask for money and they're there. You have a demonstration and now most churches are there.

The Hidden Community: Self-Help Groups

Early in the research, I met Ronnie, the 38-year-old street musician, at the local YMCA where he showers and drove him to the university to have a comfortable place to talk. When we went to the cafeteria for a snack, I was surprised to hear Ronnie greeted by about a half a dozen students. Only later did I find out that the many "Hey, Ronnies" and "Howaya, Ronnies" came from people he had met at local Alcoholics Anonymous (AA) meetings. This was my first glimpse of the relatively hidden community formed by a variety of self-help groups in North City. For some street people, self-help groups offered a rare cross-class interaction with North City's working and middle classes.

Over time we became familiar with other street people who, like Ronnie, had made cross-class friendships through self-help groups. Alicyea, a dedicated AA member, had recently met her boyfriend Drew, a salesman, through AA. An informant who discussed AA groups in North City laughed about the relationship, saying,

> Yes, that's called 13-stepping [a play on the 12 steps of AA]. That's when someone who has some time in AA, usually a year or more, makes a pass or gets into a relationship with a newcomer in the group. It happens pretty often.

Amy, who participated heavily in AA and Overeaters Anonymous (OA), as well as in the self-help mental health groups, often drew upon her memberships if a problem arose. When Larry, working as a shelter attendant, was forced to bar Amy from the shelter (because of the SSI rule that governs the first 2 weeks of the month), Amy angrily yelled, "I'm going to call my AA friends on you." (Larry is also an active AA member.) Amy has a long list of contacts at AA and also at OA who she can call when she feels distressed and is about to go on an eating or a drinking binge. These contacts evidently include professionals, white-collar workers, and blue-collar workers.

North City's many self-help groups (which occupy the largest amount of space in the major newsweekly's advertising columns, dwarfing the personal ads and club listings) meet in church basements, social agencies, fraternal halls, and health centers. In the past 15 years, the self-help movement has come to include not just AA, Alanon, and Narcotics Anonymous (NA) but also groups for overeaters, people with physical disabilities, those with physical illnesses ranging from cancer to AIDS to brain injuries, children of alcoholics (COA groups) and others who are co-dependent, people with psychiatric disorders, parents who are at risk of abusing their children, people coping with divorce, crime victims or relatives of victims, and, at least in North City, even the unemployed, artists who cannot produce art, and career changers. Since most groups meet at night in locations that ensure confidentiality, few studies have noted the presence of street people or the very poor in self-help groups.

Although active members of self-help groups did not include a majority of street people (it appeared that about a quarter of those interviewed were or had been active attendees), the impact of the widespread self-help movement was evident in the language of many street people. Conversations were sometimes laced with words such as "dysfunctional," "co-dependent," and "recovering" even when the subject appeared to be unable to define these terms or had not been an active member of a 12-step group. Cora, for example, told me that while she was spending time at the adolescent program that resembled the Drop-In Center, "They put an intervention out on me." I asked what she meant. This turned out to be a constructive confrontation between her and the staff and peers about her drinking and drug use. Beyond language, the self-help movement often merged with religion and politics, resulting in two very different reactions: Some subjects completely distanced themselves from other street people, whereas others became more committed to assisting them.

For a number of former street people, involvement in AA or other self-help groups, and the often parallel religious involvement, was a way out of the streets and into "responsibility." Lester and Alicyea, for example, were two active AA members who had left the streets and now avoided contact with street people. They viewed street people as being to blame for their own problems and frequently cited alcohol use as the key cause of homelessness. Ruth, a former street person who moved to Pennsylvania with Carla, cited religious conversion and successful alcohol rehabilitation as "making me look and take responsibility for my own life. A lot of people on the streets, they want to be there … to escape themselves and their problems, numb themselves out." Indeed, Larry, the active AA participant who was a social worker in North City, agreed that AA suggested that only "staying away from your friends" (the street buddies) would allow people to succeed in getting off substances, and in his experience, it was rare for street people to succeed in AA without totally leaving the homeless community.

Yet a number of street people—particularly those who were politically active—combined ideologies of self-help, charity, and political empowerment in such a way as to increase their commitment to help their fellow street people, even if they themselves were now stably housed. Sidney, when housed, still spent time at Checkerboard Square and provided shelter and assistance to a number of his friends: "I know where they've been at, and I feel an obligation to help them and to help lead." Roy spoke about Carlos Castenada, mystical New Age images, and his NA involvement. After he became housed, he spent time at Checkerboard

Square and the Drop-In Center and strongly affirmed his commitment to political activism.

> It's the good fight, and I've been out there since [the] May Day protest [1971 antiwar rally in Washington, D.C.]. It's a war against poverty and ignorance, and I'll be there.

The evolution of homeless activism itself (as discussed in the next section) owes much to the self-help movement because after 1988, peer advocacy came to be the dominant activist paradigm in North City.

Despite the involvement of many street people in self-help movements, and despite there being a number of subjects for whom groups such as AA worked, we found that only a small minority of self-help members actually succeeded in abandoning alcohol or drugs or in leaving the streets. Part of this results from the extreme difficulty any person has breaking an addiction plus the strong street culture supporting coping with the cold, the boredom and fear living on the streets entails through the use of substances. Additionally, AA and other groups have many limitations for street people. Larry notes:

> It really isn't easy for the street person to be in AA. I mean, yeah, the belief, the rhetoric of fellowship is there, but there's a big difference between going to a meeting and being truly accepted into the fellowship. This guy [street person] I remember, he came and he asked to have a sponsor, He asked this guy, a middle-class guy in the group, and the guy didn't even know him, he didn't blink an eyelash before he refused. ... This often happens, the street people have trouble getting a sponsor.

Moreover, many street people feel extremely uncomfortable in AA meetings because their class culture differs so much from that of the majority of the group. Larry again:

> A lot of times they [street people] come to a meeting, and the women are wearing fancy jewelry, the guys may be in jackets and ties, they're [non-street people] talking about their cars, the street person looks blankly. And in most meetings now, you can't smoke. This is a big disincentive. I mean, most street people smoke and dislike this [rule].

A number of street people who left groups like AA (often returning to drinking) expressed hostility and ambivalence toward them. "I hated going to AA. It made me real angry. The self-righteousness, the higher power. I felt like taking a drink every time I left the meeting," said Cora.

Homeless People's Political Movements and Organizations in North City

As with religious movements, there is a long history of interaction between tramps, bums, and hobos and various political movements. Being a tramp became associated with rioting and disorder in the 1870s and later decades of the nineteenth century (Ringenbach, 1973). The "Wobblies," a radical labor union, recruited heavily among tramps and bums between 1900 and 1917 (the Joe Hill song "Hallelujah, I'm a Bum" is one reflection of this). In the current epidemic of homelessness, most of the early years (1975–1985) were dominated by efforts at advocacy rather than at community organization.

More recently, however, a large number of locally based protest movements have arisen among the homeless, including the battles between Mitch Snyder's Community for Creative Non-Violence (CCNV) and the city of Washington, D.C., and the federal government, several tent city battles in Los Angeles (Ropers, 1988), the battles over Tompkins Square Park in New York City, and sporadic efforts to organize a homeless union (the National Union of the Homeless), which has had particular success in Philadelphia. Although the history and development of homeless protest are virtually unrecorded in the current academic literature, most homeless people in North City—despite obvious barriers to communication and the lack of any national or even regional organizational infrastructure—were quite well-informed about major conflicts throughout the nation. Generally, the "word" about what "Mitch (Snyder) was doing" or "what was going on down in New York" was spread by travelers who had been in the major cities and, to a lesser extent, by media coverage.

Just as I separated religious conviction from religious observance in the previous section, political activism and political ideology are also two separate entities (see Wagner, 1990), and the ebb and flow of political activism in North City sometimes involved a majority of street people and sometimes did not. For example, during the conflictual winter of 1989–1990, when the indigenous homeless advocacy group Let's Talk attracted many members, people like Brad ("I'm a revolutionary … I would like to see George Bush dead"), Roy (active since the May Day protest), and Bert (a big Jesse Jackson fan) were not particularly active. However, as we see in Chapter 7, the "Politicos" do tend to cluster together and form a subgroup of the homeless community in North City even when things are quiescent.

Although the tent city protest had initially united the homeless of North City, and despite its generally positive results (see Wagner & Cohen, 1991), to some degree its aftermath split the North City street community. After 3 weeks of protest in the summer of 1987, Mitch Snyder arrived in the city and advocated more militant strategies, including mass civil disobedience and takeovers. The Coalition for the Dignity of the Homeless and Poor eventually rejected such advice and settled the protest, achieving more shelter space, more flexibility in city welfare, and some representation for the homeless on city boards. Several militants expressed bitterness about the settlement 3 years later and blamed the coalition's leadership committee, particularly Katherine, because more changes for the homeless had not occurred:

Brad: The outcome of tent city was a joke! I mean, can you believe they [leadership] took us from city hall [where the protest started] out where we weren't disrupting the city [government]. Its b.s.! Only disrupting will change things.

Theodore: I feel as if we were sold up the river. And I take a lot of flak [because] people still think it's me [involved with Katherine's groups]. ... I'd protest again, yeah, but only if I knew [we] had [the] right leadership and [were] headed in [the] right direction.

However, a number of subjects who had participated in the tent city protest now said they would never do so again and seemed to have evolved in a more conservative direction:

Lester: It [tent city] was a bunch of malarkey. I will never hang with these folks again. They're [the homeless] to blame for their own situation, not the city or the other government. They [government] give these people [help] and they do nothing [with the help].

Kirk: I'm looking out for number one now. Hey, this [protest] did me no good, and I'm not fighting to get these bums more or all these [racist expletives] immigrants who are taking jobs from people.

Nevertheless, at the start of our research in 1989, a majority of street people were involved in a self-styled indigenous organization called Let's Talk, which Katherine and others had formed. The group was run totally by homeless and ex-homeless people, although it was coordinated with groups such as Artists for the Homeless and a local welfare rights organization. The group had ambitious and sometime conflicting goals. It sought to be a classic protest group, confronting the city, going to meetings of the state legislature, using the media, holding weekly vigils on North City's main street, and bringing in educational speakers on current issues. However, it also took on elements of a self-help social service organization. With the help of church and community action funding, a hotline was set up for the homeless, with 30 peer advocates chosen and trained by Katherine, Mitch, and other street people. Carrying beepers, the peer advocates spread throughout the city, providing information to the homeless, assisting them with getting into shelters and applying for welfare, and often confronting the city on individual cases in which clients were allegedly mistreated.

I attended a number of meetings of Let's Talk[1] in the fall of 1989 and winter of 1989–1990. The group met in a three-story building that housed an activist neighborhood organization and a food coop, appropriately called the People's Building. On a cold winter night, from 15 to 40 people would gather in a conference room. The group was chaired by Katherine, who was often mobbed before the meeting started by a number of homeless people presenting their grievances. She and other leaders scrambled to find paper on which to write down the names of the homeless people and of the social workers or city officials against whom they had grievances; such individual conferences typically delayed the start of the meeting. Katherine would finally begin her long search for another crumbled piece of paper buried in her purse that contained the evening's agenda.

An interesting assortment of people attended: some clearly homeless, scraggly dressed men, young women with children running in and out, countercultural types who sometimes turned out to be artists for the homeless (some of these people had also been homeless), and frequently, professionals or advocates in jackets and ties. The chairperson had a difficult time. Often, a homeless person would ask to speak and would quickly be recognized and then would go on and on about a personal situation and not stick to the point. Katherine, adopting her social worker role, was gentle, as, for example, when an old man who was probably mentally ill went on and on about the building he still owned that the city had "borrowed" from him, and she promised to look into it after the meeting. As newer members or less articulate older members told their personal stories, however, longer-term members—particularly militants—would give both Katherine and the speaker of the moment a hard time. "Let's get on with it. … What are we going to do about city hall? Enough b.s." was often shouted.

Although the battles between Let's Talk and the city in 1989–1990 can be judged to have had some success in improving the situation of the homeless, by the spring of 1990 two splinter groups had emerged to challenge Katherine's group. In a news article ("Advocates Leave Homeless Group," May 3, 1990), Theodore and Paula (long-time personal enemies of Katherine) charged that her group had institutionalized a homeless man who was not mentally ill and that Let's Talk was enforcing a social control strategy over North City's homeless. "[Mitch] wants to get the homeless off the street any way possible," charged Paula. The new group set up by Theodore and Paula, called Operation Crisis, promised to continue Let's Talk's peer advocacy but without imposing its will on homeless people.

Dickie, a homeless leader who had returned to North City that winter, took a different tack in announcing the formation of a third group, People Helping People. Dickie did not attack the Let's Talk leaders personally but "called [their] practice of bringing people to soup kitchens and shelters a 'Band-Aid approach'" ("Advocates Leave Homeless Group," May 3, 1990). Dickie promised macro-level political action to obtain more affordable housing and job training and believed that only a coalition of the homeless and other groups in the state would succeed in the legislature, where he declared the "action was at." According to the news article, in May 1990, Let's Talk was left with only 14 homeless advocates, Operation Crisis had 6, and People Helping People had 12.

Rather than advancing political action, the split led to a decline in homeless activism during the next year. Dickie's group could "never get it together." Indeed, I showed up at the People's Building for what Dickie promised would be an

important meeting, only to find the room occupied only by myself, a state legislator Dickie had invited, and a staff person from North City's Coalition for the Psychiatrically Labeled. We chatted amiably, and finally the legislator asked me what
I knew about Dickie, whether he was coming, and what this was all about. After
45 minutes, no one else had shown up, and the three of us departed. No meeting
was held that day, and Dickie apparently never did show up.

The other groups fared no better. A growing hostility built toward Katherine,
due in part to her dominating personality and somewhat undemocratic tendencies. Even more controversial was Katherine's growing connection with a right
wing fundamentalist political movement, which helped her secure a nomination
as a Republican candidate for the state legislature.[2] Sometime during the winter
of 1990–1991, Katherine, Mitch, and the others suspended the Let's Talk hotline.
Although Operation Crisis was still in existence, a research assistant who followed Theodore and Paula around North City's streets saw them assist several
homeless people, but over the entire summer of 1991 she never met any other
members of the group. Based on comments offered by many street people, Theodore and Paula were regarded as being too mentally unstable or eccentric to offer
effective leadership.

Although situational and strategic factors were certainly important in the decline of the homeless movement in 1990—including Katherine's personality;
Dickie, Theodore, and Paula's tendency to be very erratic; and the somewhat
risky decision to deliver a form of social services to the homeless in which the
group could be blamed if a "client" was dissatisfied[3]—I argue that the reasons for
the decline are more structural and are endemic to formal organizations among
street people. Political activity is episodic and can engage a majority of street people at times of crisis, but they see little to gain by going to long meetings, hearing
speeches, and voting on endorsements. Despite efforts by people like Roy to encourage the homeless to vote, few respond or place any faith in conventional political activity. Moreover, as is true with other formal organizations and movements, the homeless of North City are most comfortable with spontaneous,
leaderless action. As soon as a leader begins to acquire power, street people voice
suspicions. The criticism expressed about Katherine ("She's got her hand in too
many cookie jars," "She's getting too powerful") was echoed about other leaders
and would-be leaders.

A year after the split, for example, a homeless man named Gabby, who had just
returned to North City, quickly became involved in advocacy efforts and began to
research the shelters and to lead activities at the newly formed Drop-In Center
Community Group, including initiating a newsletter and developing ambitious
goals for organization. About 2 months after I first met Gabby, I heard that he
had become despondent when a homeless man attacked his legitimacy as a leader
of the homeless of North City. Although I was not present at the verbal inter-
change, the person evidently felt Gabby was becoming a self-declared leader and
asked how he "represented" him. Gabby—apparently more sensitive to criticism

than Katherine, Mitch, or Dickie—seems to have quickly reduced his advocacy efforts in response to the criticism.

Another factor in the political climate was the arrival of the crushing recession in 1990. The recession seemed to verge on depression in New England, and large-scale unemployment in the private sector, combined with state budget cuts, limited hopes for progressive change. When the governor threatened to cut public assistance, the homeless mobilized and joined advocates, city officials, welfare rights groups, and social service workers in protest rallies in North City. The strong response to the calls to demonstrate proved again the ability of North City's street people to protest and mobilize. Yet once the proposed cuts were defeated—at least temporarily—the economic downturn seemed to dampen, rather than encourage, protest. It appeared that at a time when white-collar and blue-collar workers were being laid off and many of them were ending up on welfare, and no jobs or increased state money was available to assist the poor, little was to be gained strategically by battling the city and the state. Finally, the one positive impact of the recession was a massive rise in the vacancy rates for housing and a decline in rents. This led to decreases in literal homelessness in North City in the 1990–1992 period for the first time since the start of the current homeless crisis.

Discussion

Although ethnographic studies are not directly comparable in the way quantitative studies can be, it is of interest to compare the participation of North City's street people in organizations and movements with some classic formulations of participation in blue-collar and poor communities. Some community studies have seen the primary groups of poor communities as almost being defined by their isolation from institutions and formal organizations.

Herbert Gans's classic *Urban Villagers* (1962) focused on the sociability of primary groups on the streets of Boston's Italian West End but specifically faulted the working class and lower class for "its inability to participate in formal organizations and in general community activity" (p. 265). Cynicism and suspicion of outsiders and of politicians prevented the residents of the West End from engaging in active advocacy in the political and social realms. Elliot Liebow's (1967) classic study of black street-corner men in Washington, D.C., went even further in conceptualizing the strong primary ties of these men as *replacing* other types of organization that are more common among the rest of society:

> The portion of [the] individual's energies, concerns and time … invested in self-improvement, careers and job development, family and community activities, religious and cultural pursuits or even in the broad, impersonal social and political issues … on the street corner world are almost entirely given over to the construction and maintenance of personal relationships. (p. 161)

The Checkerboard Square community stands in contrast to the almost total absence of organization and interaction with middle-class people found in Liebow and also in Anderson's (1978) study of black primary groups at Jellys tavern in Chicago and to the suspicion and antagonism of the poor Italian community toward "alien intrusion" seen in both Whyte's Cornerville and Gans's West End. Our study found interaction with a range of organizations (social service, self-help, religious, political) and a variety of middle-class people (ministers, priests, social workers, administrators, welfare rights leaders, and community organizers). The saliency of ties between street people and formal organizations in North City may represent both weaknesses of the Checkerboard community relative to the old urban village and strengths of the street community compared to other primary groups.

Unquestionably, street people lacked the ability to acquire resources and a measure of economic and social security through social networks, as could the denizens of the old urban village described by Whyte and Gans. Cut off from the extended family that Whyte and Gans described, with no access to even low-level occupational roles, and unable to turn to indigenous secondary institutions—such as ethnic organizations, rackets, or the political machines—Whyte describes, the street community is in many ways more dependent than were the old urban villages. Indeed, the necessity of meeting basic needs for food, shelter, and clothing often led street people to visit formal organizations in North City: The Drop-In Center offered breakfast, lockers, and an address; the religious groups offered food, clothes, and warmth; even the self-help groups held the incentive of free coffee and a warm place to stay for a few hours.

To some degree, the participation in organizations in North City can also be seen as reflecting a post-1960s strategy on the part of service providers and religious, political, and self-help movements to consciously do outreach among the very poor in order to attract the homeless through material benefits they presumably could not achieve independently. Although social agencies such as the Drop-In Center can be seen as following the old settlement house tradition, they also reflected the post-1960s social service theories of self-determination and rejection of the direct imposition of middle-class norms on the clients (hence, although Whyte's and Gans's subjects correctly viewed the "caretakers" as threats, the poor of North City did not need to feel threatened by these agencies).[4] In a similar vein, although there have long been church missionaries, the impact of the social movements of the 1960s can be seen to have led some church groups to adopt a more value-neutral and open acceptance of the poor, as is reflected in groups such as Carla Reets' urban ministry. Successful outreach strategies, whether by the churches or social service groups in North City, understood that the concrete needs of the homeless had to be met first, followed by the needs for social ties and community. Controversial issues of substance abuse, life-style, and possible detachment from work or social norms were (if dealt with at all) believed to be impossible to address without the existence of the "close personal relationship," as Katherine described several church leaders' views.

The street people of North City, because of their long and insightful experience with the institutions of control discussed in Chapter 5, were well able to distinguish between organizations that demanded behavioral compliance and those that did not. They were, if anything, more sophisticated than the middle-class observer in distinguishing what was part of "the system" and what was not. For example, subjects frequently verbally attacked social welfare and social workers, but when I asked about the Drop-In Center, the response was very different: "Oh no, I don't think of that as social welfare or the system, they're different," replied Telly. Sam had just finished criticizing churches and the control exercised by a fundamentalist-run shelter when, in response to his involvement in Carla's Living Presence church, he distinguished "bible thumpers" and enforced religion from Carla Reets' humanitarian aid and commitment to the homeless. Subjects frequently denounced national, state, and local political leaders, but when asked about people like Bruno Pickard, an activist welfare rights organizer who was on the coordinating board of tent city (and who has also run for political office in North City), criticism ceased. "Oh no, I don't mean him," said Bert, "he's good people. He's on our side, not the system's."

However, the participation of street people in organizations and movements in North City suggests more than the need for resources and outreach strategies on the part of social workers, ministers, or political organizers. In comparison to the urban villagers Whyte and Gans talked with and Liebow's and Anderson's street-corner men, the North City street people seem far more sophisticated, less insular, and more oriented toward social movements. Although conclusions about the homeless everywhere cannot be drawn from those in North City, it is apparent that several strengths may exist among street communities that may be underreported or unrecognized.

The Checkerboard community was far more open to new information and political and social developments than was the insular urban village. Quite a few of the street people traveled and were fond of talking about developments elsewhere. Some even kept notes about shelter conditions in other cities, conveyed news about political movements, and provided word-of-mouth information about social benefits and programs around the country. Moreover, the community had a sophistication about social movements that is not apparent in the older ethnographies (although this was not one of the research foci of those studies). Many members of the homeless community in North City could discuss political strategies in an intelligent, experienced fashion; many were familiar with self-help movements and critiques of the medical model of mental illness; most were implicitly (if not explicitly) aware of critiques of the Reagan-Bush presidencies, particularly their treatment of the homeless issue.

It can be argued that the street community—detached from the social organization endemic in the old urban village that was based on neighborhood and family ties and indigenous secondary organizations, such as the ethnic political machine and voluntary organizations—has replaced these ties with loosely organized post-1960s social movements. That is, the association over time of local poor people with ex-middle-class countercultural types, critical mental health clients, angry Vietnam veterans, and others has bred a somewhat oppositional world view that accepts as natural homeless political activity and opposition to the government, as well as opposition to establishments such as the mental health system and other bureaucracies. Group norms are influenced not just by oppositional political stances but by the symbolic examples of people like Mitch Snyder and by less oppositional but still social movement–like influences such as the self-help movement, which locates the origin of personal problems within dysfunctional families and looks to the person or group—rather than just to professionals—for change.

Street people's long-term ties to formal organizations and institutions should not be overrated, however. As compared with the earlier ethnographies, some studies conducted in the 1970s (particularly Kornblum, 1974; Susser, 1982), in arguing against the myth of social disorganization and against the view that working-class and poor people are apathetic, seem to present organizational life and political involvement not only as existing but as long-term, consuming commitments within the communities they studied. Of course, Kornblum and Susser studied far more stable communities than North City's Checkerboard Square; perhaps more important, they studied, respectively, Chicago at the time of the Sadlowski challenge in the United Steelworkers Union, and Greenpoint-Williamsbug (Brooklyn, New York) at the time of the New York City fiscal crisis. In comparison to those communities at the times studied, our research over the 4 years (1987–1991) of North City's homeless community suggests that involvement in organizations and movements is far more episodic than was found in these two earlier studies.

If the Checkerboard Square community had been studied only in the summer of 1987 or the winter of 1989–1990, it would appear to be far more mobilized and involved with formal organizations than it was at other times within the 1987–1991 period. I have suggested that despite a strong interest in formal organizations and movements, North City street people are ambivalent about long-term commitment. They are suspicious of leaders and told me so (several quoted the Bob Dylan song, "Never follow leaders, watch the parking meters"). As noted, when political leaders became too powerful or too entrenched, suspicions and criticisms spread widely ("hands in too many cookie jars"). Second, street people did not see long-term gains as resulting from activities such as voting, following agendas, sitting through long meetings, or passing resolutions. Following Piven and Cloward's (1977) view of protest among the poor, I suggest that the poor are mobilized only at episodic intervals when a particular political opening exists or when events propel spontaneous uprisings. When organizations seek long-term members and participants, they tend to develop a more bureaucratic organization, and spontaneous protest declines. Street people in 1991 saw little to be gained from the government during a deep recession in which benefits were being cut or frozen and in which sympathy for the poor had lessened.

The Checkerboard community's culture of resistance blends with an anarchistic spirit in terms of long-term commitment. Not only are political groups held at a distance when permanent leaders arise and positions are filled, but church groups, self-help groups, and the other organizations I have discussed are subject to the same response. Many churches had a following among street people until particular lay leaders or clergy demanded membership or increased involvement; several subjects had left the Coalition for the Psychiatrically Labeled when formal job duties were attached to their stipends (Jack: "I liked hanging out there, writing some poetry ... but then they wanted a number of hours a day, sign in and out. Not worth it to me"). Other subjects were apathetic about social agencies' efforts to involve the homeless in their operations; for example, the effort by the Drop-In Center to form an advisory board of clients faltered in 1991.

Although suspicion of leaders and ambivalence toward formal organization can be ascribed to different sociological facts about the poor, I wonder to what degree this suspicion and ambivalence is not close to that of average Americans. The decline of the U.S. party system and distrust of government, media, trade unions, and churches endemic in the 1990s seems to suggest a degree of similarity, rather than difference, between the view of most of the Checkerboard Square community and that of other Americans.

Finally, my generalization—that there exists an interest in and curiosity about organizations and movements without wanting to make long-term commitments—is one whose exact contours differ among subgroups. The Friendly Social Club and a group I call the Politicos were particularly attached to and interested in formal organizations, whereas other subgroups were more distant. In Chapter 7 I follow the relationship between the formal organizations and the different subcultures on North City's streets.

Notes

1. "Let's Talk" appeared to me to be an odd name, but it seemed to reflect the quasi-religious self-help ideology that came to characterize both the group's and Katherine's own political views. Although the group engaged in a lot of conflict for one with such a name, Katherine initially saw it as an effort to achieve consensus and harmony between homeless and poor people, on the one hand, and city officials and the general public on the other through an open exchange of views.

2. Katherine did run as a most unusual Republican candidate, remaining rather militant on issues relating to homelessness and the poor while opposing abortion and gay rights. Evidently, Katherine was caught up in a power struggle between two wings of the GOP in which a conservative group sought to wrest power away from the dominant moderate faction. The race was for a safe Democratic seat, and her opponent in the November election

won easily. Katherine told me she "was used by the party [GOP]" and does not regard herself as a conservative GOP activist.

3. I had warned Mitch—who frequently called my house during this period—that getting involved in service referrals, assessment of social and psychological issues, and other social service–related roles might be dangerous to the organization. In addition to the question of competency, which was inevitably raised, the group risked the displacement of broader strategies and issues by day-to-day grievances, and it would bear the blame for any mistakes. Indeed, the city, although initially extremely hostile toward groups such as Let's Talk, eventually gave it the equivalent of union status and began to refer clients to it. Katherine, Mitch, and other leaders were then blamed by the city, professionals, and some homeless people when assistance was not secured or when "the system" failed to respond to their advocacy efforts.

4. This is not to say that the workers at social agencies like the Drop-In Center do not hope clients will ultimately adopt middle-class norms. However, since the 1960s the principles of social advocacy and engagement in social work practice have stressed "meeting the client where he or she is at" and accepting diverse life-styles. At the least, I view this as showing respect for religious, political, life-style, and ethnic differences and refusing to openly impose middle-class beliefs and values on clients, as was frequently done by the old settlement house workers.

7

Subcultures and Patterns of Association Among Street People

In order to examine the patterns of living and association, the dominant norms and values, and the social networks on the streets of North City, it is necessary to explore the informal organization of the Checkerboard Square community and its links to the formal organizations discussed in Chapter 6. Street people do not associate or "hang out" randomly but develop social ties within several subcultures. Two of these subcultures—the skid row–like Street Drunks and the crowds of scraggly youth, or Street Kids—are familiar types in most U.S. cities. Two other groups—the Social Club, composed of mentally ill street people, many of whom are or have been members of the Friendly Center, and a group I call the Politicos, whose members organize their lives around advocacy and assistance to other homeless people—may not be as familiar in other cities or may simply be less visible.

The Whole as Greater Than the Sum of the Parts

Because of the widespread tendency to divide the poor according to diagnosis and classification, it is important to begin by noting the primacy of the overall street community. Although different patterns of association and daily life do emerge from my discussion, the Checkerboard Square community is united by daily face-to-face contact, including spending time at the square, at soup kitchens and the Drop-In Center, at the shelters, and so on. Many personal ties cross the different subcultures. Accommodations must be made between groups that are sometimes wary of one another. And they all share overall similarities that flow from their socioeconomic situation and their exclusion from the overall dominant culture.

All groups within the street community suffer from strong social stigmatization by the public and, to varying degrees, by the social welfare system. As noted in Chapter 1, street people who are not in traditional families have long been viewed as the least deserving of the undeserving poor. Societal hostility unites the group and forces structured patterns of organization to survive in economic, political, and social welfare contexts that generally deny these people support and benefits. Second, as I explored throughout Part One, the community can be characterized as a culture of resistance whose adaptations to mistreatment in the family, in the workplace, and by the state are structured around its insights into societal hostility and its rejection of the conventional wisdom about the family, the work ethic, and the "American Dream" generally.

Third, as noted in many ethnographies and community studies of the poor (see Anderson, 1978; Gans, 1962; Horowitz, 1983; Liebow, 1967; Stack, 1974), a strong norm of sociability, including dense social networks, characterizes the community. That is, street people actively seek each other out to spend time together and to participate in various primary groups. Not only do these groups become a central organizing principle in their lives, but street people often suffer depression, anxiety, and boredom when placed in flophouses or other circumstances that geographically separate them from their peers. As Suttles (1968, 1978) has noted, life in the slum tends to lead to "ordered segmentation" in which social groups form and then protect themselves by organizing around territory, ethnicity, age, sex, or other similarity. Indeed, socioeconomic similarity (homelessness) is the overall ordered segmentation of Checkerboard Square, although, as we will see, many of the primary groups also form according to age, sex, and other personal similarities.

Fourth, implicit in this sociability is the presence of mutual aid within the community. The norms of sharing food, cigarettes, alcohol, drugs, information about social services and benefits, money, and housing (if and when available) existed in all subcultures of this community. Of course, frequent disruptions of this norm of reciprocity occurred when different street people felt exchanges between them were unfair.

Finally, the community was capable, within limits, of achieving an overall social solidarity. As was most vividly displayed by the tent city protest, the community saw itself as an oppressed group and under certain circumstances was capable of uniting for joint action. As I explore in the discussion of each of the groups, however, the subcultures differed in their degrees of social solidarity and in their tendency to support mobilization through social or political action.

Classification Versus Association

Although some subgroups among the homeless are joined together—and then come to associate together—based on a diagnosis or a condition, this process should not be confused with the tendency of many experts to subdivide the homeless by diagnostic category or to impute causation (why they became homeless) to these conditions. No simple causative relationship can be determined from the fact that a street person drinks alcohol or is diagnosed as mentally ill. Thousands of residents of North City are alcoholics, for example, and they are not and probably never will be homeless. Similarly, relatively few poor people who drink to excess become homeless. Thousands of people are labeled mentally ill, and most will never become homeless. This alone should give pause to a tendency to overdetermine the causes of homelessness. As has been pointed out by several critics (Johnson, 1990; Marcuse, 1988; Snow et al., 1986), social scientists are unable to distinguish cause and effect; that is, once homeless, many people start to drink, and many begin to exhibit signs of depression and even bizarre behavior rather than having become homeless because of these behaviors.

Moreover, diagnosis and classification, when related to association, are related in a very complex way. A street person may drink heavily, for example, and not be a "Street Drunk." The street person, although he or she drinks may not be drawn to associate with this subculture because he or she does not share other norms and values of that group or may be the wrong age or gender. Others who may be labeled mentally ill aver social ties with the subculture organized around mental illness because, for a variety of reasons, they feel more comfortable spending time with other groups and do not identify with such a label.

In North City, then, association is influenced, but not determined, by social problem or diagnostic classification. For example, members of the Social Club came know each other through similar experiences in the mental health system and through activities at the Friendly Center and other organizations, such as the North City Coalition for the Psychiatrically Labeled. However, not all mentally ill street people are attracted to this group. The norms of the group push some away while inducing others to join. We frequently found people who associated with a group in which they did not fit by classification. For example, Brian, a 29-year-old street person who was first interviewed at the Friendly Center, had no psychiatric diagnosis and did not receive mental health services. Yet he appeared to be spending time with the Social Club group, possibly because he was interested in a number of its female members socially.

Most important, homeless people face limited structured alternatives. The case of Tiny is a good example. As a man in his mid-50s, Tiny became homeless in North City in the mid-1980s. He had moved to North City from Connecticut at the suggestion of his grown son after losing his job because of a layoff. He initially worked at North City's fish piers but lost his job when he hurt his back and legs. While awaiting disability benefits, Tiny became homeless and began "taking up" with the Street Drunks who associate with each other near the piers.

Tiny's association was due in part to his own circumstances: His son was already spending time with the drunks, the Street Drunks are highly visible at and near the piers—often watching the ships and helping unload fish—and Tiny had begun to drink heavily. More to the point, however, assuming that Tiny could not obtain housing at this time and chose not to leave North City, with what other group could he affiliate? He would not be welcome among the Street Kids at age 56. He certainly did not consider himself mentally ill, and he would to have not have been a likely candidate to join the primarily baby-boomer, politically or religiously influenced Politicos. According to Tiny, he was not a heavy drinker prior to his association with the drunks, which, if true, suggests that alcoholism alone was not the determining factor in his association.[1]

Association is complex, based in part on chance, on subjective self-concept, and on demographic characteristics but also on the overall limited social roles that exist within the street community. These roles, as I explore in the remainder of the chapter, are heavily influenced by society's broader organization. For example, Tiny's rejection for social benefits and shelter probably reinforced his role as a Street Drunk. The stigma and hostility directed toward a male street person in his mid-50s and his separation from the social benefit and service system reinforced an outsider identity for Tiny, as it would for other Street Drunks.

Description of Subcultures

Although, as noted, not all homeless people in North City spend time together, and not every role or orientation can be categorized, four major subcultures appeared to exist among the street people: (1) the Street Drunks, a predominantly older, male, highly resistant subculture whose members accepted the labels of "bum" and "drunk"; (2) a large number of youth, ranging in age from 13 to their mid-20s, that I divide between the younger Street Kids and the older Young Turks, the latter continuing to spend time in the same general areas as Street Kids but who generationally distinguish themselves from the younger group; (3) the Social Club, composed of the mentally ill who are often connected with the Friendly Center and other mental health groups, composed of both sexes and a variety of ages, although baby boomers (30–45 years old) predominate; and (4) the Politicos, a group of homeless and formerly homeless people who tend to be baby-boomer age (30–45 years old) and who engage in research, advocacy, and service to the homeless community.

Table 7.1 provides a short description of each group and its core value orientation, and Fig. 7.1 indicates a continuum in degrees of social solidarity and ties between the informal groups and the formal organizations discussed in Chapter 6. I describe the different patterns in each group and then examine their relationships with one another.

The "Street Drunks": Macho Toughness

Street Drunks are well-known to North City's populace. These unbathed and unshaven older men who resemble skid row bums are hard to miss throughout North City and, to the consternation of advocates, are frequently seen as representing all homeless people. (Some drunks such as Solly, moreover, love to take

TABLE 7.1 Subcultures Among North City Street People

	Description	Core Value Orientation
Street Drunks	Generally older male alcoholics (45+) who identify as "bums" or "drunks"	Toughness, machismo
Street Kids	Kids 13–18 (both sexes) who spend time at Checkerboard Square	Toughness, invulnerability
Young Turks	Young adults (19–27) of both sexes who usually came to the streets as street kids and stayed	Survival against the odds
Social Club	Accept label of mentally ill, usually involved with Friendly Center and other self-help groups; varying ages but most baby boomers (30–45); women more dominant	Therapeutic sociability
Politicos	Self-declared advocates and travelers, usually baby-boom age (30–45); influenced by political, religious, hippie, or mystical beliefs; both men and women	Selfless commitment

FIGURE 7.1 Continuum of Social Solidarity Between Subculture and Overall Homeless Community and Ties with Formal Organizations

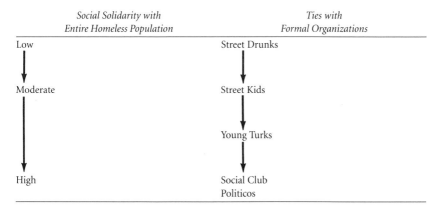

on the role of spokesperson and give frequent press interviews in which they voice rather idiosyncratic opinions.) Although Street Drunks spend time at Checkerboard Square and service agencies such as the Drop-In Center and soup kitchens, they are generally independent and are highly resistant to the "civilizing" influences of professionals (social workers, mental health workers, clergy) and advocates. They often sleep in out-of-the-way encampments such as "Hobo Jungle," a small, rambling woods with some cleared trails near the railroad tracks. In Hobo Jungle, one can see a variety of makeshift accommodations such as lean-tos, used furniture, and a variety of tents—a few of which appear to have been quite expensive but are now badly battered by the elements. These men can be seen during the day collecting refundable bottles throughout the city, begging or "stemming" as they call it—and spending time at the fish piers and at the main branch of the public library, which they use a place to sleep, rest, and sometimes read.

Almost all of the Street Drunks are male, although two or three women joined their circle at times. For the most part, Street Drunks socialized and had sexual relationships with women outside of their immediate group, who were often labeled mentally ill. Street Drunks almost always look older than they are: Many we interviewed were in their 50s but could pass for 70 or 75. Although most were over 45, some were younger, although they too appeared far older (often a 30-year-old looked perhaps 50).

Service providers are usually hostile toward the Street Drunks, regarding them as incorrigible and beyond help. Because of drunkenness or behavioral problems, many of the drunks are frequently banned from shelters, soup kitchens, and other service agencies. Even some political advocates in North City find the Street Drunks to be problematic and sometimes say they "get nowhere" after years of trying to assist them. Police are particularly hostile toward Street Drunks. Street Drunks are frequently arrested for minor infractions such as spitting, obstructing a public way (such as a doorway), and interfering with a police officer (refusing to move). Larry spoke of a Street Drunk who, whenever the police saw him, was stopped and asked where he was going. Such constant and intense pressure inevitably provoked this man to make angry responses, and he would often then be arrested. The older and weaker Street Drunks were also the most preyed upon of the street population. Local skinheads have been involved in numerous incidents of violence against the Street Drunks, and several deaths have been reported as a result. Often the Street Drunk carries all his possessions with him, so a robbery may net the perpetrator a check or some food stamps.

The hostility of the public and providers toward the Street Drunk is returned in kind. Most Street Drunks embraced their role, stating, "Yeah, I'm a bum and I'm proud." They devalue the institutions of control, such as shelters and welfare; attach little importance to possessions, including money and housing; and are frequently skeptical about organizations, including political and religious groups. They infuriate the public and social workers because at the beginning of a month, some will use their checks (if they are on welfare or Social Security) to buy a large amount of alcohol, secure a motel room (or sometimes housing through a service agency), and invite all their friends to party. After the binge, they are sometimes evicted from apartments or run out of money to pay for another motel room. They then show up at the alcohol shelter for detoxification and remain until the next month's check comes. Despite their hostility toward "the system," some seek public assistance when their checks or underground earnings are gone.

Despite the poor image of the Street Drunks, they participated in their own close-knit community, with its own internal norms and culture. Street Drunks usually spent time in small groups, forming particularly tight pairs. Friends such as Solly and Lindy or Tiny and Horse were inseparable and even claimed to be "cousins." This use of "fictive kin" was an interesting carryover to this mostly Caucasian group of what has often been found in black or Hispanic cultures (Horowitz, 1983; Liebow, 1967; Stack, 1974). The drunks were very reliant on each other for mutual aid; a bottle of liquor, cigarettes, spare change, and information on where to get services or a meal were expected to be exchanged, and a refusal to share was considered an affront. Even women were seen as communal, and frequently a female partner was passed around to friends. As noted, obtaining housing usually did not result in separation from the group; rather, the apartment was considered common ground where friends could sleep on the floor, drink together, or bring women and have parties.

Most of the tactics for survival—"shadow work"—were also based on teamwork. For example, drunks could receive fairly good money by stripping copper from old abandoned buildings and warehouses. This was usually a team effort in which a few men would locate a building and others would study the entrances and plan how to get in. Once the "scrapping" was done, the men had to find ways to haul the copper to dealers who would pay for it. This usually required borrowing a vehicle and hiding the copper until it could be cashed in. The Street Drunks also formed a community at the fishing piers ("the waterfront is where I fit in," they often said). Evidently the past experiences of many Street Drunks as fishermen or sailors and the macho culture of the fishermen seem to mesh. Street Drunks are invited onto the boats and may be hired to watch the boats while they are docked, and drunks and fishermen trade stories and drinks. Drunks also work together to get money by stemming cooperatively, by collecting bottles, and through trading in food stamps at local stores.

Street Drunks gained status within their own subculture by "pulling one over." For example, Denver was known as the best stemmer. He pretended to be a Vietnam veteran and—based on his particularly pathetic appearance and his ability to articulately relate his "life story"—sometimes made $30 a day through begging. Pulling one over could also include minor theft of money, called "rolling'" in which tourists or other strangers had their pockets picked or were conned out of change. Those who were best at stemming and rolling were seen as tough and independent and were emulated by the group.

The drunk's core value of machismo, toughness, and independence parallels that of the oppositional male subcultures among Willis's "lads" (1977) and MacLeod's "Hallyway Hangers" (1987). Like the tough youth, the Street Drunk would never admit fear or pain and waxes romantic about danger and excitement. Larry, now working as a street counselor with this group, tries to use the violent attacks on older drunks and similar frightful incidents that take place on the streets as opportunities to reach out to the drunks and to offer counseling and rehabilitation:

It's tough. It doesn't usually work. They say, "We're not scared of anything. We love this life." It's not cool [for them] to admit to fearing anything. It's an "I'll die with my boots on" attitude.

Katherine notes that trying to get the drunks involved in political action is hard because their first response to the service system is to say, "What the hell do we need their help for?" The macho attitude is also reflected in the Street Drunk subculture's antagonism toward homosexuality. Their conversations are frequently laced with anecdotes about gays and fears that "they'll fuck you while you sleep." A number of fights have broken out at the alcoholics' shelter when the drunks discover or assume that someone is gay.

Despite the drunks' protestations of complete independence and noninvolvement in any part of society, they should be regarded as having a low level of contact with formal organizations in North City and low degrees of social solidarity with other homeless people rather than as being totally isolated. Many drunks enjoy long talks with social workers at the Drop-In Center and other service agencies in North City. Once they find social workers and other providers who accept them as they are, they can be warm and friendly, even participating in some group activities. A large number of Street Drunks had been to AA and other groups and had achieved periods of sobriety. Although they had little faith in the efficacy of political action, they did join the tent city protest. "They were the last to arrive, coming in at night, and sometimes the first to leave when all the meetings started. But they were there and were supportive," reports Katherine. The Street Drunks follow events and "like to philosophize about government," says Larry. Recently, the governor's proposed budget cuts created fear at the alcoholics' shelter, and a number of Street Drunks joined protests against cuts in welfare. Many of the drunks have also attended the church services and religious functions mentioned in Chapter 6.

The Street Drunks can be distinguished from the other subcultures by their extremely strong self-concept of independence and pride and by their relatively marginal role in formal organizations and low participation in the overall street community. Their relationship with other subcultures is ambivalent. They can provoke hostility from other street people, and yet they often evoke their sympathy, aid, and advocacy. In their own way, the drunks are very knowledgeable about street life and about how other homeless people feel. Since they do not worry about manners or about how they are perceived, they often voice opinions that many others share but are afraid to express. When confronted by the group of employers who came to tent city or by the hostile comments of the public, they did not hesitate to tell people off—to the delight of other street people. In the comments they made to me in the course of this study, they often provided cogent analyses of the social service system. They were also quick to point out the people who were most in need of help (their own sense of independence led to a kind of modesty in which they urged social workers and volunteers to help women, children, the mentally ill, and others who they felt were more in need than they were). Because they were "armchair experts" who were often ignored or discredited by the representatives of "the system," they served in a way as the "eyes and ears" of the street community, frequently whispering some piece of news into the ears of homeless advocates and then going on their way.

"Street Kids" and "Young Turks": Surviving Against All Odds

In contrast to the stark visibility of the Street Drunks, the many homeless young people of North City generally look like other kids. As they congregate in Checkerboard Square or on street corners or in parks, listening to loud rock music on a boombox—the guys sporting long hair, T shirts, and jeans and sometimes enveloped by the smell of marijuana—it is possible to feel one is among any group of U.S. youth. Even listening to their conversations—about music, bikes, or cars, about who is dating whom, or about popular icons of the music and entertainment world—it is hard to separate them from other kids who are hanging around after school or on summer break. A close look at the Street Kids might reveal more matted, unkempt hair, extremely smelly and soiled jeans, or an unmatched set of shoes, but from a distance they could be the sons and daughters of any North City parent.

Unlike the Street Drunks, but like the other two subcultures I explore, the Street Kids also blend into the community through social network ties with a variety of housed citizens of North City. The kids are likely to have been born in North City or in surrounding towns and to have gone to school nearby. Although some of their ties—particularly with adults—have been severed, they often maintain enough friendships to be able to sleep overnight at various people's homes. Although these arrangements are often short-term, some succeed in living on others' floors or in their guest rooms for long periods of time. The youth also have more resources than the Street Drunks in terms of going in and out of North City to neighboring towns and suburbs and journeying elsewhere throughout the state in order to stay with a friend, to pick up some drugs or clothes or musical equipment, or to take a temporary job or a job training slot (a number of the youths had been in and out of the Job Corps site upstate).[2]

Although I grouped together North City's youth, ranging in age from as young as 12 to about 26 or 27, because they share a very similar experience—usually coming to the streets after suffering abuse and neglect in their families and after having had contact with the child welfare system (see Chapter 3)—there are obvious developmental and generational differences within this large grouping. For this reason I have divided the group between the young Street Kids, age 18 and under, and the Young Turks, the older (19–26) cohort who still mingle at the same street corners but who maintain somewhat different values and social organization than those of the younger group. In fact, it was amusing to hear 21- and 22-year-old Young Turks complain about the "kids today," referring to youth only a few years their junior:

Cora: These kids [on the streets] today. They're given everything from Nintendos to pool tables. They're carefree … and [they] don't realize that they get stuff because of what we did [the protesters at tent city].

Harry: These kids! All they care about [is] getting high, getting laid. They think they're cool until [they eventually] realize what it's like to be on the streets a long time.

Although this generational or cohort cleavage was in part the result of the politicization of the now-twentysomething group that had participated in tent city in 1987[3] and also of that group's jealousy about the development of services to adolescents that had not existed at the time they were young street people (particularly the Porthouse Shelter, which the Young Turks thought of as a "party house" with its VCRs, pool tables, and computer games), this distancing appears primarily to reflect the influences of aging and street experience. When we talked to the now-older Young Turks who had been on the streets when they were ages 14 to 18, they described themselves retrospectively as having the same "devil-may-care" attitude they impute to the "kids of today":

Ruth, interviewed at age 24, discussing her teen years on the street: I felt pretty invulnerable, really, as a kid, indestructible. It wasn't hard living on the streets … hang out with my friends, whole bunch of us. High most of the time. Didn't have too many cares.

Jamie, interviewed at age 23, discussing his teen years on the street: I didn't mind being on [the] streets [of North City]. It was cool. Hung out with [names several guys] and slept under the bridge. [Some] people tried to get me in[to housing], but I had more freedom outside.

Taken together, the quotes from the street people indicate that typically, the young teens on the streets of North City had a feeling of invulnerability and a general subcultural norm of toughness, which although less antisocial that the Street Drunks, mirrored much of the Street Drunks' machismo. In many ways, the Street Kids' attitude mirrored in an exaggerated way the norms and abandon of most adolescents. However, once the kids turned 18 or 19 or 20, they tended to become more critical of street life and more hesitant to embrace aspects of this existence. The Young Turks were generally divided between two orientations in their efforts to leave the streets (and in some cases straddled both orientations). The minority embraced the tough street attitude and entered a more "professionalized" life of crime with the hopes that they would not be caught by authorities and that one more "deal" or "trick" would bring them financial security. The majority, particularly of the females who were now over age 18, went in a very different direction. Young Turks such as Agnes, Cora, Cheryl, Eric, Jonathan, Ruth, Lois, and Sylvia attempted to utilize their contacts with social agencies to gain social benefits and counseling, to work at casual jobs or obtain other employment, to enter the Job Corps or secure a GED, or to join AA or other self-help groups.

Many Young Turks were still undecided about their direction and showed evidence of both tough street values and more middle-class social norms. Brad, at age 21, "could go either way," commented the researcher who interviewed him, with "either" referring to a life of hard crime or a successful college career. Very tough and macho, Brad bragged about his life living on the streets since age 12 (in New York City as well as North City) and claimed to maintain Mafia connections. Yet he had also become a favorite client at several social agencies, had worked at the fish piers, had obtained his GED, and spoke of attending college. His comments reflected aspirations ranging from being a revolutionary to being a college student and having "a house with a yard and a garden" to becoming a "hit man." Brad was emblematic of the Young Turks in that whatever direction he went, he felt a strong confidence that he would survive and "make it" on his own terms.

Interestingly, the Young Turk cohort had a degree of optimism not usually reported among the poor or the homeless. Although they did not hold hopes that they would achieve a middle-class life-style, most felt that the worst part of their lives was over, that having suffered at the hands of their families or foster or adopted families and having lived on the streets for some years, they could now cope with anything. This survival ("I will make it on my own terms") orientation united both the more resistant bravado value orientation that Rudy, Jamie, Harry and Dennis, and others had with those who had embraced a more cautious strategy of being a client of social agencies or other institutions.

The life chances and norms of the subculture were structured to a great degree by the economic, social welfare, and criminal justice implications of being under or over age 18. For kids under 18, as I have indicated, life on the streets was regarded as representing freedom and a relief from abusive parents, foster homes, or child welfare institutions. These kids usually could not work in the regular economy or even collect social benefits because of child labor laws and social welfare regulations; they were outsiders who used their peer group as a central organizing mechanism to protect themselves and gain status and community. The combination of free time and lack of opportunity meant that they frequently spent the day wandering around, visiting soup kitchens and other service centers, and engaging in petty crime and in a variety of underground money-making efforts such as selling drugs, "going down to the Oaks" (a code for prostitution in the park), trading in hot goods, or gaining a day's work at the fish piers or carnivals. When arrested as juveniles, they generally risked at most a sentence at the youth center, a fate many of them considered to be an acceptable risk.

The crowd over age 18 enjoyed the same camaraderie and similar music, clothes, and dating patterns as the younger group. However, they had some advantages over the younger group (they could be hired for jobs or collect social benefits) *and* a host of disadvantages if they continued to engage in certain deviant behaviors. The disadvantages stemmed in part from what might be regarded as the limited window of opportunity provided by the service system and other institutions in North City. That is, Street Kids can be seen as having more human capital than do the down-and-out Street Drunks, and social workers—and sometimes educators and job trainers—often take an interest in them. Many social workers, priests, ministers, and community members tried to "save" particularly attractive and articulate young people (Cora and Cheryl were helped in securing housing after tent city by the Drop-In Center and a group of clergy; Ruth was literally taken in by Carla Reets after tent city; Louise, a 16-year-old street person, was aided by a volunteer who sat with her every night so she would not go down to the streets and continue "hooking").

But such "saving," even if possible, comes as a limited offer. If the Young Turk continues to gravitate to the streets, to engage in drinking or using drugs or to otherwise disappoint service providers, he or she will not only lose this window of opportunity but may experience hostility. Subjects like Jamie, Rudy, and Dennis, when they did not comply with various rules or expectations, were denied social benefits or refused services by different social agencies. Most important, as opposed to juvenile offenders, if they are arrested now, as young adults they face the full weight of the criminal code. For these reasons, as well as perhaps because of the aging process and length of time on the street, a number of Young Turks struggled to remain as "straight" as they could, particularly if they were also encouraged by counselors or others to think that their compliance with rules or attendance at school or at training could lead somewhere.

The Street Kids and Young Turks formed loose-knit groups of three to five members that included both males and females. Often the informal leaders were attractive young men or boys like Brad who had "street smarts." Young girls and women could also achieve status through good looks, "sharp dressing," and access to cash or vehicles. Louise was popular at the time of tent city because of her looks, dress, and street smarts. Cora, like Brad, seemed to stand out as a leader of the kids around this time also partly because of her looks but also partly because of her intelligence and strong voice in defending the homeless. Heterosexual partnering was key to the social organization, and "messing with a steady" was a serious offense that could invoke a violent reaction. Generally, the kids engaged in serial monogamy and "went steady" but then often split up as a result of a fight or because of one partner or the other straying. Although there were many more females in this group than among the Street Drunks, and they were able to achieve some status, the subculture remained fairly macho and sexist. A double standard existed concerning sexual promiscuity, for although male Street Kids slept around without penalty, this was serious offense for a young woman. Katherine reports that Serena was ostracized from the group at the time of tent city because she was known to go "from tent to tent" having sex with many males.

As with the Street Drunks and other groups, a norm of mutual aid and reciprocity existed within the subculture. Food, cigarettes, alcohol and drugs, small amounts of cash, and access to any shelter—whether makeshift, like the abandoned rail boxcars street kids slept in, or actual apartments or houses—were expected to be shared. The kids were very innovative at securing goods, which could range from Eric's ability to enter gas stations or convenience stores and, while applying for a job, steal a carton of cigarettes or some food, to Judge's ability to go into a store and try on clothes and leave with a stolen leather jacket. Despite the obvious poverty of street life, quite a few goods—from expensive leather jackets to CDs to sums of cash—sometimes filtered into the community as a result of theft and other activities. Of course, access to housing, expensive goods, or cash sometimes caused conflict rather than mutual aid. When Eric and two of his friends acquired several hundred dollars from a heist, they had a bitter fight while trying to divide the money. Although the kids were far more endearing than the drunks, their loud behavior and arguments, drinking and drug use, and "devil-may-care" attitude often led people to give up on them completely.

Katherine, Nina, Trudi, and Lucky—some of the mothers of the street—now had mixed feelings about having housed a large number of street kids in the past. Katherine described herself as "an easy touch":

> They used to come [to me] and say, "Hey Katherine, this is my girlfriend, she's pregnant, we have nowhere to stay," and I'd house them. It would turn out that the girl was not pregnant, of course.

Katherine remarks that she had about 10 kids staying in her two-bedroom apartment, and after awhile she found she had no food left in the mornings and "no place to call my own." Nina, who still shelters a number of the Social Club street people, is now somewhat bitter about the Street Kids: "They used us and particularly Katherine. Got her in trouble with all their booze and drugs and sex."

Compared with the Street Drunks, the Street Kids and Young Turks displayed a strong social solidarity with the homeless generally and strong ties with formal organizations. The kids were fond of social workers and other employees of local agencies and frequently maintained more than one worker or counselor. Judge and Harry, who hugged their respective Drop-In Center workers with delight, were also very close to their counselors at an adolescent program. The kids had much more awareness than the drunks of the services in North City and felt positive about them. The Street Kids and Young Turks also provided probably the largest number of foot soldiers for the homeless political movement, particularly at the time of tent city. A number of kids and young adults ages 17 to 26, particularly the men, were the most militant of the homeless studied (see Cohen & Wagner, 1992). The Young Turks in particular were also far more likely to use the self-help groups described in Chapter 6 than were the Street Drunks.

However, in comparison with the older subjects classified as being in the Social Club group or as Politicos, the group's feeling of solidarity and involvement with formal organizations were lower; hence Figure 7.1 reports them as moderate in these areas.[4] Although they verbally avowed strong support for all homeless people, the kids frequently clashed with other groups, particularly the Street Drunks. They were often likely to distinguish the "good" homeless from the "bad," to the detriment of a few street types such as the drunks or the severely mentally ill. Moreover, perhaps typical of youth in general, their patience and ability to commit themselves strongly to organizations or movements were weak. Of the homeless organizations in North City discussed in Chapter 6, they were attracted by conflict and excitement but drifted away from meetings and talk of organizational issues. Finally, their very ability to go in and out of town and to seek adventure, work, or relationships elsewhere caused many to not be consistent members of local organizations.

The "Social Club": Therapeutic Sociability

I introduced the group that spends time at the Friendly Center's Social Club in Chapter 6; it should be noted, however, that the subculture that forms around the Social Club is not identical to membership in the center. Although most of the members of the social group discussed here are active in the center, a number have quit the center yet remain actively involved with their center friends and within this subculture.

As is clear from the earlier descriptions of the Friendly Center and subjects such as Amy and Nina (profiled in Chapter 2), this group hardly fits the public "bag lady" stereotype of the mentally ill homeless. As with the Street Kids or Young Turks, most of the Social Club group could pass for ordinary poor people on the street. Traveling in groups to soup kitchens or occupying benches at Checkerboard Square, they appear from a distance to be average citizens. A close look at these individuals, however, may reveal physical manifestations of poverty and psychiatric treatment such as the prevalence of obesity and the large number who are missing teeth. Additionally, they wear old and sometimes unmatched apparel, and some of their expressions may seem a "little off," such as a fixed smile or unfocused eyes. The street people in this group sometimes do have severe psychiatric crises, including hospitalizations, but on a day-to-day basis, most are medicated and do not display bizarre or psychotic behavior.

The Social Club group has many advantages over the untreated mentally ill street people. Without even addressing the merits of medication or counseling, the street people's contact with the Friendly Center and with case managers at the mental health center or the Psychiatric Coalition usually means that they have far more resources available to them than do isolated homeless people. These agencies link subjects with the Social Security office for disability or SSI benefits, with city and state social service agencies for welfare, AFDC and food stamps, and with subsidized housing programs. Moreover, the group is exposed to a wide array of activities and programs, not only through local programs such as Friendly Center but also through a statewide network that includes special dances and socials with other psychiatrically labeled people. The Social Club group had a better chance to obtain housing in the early 1990s than in previous years. However, problems such as lost checks, difficulties with payees (many subjects had been given guardians by the courts), layoffs from work, psychiatric breakdowns, breakups of relationships, and eligibility changes in benefits that caused them to be cut off often led to literal homelessness for about half of the people followed during the 1990–1991 period.

To a far greater degree than the Street Drunks or the Street Kids, the Social Club's tightly knit subculture shared norms of therapeutic involvement with organizations and agencies, with "working through" personal issues, and with participating in activities. Some subjects were, like Amy (described in Chapter 2), virtual whirling dervishes, participating in so many social events and outings, self-help groups and therapy, church and political affairs that they were hard to catch up with. Once I got to know the people in this group, I began to notice them throughout North City; I met them at movie theatres, the beach, political demonstrations. summer festivals, and local ball fields. To a great extent, their participation in activities and their norm of emotional sharing can be judged to have been positive outcomes of their experience with the mental health system. Larry, who worked at the Friendly Center, agreed that the norms of this group reflected the philosophical goals of the mental health providers:

> They hang out together, they are committed to show their emotions and share their feelings. They are tight. ... So you have to say the model works on [these] people. They've been taught this at [the state mental hospital], at [the private psychiatric hospital nearby], at [outpatient clinic], and it kinda works.

A second reason why therapeutic sociability rather than the macho toughness of the Street Drunks or Street Kids dominated the Social Club was the prevalence and dominance of women in this group. As is true nationwide, women prevail numerically among the mentally ill homeless (Bachrach, 1985; Cohen, 1988; Crystal, 1984). Coupled with the numbers is the fact that women had more status here. The Social Club was socially dominated by several women who had been homeless but who were now advocates or street people with expert knowledge of the labyrinthian social service system. Katherine and Nina, for example, talked of the group as "their people." Whether for attending a demonstration, going on an outing to a church, or planning a social, Katherine or Nina could gather a number of group members and ensure their attendance.

The social dominance of the women and the therapeutic norm of the group created several differences with other street subcultures. Conversations were frequently spiced with antimale references even when men were present, and strong sanctions against male violence and strong support for legal abortion were evident. The family violence discussed in Chapter 3, both in families of origin and in frequently stormy current relationships with men, was often talked about in an atmosphere of solidarity. The women defended themselves well, both in terms of individual perpetrators (recently a man who had violent tendencies was thrown out of the Friendly Center and turned over to the police at their urging) and of their contact with other homeless people on the street. By traveling in large groups and having the capacity to become very loud (and even threatening), the group staved off violence and harassment. Further, although prejudices such as those against homosexuals were strong among Street Drunks, alternative life-styles were generally accepted within the Social Club group. As we saw with Telly's suspension from the Friendly Center in Chapter 6, a number of the women were greatly upset by his verbal attacks on gays. They frequently defended the right of gays to participate in their outings and events.[5]

Except for some male activists, such as Ralph and Jack, who had left the Friendly Center and were now active in the North City Coalition, the men involved in the group—such as Bert, Randy, Ronnie, Darryl, JoJo, and Ben—were relatively passive and accepting of the women's dominant role. Although they sometimes sided with the male in the many debates about relationships that dominated conversation, they also openly admitted their problems and their own failures. "I had to learn to talk about my feelings. It's taken a long time," said Randy, for example, and he seemed sincere in wanting to work out problems he had in relationships with both men and women.

Group norms supported the sharing of goods as well as feelings. Social Club subjects loaned one another money, borrowed toasters, mattresses, and clothes from one another, and almost always tried to shelter each other when someone was homeless. As with the Street Kids, this norm sometimes led to conflict when exchanges were not reciprocated or agreements were violated. For example, Amanda and Sara frequently became homeless and were allowed to stay at Nina's or Barbara's. But they often reneged on promises to leave, and Barbara recently evicted Sara after she overstayed her agreed-upon limit of 5 days by weeks. "She was doing nothing to get housing, dammit, and [my] landlord would throw me out if I keep her here," Barbara stated angrily. Long periods of tension could develop between subjects when norms of reciprocity were not observed by one party failing to return loaned items, overstaying his or her welcome, or "stealing" partners (as, for example, in Chapter 3 when Amanda went off with Sara's husband).

Although the Social Club was far less involved in criminal activity than were the Street Kids, some of its members had engaged in petty theft, panhandling, drug use, and prostitution. Several of the men had arrest records—one for child molestation, others for drugs or theft. Although the social agencies had numerous rules (for example, the Friendly Center prohibited use of alcohol and drugs), the group members supported secret use of substances. They generally, however, seemed opposed to violence, major theft, and drug dealing.

The norm of sharing feelings and keeping no secrets did not lack problems. The group was often loud, disruptive, and even "badgering." Larry felt that the constant bickering and self-examination of feelings and perceived wrongs that took place at the Friendly Center caused some people to leave:

This client, he was a pretty good guy, but he smelled from the street, he used to stare a little vacantly. … The [Social Club group] harassed him no end. … "When are you going to take your next shower? Why are you staring so much?" It got ridiculous, and the guy finally left [the Social Club].

Subjects sometimes prided themselves on their ventilation of feelings such as anger and hostility. For example, Nina was frequently angry and critical, and, like other Social Club members, she sometimes used her disability to justify making harsh attacks on people: "It's my disability, so sometimes I don't think [about] what I'm saying." Nina, in fact, liked the Friendly Center because her verbal attacks or outbursts were usually ignored or forgiven.

As indicated in Figure 7.1, the Social Club (along with the Politicos) had the strongest involvement in formal organizations among street people and felt a deep sense of social solidarity with all homeless people. The members frequently used a wide variety of social service agencies and self-help, religious, and political groups. The group shared a strong sense of "entitlement" to social benefits and to better treatment from homeless shelters, psychiatric facilities, and city and state governments. A number of subjects had gone to the Washington, D.C., demonstration for the homeless in 1989 and had participated in the march against George Bush in Kennebunkport, Maine, in 1991. Many sported various political buttons. Other subjects seemed less committed politically or religiously but went to events out of loyalty to people like Katherine or Nina.

As I discuss in "Culture and Association Among Street People," the higher levels of social solidarity and of resources available to the Social Club lead them to develop a different kind of culture of resistance than that of the Street Drunks or the Street Kids. Members of the Social Club are less embittered personally and less obviously at odds with the normative bounds of behavior as expressed through activities such as crime, but they are nevertheless both politically and culturally oppositional. They generally see themselves as oppressed by "the system" and as estranged from the family and work ethics. Indeed, in organizing their lives, they substitute a therapeutic community for the structure of the work world and the nuclear family that many Americans use to organize their time. Such organization substitutes friendship and community for what subjects tended to see as an overly competitive and materialistic world. Interestingly, their disability sustains this alternative life-style because the severely mentally ill are not as normatively expected to work full time or to live within their families of origin.

The "Politicos": Selfless Commitment

As with the Street Kids and the Social Club, the subjects classified as Politicos are not easily identifiable from afar: They include both men and women—usually of baby-boomer age—who spend time at Checkerboard Square, the soup kitchens, and social agencies and who, despite their shabby attire, could easily pass as ordinary poor citizens. A closer look may reveal some idiosyncrasies such as the tendency to be jotting notes into notebooks or onto scraps of paper or to be wearing political buttons. Some members of this group adopt Bohemian touches, as with Joel and Gabby wearing cocked berets.

Although some street subcultures (such as the Social Club) are heavily structured by agencies within North City, Politicos meet each other relatively independently and often have come to the streets with a prior orientation to social action. Even during periods of relative quiescence within the broader homeless political movement in North City (see Chapter 6), people like Theodore kept copious files of "cases" in large boxes, some like Mitch always seemed to have plans to speak at media events, and others like Tobi planned to write a muckraker book. As with the Social Club group, the Politicos had some resource advantages over many other street people. Many were from middle-class families of origin and were generally better educated than the majority of those on the streets. Their knowledge of the service system and contact with political and social service leaders led them to at least try to maximize the social benefits for which they were eligible. And although they were more able to secure housing than were the Street Drunks or Street Kids, as was true with the Social Club group, many were episodically homeless—some, like Joel and Arnie, because they left to travel and to live out of their vans and others, like Dickie or Tobi, because of problems with landlords, with the welfare system, or with the mental health system.

No one is born a Politico. The subculture develops from several different sources: the hippie countercultural movement (typified by Joel, Arnie, Roy, and Gabby—some of whom have been traveling since the Haight-Ashbury days), the Vietnam veteran experience (overlapping with the previous influence but also including folks such as Mitch or Herb who are not countercultural), and the mental health movement (typified by Mitch, Tobi, Ralph, and Theodore). Not surprisingly, despite their unity in pressing for social change in conditions for the homeless, the divergence in their backgrounds led to considerable variation in the specific political views (sometimes ranging from far left to far right) and in their personal styles and norms.

Given their strong commitment to political action, they were, along with the Social Club, the most involved in the formal organizations in North City—religious groups, self-help groups, and social agencies—as well as in political groups. They took as their raison d'être to achieve unity and solidarity among the poor and homeless people and often mediated disputes between other homeless subcultures, such as when the Street Drunks clashed with some the mentally ill. Generally, the Politicos refrained from most of the deviant activities that dominated the lives of the Street Drunks and the Street Kids. There was some variance, however, between the hippie element, who did use drugs and were more prone to violate societal norms they disagreed with, and the more religiously motivated Politicos, who were generally—as far as I could tell—more "straight."

Politicos explained their daily actions and even their status as street people as being based on a selfless commitment that centered on ideological, religious, or even mystical purposes. Most were extremely sensitive about their reputations and commitments. Gabby, for example, tells how when he planned a demonstration that fizzled out, he attended anyway because otherwise "[local newswoman] would have lost confidence in me, and [I] can't have that happen." Dickie claimed his decision to move to a nearby city was caused by the demands of the homeless movement, although others insisted his reasons were more personal, including having a partner there. At times, it was difficult to untangle these subjects' motivations since they explained a wide variety of daily activity that others would see as just being representative of homelessness as being research or observation (for example, the frequent explanation of shelter stays as being necessary to look around and take notes). Generally, however, I had the impression that their commitment was always sincere, even if their attribution of some daily patterns to broader objectives was sometimes less clear.

Politicos distinguished themselves not only by continued reliance on political explanations for where they went and what they did but also by their need for approval from middle-class and mainstream figures. Almost all of the group members talked about their relationships with newspeople and broadcast journalists; many others spoke of city council members, state legislators, or other political leaders as personal contacts. In some cases, Politicos were able to use higher-power actors—from political leaders to community organizers to social workers to university professors—as mentors and advisers. In other cases, however—such as with Dickie, Paula, and Theodore—it was not clear that the political leaders and others they cited actually returned their respect or would even remember talking with them (for example, in the meeting set up by Dickie described in Chapter 6, a state legislator attending asked me who this guy was, and why he had not shown up for his own meeting).

Politicos were more isolated than the other groups in the sense that they either consisted of pairs—such as Mitch and Katherine, Paula and Theodore—or were "lone rangers" like Joel or Arnie. Although highly committed to helping and organizing the homeless, most did not engage in serious personal relationships with the other street people. Although this was never stated, the Politicos may have regarded many of the homeless, particularly the Street Drunks, as being beneath them. They seemed to orient more toward advocates and middle-class people. It is also possible that their somewhat higher levels of education—both formal and informal—created some isolation.[6]

Despite frequent disagreements among Politicos, as reflected in the splits within the North City homeless movement discussed in Chapter 6, they did form a distinct subculture. They saw their role as that of gadflies and participated in a whirlwind of activities from which they did not gain personally. In fact, these activists were often looked at with hostility by city officials. Gabby was recently barred from municipal shelters after asking too many questions and writing down a great deal of information. Theodore, Mitch, and Tobi feel they have suffered as a result of their advocacy efforts, particularly in their ability to move freely within shelters and within other offices such as welfare, where they must go to secure their benefits.

Another strong norm of this group involved frequent travel to a variety of cities, near and afar, for the purpose of gathering information. Katherine and Mitch traveled throughout the United States in 1989 to take notes on how different cities treat the homeless, and they stayed in numerous shelters. Dickie left North City in 1991 to visit shelters for the homeless in the state of Washington. Arnie was leaving for the West Coast in 1990 to do research on services in California. Although to my knowledge these surveys and experiences have never been fully organized or published, the Politicos served a key function within the street community by bringing in new ideas, news of political movements, and alternative strategies for change.

For example, during a visit I made to a meeting of the newly organized consumer group at the Drop-In Center, I was impressed with the scope of knowledge of several Politicos regarding services and resources around the country. During a discussion, Gabby mentioned experimental shelters in San Diego that were only later profiled in the national media. Dabney, a Politico who had only recently arrived in North City, discussed the availability of a clearinghouse on homeless groups throughout the nation and the existence of a computer data base. The vast store of knowledge of some Politicos made them central to the social organization of the street community, although at the same time it led to some personal isolation. They were relied upon and were well respected as informants and leaders, but their discussion of computer data bases, case files, and political strategies may have caused other street people to feel that they were a bit peculiar.

Relationships Among the Groups

On a day-to-day basis, these four groups came into frequent contact at service agencies, in other formal organizations, and through their common use of public space. However, even when they were physically proximate, some groups maintained their distance, whereas others developed close ties.

The Street Drunks generally had the most distant relationship with other groups unless a major mobilization or crisis was occurring within the community. Street Drunks often avoided (or were banned from) local shelters and other service agencies and were either forced into or preferred out-of-the-way locations in which to sleep and spend time. This isolated them from the Street Kids and the Social Club, as well as from short-term homeless individuals and families. Street Drunks also spoke with contempt of "wing nuts," their derogatory term for the mentally ill. Just as they felt a macho contempt for gays, the drunks apparently saw the severely mentally ill as unmanly and as people who could not care for themselves. Street people who were psychotic or severely mentally ill may also have threatened the drunks' sense of security because, as with their fear of sexual attack, they often believed the mentally ill would attack or disturb them if they were not vigilant. Interestingly, both my experience and the comments of informants revealed that the Social Club members were, for the most part, not regarded as "wing nuts" since they could take care of themselves, were known personally to the drunks, and did not seem flagrantly mentally ill. Nevertheless, the highly different norms and culture of the two groups, as well as the very different activities in which they engaged, kept the Drunks and the Social Club very separate. They tended to avoid one another when they were in close proximity, and no close friendships existed across these two groups.

The relationship between the Street Kids and the Street Drunks was more complex. Although the wide age difference and extremely different interests and culture usually precluded friendship, many drunks and Street Kids understood each other's backgrounds, and kids often aided the Street Drunks. Young Street Kids, particularly females, often brought coffee or food to the drunks. Others helped the Street Drunks obtain medical attention and served as advocates for them with social workers and others. When Wally (the Street Drunk who died of cancer in 1990) was alive, he became a father figure to many homeless Street Kids. In turn, he was "taken under the wings" of the younger kids and given food, spare change, and help with shelter. At the time of tent city, the kids demanded that Wally receive social services and health care from local officials.

At times, however, tensions arose between the two groups. At tent city, Katherine remembers the Street Kids complaining about how little the drunks did to contribute to the maintenance of the encampment (including helping with chores and the security patrol, and similar tasks) and how they seemed to be getting a "free ride." Kids would ask, "Why should we share our food with these guys? They just get money and drink it away." Because both groups were dedicated to toughness, fights occurred over space at abandoned buildings and places in the lines at soup kitchens. Often one group or individual perceived the other as being disruptive. Solly, a Street Drunk, had the habit of singing old songs at a very loud volume while in line for the Drop-In Center's breakfast. This often provoked an angry response or a fight with some Street Kids who, sleepy or hung over, were outraged at such noise early in the morning. However, the Street Drunks hated the kids' loud music, drug use, and sexual antics. A loud boombox or public display of sexuality sometimes provoked a fight. So, as with the Street Drunk–Social Club relationship, when they were not forced into close contact (such as at soup kitchens), the Street Drunks and Street Kids usually maintained a distance from one another.

The Politicos and the Social Club group, however, maintained close ties. The strong commonality in values and attachment to formal organizations provided them with similar activities and patterns of using the shelters and service agencies. Moreover, activists like Katherine, Mitch, Trudi, Nina, and Joel had often participated or volunteered at the Friendly Center or had experience with mental health organizations (the Social Club members and other mental health activists sometimes became Politicos as a result of this association). The Politicos were also able to maintain a close working relationship with the Street Kids, particularly the Young Turks, whom they had gotten to know at tent city. Street Kids generally looked up to the Politicos, particularly those like Joel and Roy, who to them represented the hippie days of the 1960s. This did not prevent some culture clashes, however, and the Politicos did not always approve of the Street Kids' behavior, nor were they likely—because of age and other reasons—to actually share in their friendships, sexual pairings, or networks to secure drugs or "hot" goods.

On a daily basis, the Street Kids and the Social Club group traveled in very different places, interacting with different service bureaucracies and institutions. Although numerous links existed between the two groups (Del, the son of Nina—who was a major figure at the Social Club—was a popular Street Kid; Karl, a Young Turk, was being housed by a staff member from the Friendly Center and was close to a number of Social Club subjects), age segmentation and its attendant cultural differences, as well as a milder version of the Street Drunks' contempt for the mentally ill that prevailed among some tough male Street Kids, generally prevented close ties from developing. Yet overall the Street Kids accepted the Social Club group well enough to cooperate with them at tent city and other political demonstrations and to interact with them at service agencies and soup kitchens, where mutual aid was often exchanged between members of the two groups.

During the 1987–1990 period, the overall street community was linked together by the Politicos, as well as by a small number of people not classified above who might be regarded as Sages. Sages were middle-aged (age 30 to 50) episodically homeless people who were long-term North City residents, were usually employed, and had a strong knowledge of the social service system. Although not necessarily advocates in a political sense, they were committed to helping homeless people and often sheltered them at their apartments when they were housed. Sidney, for example, the on-and-off construction worker, was central in involving Street Kids Harry, Roland, and Seth in the tent city protest and even loaned them a tent to stay in. These kids (now Young Turks) still go to Sidney for advice, assistance, and sometimes shelter. Donna and Mickey, an older couple who moved from trailers to family shelters and back to trailers with their children, were Telly's aunt and uncle and had some influence with him and some other Social Club members. Herb, the 48-year-old American Indian craftsman, was well liked by a group of Street Kids and Social Club members, and he got a number of people involved in tent city.

Culture and Association Among Street People

The public has a strong tendency to view associational patterns as separate from historical, economic, and political contexts, to conclude generally that "birds of a feather will flock together"—such as the Street Drunks spending time together. Generally, within the social science literature, primary groups among the poor have been seen as reacting to low self-esteem and "low life chances" that characterize their lives. For example, Anderson (1978:212) approvingly quotes his street corner men as saying "cats hang with the studs they can handle," indicating that association is primarily a protective device for achieving status within a primary group in light of the exclusion and rejection of the street-corner men from other parts of society. Suttles similarly sees life-styles and association in the slum as a process by which individuals "insulate themselves from destructive stereotypes of the wider society" by grouping together in their own informal organizations (quoted in Horowitz, 1983:17).

There is much truth in the observation that lower-class people, having been excluded from other social arenas, try to compensate by gaining prestige within primary groups. However, they do so only in a historical context that makes available certain forms of identification and not others and in a political-economic context that structures their identifications and helps them to see these cultural patterns as making sense. Susser (1982) makes a similar point when stating that subjective traits or life-styles should not obscure the broader social trends in society that tend to group people together or to separate them.

First, it should be noted that the street people of North City do not create their patterns of identification de novo or in isolation from a historical context. In fact, they follow consistent trends of making sense of their lives through the use of known oppositional stances and sense-making devices.

At least since the early twentieth century (see Anderson, 1923; Miller, 1991), the closing of the American West, the decline of migratory labor, and the spread of urbanization have led to the detachment of the social role of "hobo" or "bum" from the labor market and other productive roles. As I note throughout, single men of working age have been particularly repressed by the social welfare system and other institutions, and they lack the limited access to "the system" that even single mothers or the elderly poor now have. Although the role of bum and hobo seems to be as negative a stereotype as the public could imagine, for the older street people that role is a sense-making device that explains their situation by inverting normal social status and embracing an oppositional role. As noted earlier, the fact that at times in U.S. history, hobos and bums have also been heroes (the "Hallejuah, I'm a bum" tradition of the Wobblies, for example) adds a romantic flavor to this stigmatized role.

Although street kids have been present in major urban areas for centuries, economic and social forces in the twentieth century (compulsory schooling, abolition of child labor, Social Security benefits for orphans) initially led to a reduction in the number of "street urchins." However, new cultural trends that accompanied the now-extended adolescence in the United States began to produce an identifiable youth culture in the post–World War II period (see Brake, 1985). Social trends such as increased poverty, youth unemployment, and the breakup of the family have combined with varying generational revolts and separate streams of youth culture to produce a highly identifiable worldwide oppositional youth culture. Although Street Kids in North City were rarely gang members, they drew on the symbols of low-income youth throughout the United States, including phrases, T shirts, and rap music from urban black youth culture. As with the Street Drunks' embracement of the "bum" label, a Street Kid or Young Tough role is a sense-making device that gives cultural credence to the kids' detachment from the norms of the adult world and that adds status and élan to their daily lives.

The Social Club and Politicos' identifications and subcultures are products of much more recent historical developments. Deinstitutionalization of the mentally ill in the post-1950s period produced for the first time a large number of visibly mentally ill people who were not segregated from society in locked wards or private homes. Although much attention has necessarily been given to the severe problems of the deinstitutionalized mentally ill, the potential for a positive role embracement of a psychiatric label has received less attention. The Social Club group draws from the civil rights ideology of the 1960s, which led to a small social movement of the psychiatrically labeled—particularly in the 1970s—with groups such as the Mental Patients Liberation Front (see Chamberlin, 1978). Again, as with the Street Drunks and the Street Kids, the Social Club inverts normative social status to view psychiatric status as a positive identity.

For the Politicos, the countercultural movement of the 1960s, the antiwar movement of the same period, and the loosely connected and developing homeless movement of the 1980s have been very influential in producing a more slowly evolving social role as street people who are political advocates or traveling researchers. The subculture finds strong identification with both the hippie movement of the 1960s and the more religious influences of the homeless movement, such as Mitch Snyder's powerful influence in the 1980s. Cultural factors alone, however, do not completely explain the embracement of this role since it also requires a core of impoverished street people, many of them downwardly mobile compared with their families of origin in the 1970s and 1980s

The potential identifications—bum-like Street Drunks, Street Kids, self-identified ex-mental patients, Politicos—then, are well-known cultural types. Although these roles include a number of complex requisites such as age, life-style, and behavioral norms, they are also linked in an organized way to different degrees of societal hostility and to the different degrees of access the groups have to social resources. In other words, if "cats hang together," as Anderson (1978) says, it is not just that as a subculture they share similar life-styles and norms but also because these life-styles seem to be rational stances, given the treatment society metes out to each group.

Among the undeserving poor, distinctions are drawn that are both formal—within the social welfare system and the criminal justice system, for example—and informal, such as the attitudes of social workers, mental health professionals, and charity officials. These distinctions, formal and informal, serve to place the older street person at the greatest disadvantage, with the street kid next and the mentally ill last.

The "older" man (often as young as 40) who becomes homeless is ineligible for most social benefits and is subject to extreme levels of discrimination from employers, landlords, shelter providers, and charity officials. As he becomes unshaven and unwashed and is clad in tattered clothes, he is likely to be identified as a skid row type regardless of whether he drinks. Before the Street Drunk gives up entirely on the "system," he may already be stigmatized and be isolated from those few resources that might help reverse the process of decline.

The Street Drunk in North City, who had usually worked on farms or in rural mills, lacked the education or prior cultural associations that could cognitively explain his down-and-out status through a political or other organized conceptual system of thought. Indeed, Street Drunks, when questioned individually about their political views, were sometimes conservative and ironically believed in the goals of the "American Dream" (although they noted that the dream had long passed them by) far more than did other homeless people. Almost completely locked out of all systems because of age, appearance, and lack of skills, the older bum usually blamed himself for his downward fall and adopted the Street Drunk identity as a way not only to make sense of what had happened to him or to gain companionship and community but also to obtain some resources in an economy and social welfare system that seemed impenetrable.

True, the Street Drunk compounds his stigmatization by drinking, spending time with other drunks, and sometimes behaving crudely, but given the lack of opportunities available to him, the sharing of goods among the Street Drunk community and the access to group "shadow work"—which can sometimes be fairly lucrative—may more than compensate for this. That is, if other strategies of success, such as access to legitimate work, are blocked, the Street Drunk pattern makes some sense.

Street Kids face similar barriers to those of the drunks, but they also have more resources than do the older men. As noted, the legal and social welfare system cuts off those under age 18 from almost all of the legal privileges of adulthood and from access to most social benefits. When they become homeless, kids under 18, like the Street Drunks, are shocked to learn that few resources are available to help them and to find that they are likely to be harassed and arrested by police since so many status offenses (running away, truanting, delinquency) criminalize the behavior of the young, placing them in a running battle with authorities.

Street Kids, like the Street Drunks, are reinforced by "the system" into an oppositional cultural identification as they find alternative ways to survive based on the group and on various illegal ventures. However, since Street Kids realize that their complete exclusion from work roles and social benefits is temporary (at age 18 they do gain more rights) and that many social service and mental health professionals or clergy are anxious to "save" them, they are placed in a different position. Some Street Kids see alternatives, which explains why this subculture bifurcates into those who gradually give up some of the more deviant aspects of street culture and others who become so embittered at their treatment by the system that, seeing few real alternatives, they turn to careers in crime.

Those labeled mentally ill in North City, in contrast to the drunks and kids, have access to many more resources from the service system, are treated more leniently by police and landlords, and find more sympathy from social workers, clergy, and other members of the middle class. In response to a question about how she saw herself in comparison with the other homeless, Amy made this point:

> I've had more resources. The general poor have not necessarily had, you know, the Friendly Center, the [North City] Coalition [for the Psychiatrically Labeled]. Being mentally ill and a resourceful person, I have made use of a lot of things available [to me]. Others cannot.

Larry, the informant who has worked extensively with both Street Drunks and the Social Club, believes the mentally ill—at least in North City—have it "good" compared with the Street Drunks. Those diagnosed as mentally ill were usually able (in 1990 and 1991) to secure SSI or Social Security disability, which can at least pay for an SRO hotel room or food, and subsidized housing can often be obtained for this population. Larry also notes that the community, although hardly immune to discrimination against the mentally ill, comparatively speaking gives them more consideration than is shown to the drunks:

> So the landlord up on [street], he's had drunks placed there, but as soon as they present a problem, they're out [evicted]. But the other day, he had this guy who was mentally ill. He [the tenant] went off his meds and started having a [psychiatric] break[down]. Last Thursday, he was in the kitchen with a butcher knife and tapping it, saying he was going to kill someone. [He] went to [psychiatric hospital]. So I asked [landlord] if he would hold his room [for the tenant]. He says, "Oh sure, of course!" I was amazed 'cause he'd [landlord] never do this for a drunk. The guy would be out on his ass, and he'd be glad. But he sees mental illness as a sickness and also has a good appreciation for that three-letter word spelled "SSI."

It may seem ludicrous at first to talk of advantages of mental illness when society continues to stigmatize the mentally ill and communities mount "not-in-my-backyard" movements. Also, any generalization is limited to particular conditions as well as to market alternatives landlords and others have. But within groups that are stigmatized, it is evident that, comparatively speaking, the medicalization of mental illness in the twentieth century has led to some recognition that the homelessness, poverty, and other problems of this group may be due to a "sickness" that is beyond the control of the individual and that the individual is not to blamed for. As negatively as the psychiatrically labeled are viewed, they are treated more kindly than are the Street Drunks or the Street Kids. More important, although the legal and social welfare systems have been mandated to provide benefits to all homeless people, they regard this mandate with ambivalence when it comes to substance abusers or disorderly youth.

Politicos present a more complex example of differential societal hostility and access to resources since they are not a class recognized either by law or by rules. As noted, the Politicos are somewhat more likely to be of middle-class origin and to be educated, so they have more resources from the start than some of the other street people (money from family members or friends, some job skills, and the like). Further, since many have had social problems that are arguably felt by society to entitle them to a "deserving poor" label (particularly the veterans) or have been diagnosed as mentally ill, they may have experienced the social service system, legal system, and other societal institutions in a way that—although hardly benevolent—is not as totally closed as it is to the Street Drunks.[7] In a self-reinforcing fashion, the comparatively lower degree of societal hostility toward the Social Club and the Politicos combines with other attributes of these two groups—their willingness to join formal organizations, to cooperate for the most part with service providers, to engage in collective action—to encourage them to associate together within their own groups and subjectively to see some degree of efficacy in fighting for political and social rights.

If my argument—that late twentieth-century societal hostility and corresponding access to resources have a great deal to do with association and culture among these four subcultures—is correct, then it is an ironic truth that those most excluded from "the system" will in some ways be the least likely to engage in formal protest or advocacy, whereas those who have seen at least minimal gains will identify problems in a more political fashion. The Street Drunks and young Street Kids often see little hope for change in their lives through group efforts to improve the welfare system, the shelter system, or various social policies in North City. The Politicos, the Social Club group, and some of the Young Turks, however, have often had experience with and knowledge of successful protest or have witnessed changes (sometimes subtle) in their own lives based on policy changes in city welfare, Social Security, veterans' benefits, or AFDC benefits.

In this sense, the culture of resistance I have described differs within the Checkerboard Square community. The Street Drunks and Street Kids who adopt the culture of "macho toughness" (as described by MacLeod, 1987; and Willis, 1977) are less likely to turn their insights about "the system" into organized collective protest or to adopt a political orientation, whereas the other groups, to varying degrees, tend to meld their cultural resistance into more organized forms of political resistance.

Notes

1. Since the data are based on self-reports and I have no way of verifying any cause-and-effect chains, I can make no general statement that would definitively contradict the view

that Tiny or others did not drink before becoming homeless or that alcoholism is or is not a major contributor to homelessness.

2. Transiency differed considerably among the four groups discussed. The Street Drunks usually stayed in North City unless things became intolerable; when, for example, they were thrown out of most available shelters or service centers, some left town, never to return. Street Kids and Young Turks, however, tended to use North City as a base even when they traveled or left for work, training, or other reasons. A Street Kid would almost certainly return, even if he or she had left town for awhile, but the Street Drunk who left might never come back. The other two groups—the Social Club and Politicos—were more stable than either the Street Drunks or the Street Kids; although the Politicos did travel, they could be counted on to return. Generally, the Street Drunks tended to not be from the North City area initially; thus they lacked the local ties members of the other groups had. Their more hostile relations with the service system and other institutions of North City often made them feel it was easier to sever the few ties they had and move on.

3. Because this study was originally embarked upon as an attempt to locate and interview the tent city participants, most of our contacts were with people no younger than age 17 or 18 (since we started 3 years after tent city, the youngest subjects we had in our records were 14 or 15 at the time of tent city). Although we had contact with some of the new cohort of street kids (who were under age 17 or 18 in 1990), we have less data on them than on the original cohort.

4. Note, however, based on some of the discussion, that in the figure the Young Turks are placed closer to the Social Club and Politicos in their solidarity and ties with formal organizations than to the Street Kids.

5. See Chapter 3, note 4, on the lack of identified lesbians within the sample.

6. There are exceptions to this generalization, particularly in the partnering of Politicos. Mitch was undoubtedly aided in the process of moving from being a rather isolated street person to becoming a Politico by his relationship with Katherine, for example. I do not mean, then, to imply that the Politicos did not meet partners or lovers among the street population or train interested street people in the ways of being a Politico; rather, they generally kept their social lives separate from daily interactions with most other homeless people.

7. This argument is raised with caution. As described elsewhere, many subjects classified as Politicos and Social Club members have had horrific experiences with service providers, employers, and landlords. So the argument is either true only comparatively speaking (they have greater access than do Street Drunks or Street Kids) or perhaps is only another way of saying that societal laws and institutions ultimately stratify the homeless population.

For example, we do not know how many mentally ill people give up on securing benefits to which they are entitled, such as SSI or Social Security disability, or how many veterans give up on the long bureaucratic battles with the VA. Perhaps those subjects who remain in North City or who have become Politicos or Social Club members are unusual in their degree of psychological strength and "staying power" to fight for the benefits most of them eventually did accrue.

8

Checkerboard Square and a Radical Critique of Homelessness

By intensively studying a group of street people, I have looked at the poorest and most heavily stigmatized members of U.S. society through a different lens. Despite grinding poverty caused by the failure of the U.S. economic system, and despite the historical patterns of repression against the poor, such poverty did not make our subjects isolated or pathetic. The voices from Checkerboard Square suggest that street people can develop their own culture, values, and community. Their way of life is a rational response to their social and economic conditions. Although stripped of the basic components the public believes are essential to life—home, family, property, secure jobs—street people not only participate in a community life but continue their associations even if they secure housing. Their understanding of society—sometimes instinctive, sometimes more politically sophisticated—leads them to resist various demands made upon them and to develop alternative ways of getting basic needs met.

The radically different account of a group of homeless people presented here raises the issue of why Americans of most social classes and at most points in the U.S. political spectrum do not view the homeless as part of a culture, community, or collectivity. Further, the study has implications that not only challenge the dominant individualist paradigm of most Americans but that raise challenging questions for reformers, advocates, and social scientists who have sought to foster sympathy and support for the homeless and the very poor.

Perspectives on the Homeless and the American Culture of Individualism

Americans seem to view the homeless in one of three ways: (1) with a hostile, judgmental view (sometimes labeled "blaming the victim" by social scientists, advocates, and liberals) in which the poor are held responsible for their own fate and are seen as disruptive of the public order; (2) with a charitable view that crosses the political spectrum and is supported by both religious and secular traditions, which require that assistance be given to those in need and that (when charity is accepted) offer compassion; and (3) with a liberal, therapeutic view, which sees the very poor as clients who through proper classification, treatment, and amelioration can rejoin society and regain their self-esteem.

Despite the important differences among these views, they have strong similarities. Each tradition—roughly speaking, the rugged individualist, the religious, and the social service view—sees the down-and-out person as an individual (or a family); that is, as a disaggregated unit cut off from the social order. The poor person or family is examined regarding psychological or physical health or moral or religious worthiness. He or she is then alternatively blamed or bemoaned, helped and supported, or diagnosed and treated, depending on the ideological tradition (or professional role) of the examiner. Even when the sociological, economic, political, and other macro-level causes of poverty are understood, most Americans respond by saying "OK, but what can we do now for one person?" or "But he or she shouldn't act that way." It has been my experience, for example, that even when students or social worker audiences understand the broader social structural reasons for homelessness—lack of affordable housing, underemployment and unemployment, low amounts of social benefits, and so forth—they prefer to discuss individual case histories or the impact of alcohol, drugs, or child abuse on individuals. Or they often acknowledge broader issues only to dismiss macro-level action in favor of individual action, such as volunteering at a soup kitchen.

Perhaps at some level, Americans simply understand and even enjoy discussing personal issues more than they do broader social or political issues. We not only attribute causation to individual circumstances, but we seem to enjoy the process of analyzing character and personal history rather than looking at the more global cultural or historical aspects of problems. Political questions and competing political parties are seen as a bore in the Unites States, and media coverage of the personal lives and attributes of politicians seem more enticing to the public. Large-scale problems, such as the environmental crisis, are seen as overwhelming except when reduced to personal actions such as "buying green." Problems such as crime or single-parent families are debated through individual surrogates and metaphors such as Willie Horton or the "Murphy Brown" television show. No doubt, as Bellah and associates (1985) note, the popular culture has deeply expanded American individualism into a "culture of separation" in which fragments and snatches of information are provided to us in discrete and idiosyncratic parts, making a coherent view of U.S. life and its broader fabric even more difficult to visualize. Problems such as poverty are divorced from a social context and are reduced to anecdotal snippets from the 6 o'clock news. Paradoxically, the expansion of information and education in Western life has allowed almost everyone to feel he or she is an expert on what the poor (and other issues) need because he or she saw it on television last night, yet the broader context of people's culture and community is obscured by most of the 60-second interviews and talking heads on television.

Bellah and his associates' (1985) path-breaking book on U.S. individualism suggests that across the political spectrum, Americans share a "first language of individualism," which explains reality through a lens of personal life, individual will, and personal morality. In Bellah and co-workers' classifications, our first two views—those of the rugged individualist and the charitable—emanate from the biblical and Republican traditions of colonial America, which they conceptualize as utilitarian individualism. They see the third dominant view—the social service–psychotherapeutic view—as modernist tradition, which they label expressive individualism and consider to be a variant of romanticism. Undoubtedly, at different historical junctures, all of these traditions represented progress: Bourgeois individualism advanced Western cultures from feudalism, monarchy, and the medieval church; and the therapeutic culture advanced the acceptance of different kinds of behavior, converting people who had been believed to be "bad" or immoral into those suffering from "conditions" or diseases that could affect any of us.

Bellah and co-workers (1985) contrast Americans' individualism with the older tradition (more common in other cultures) they call the "community of memory." Whether community is embedded in social class, race and ethnicity, geography, religion, or some combination of these factors, social interdependence, group practices, and tradition are central to this view of life. American Indian culture or African cultures, for example, would explain people's behavior yesterday or today as based on the actions of their ancestors, of their tribe, of their religion, or of the needs of their community, not because "they felt like" doing this or that or because "they were doing their own thing." In some ways, the homeless subcultures identified in Chapter 7 can be seen as different "communities of memories" based on historical identification, age and gender segmentation, and social class and political identification.

Given what Bellah and associates (1985) call Americans' "ontological individualism," it should not be surprising that even compared with European cultures, Americans tend either not to see the social, cultural, political, or economic nature of issues or to see them but to prefer to talk about and act on more personal, individual aspects of issues. To accept the fact that street people have a set of norms, a culture, and patterns of life that are not random but are structured, of course, implies that all Americans have certain norms, cultures, and structured patterns that are based on social class, age, ethnic cultures, or regional cultures. Americans tend to reject these thoughts as not representing their conceptions of free will and autonomy and therefore tend to reject or ignore most sociological or social structural critique. American individualism has long ceased to be a progressive force both because it denies community and culture and hence what ultimately brings people together, producing an atomized notion of happiness and the good life, and because—even compared with cultures that have similar economic systems—all efforts to systematically control rampant individualism are viewed as restricting individual rights.

What I am suggesting is that although the nature of our economic system—the most individualist capitalist system in the world—is certainly the major factor in the treatment of the poor throughout the last 300 years, such a system could not sustain itself without widespread cultural support for individualism and an individualist paradigm for conceptualizing virtually all human behavior. Despite the many recent books on and analyses of the impact of deindustrialization, housing gentrification, and other social causes of poverty, Americans often seem to be unmoved (beyond engaging in charity or social service) to tackle such social problems. Although in the abstract Americans certainly wish each other well, the tools to radically change the society, such as a major redistribution of wealth, do not seem to capture an audience.

In many ways, the categorization of "homeless" is itself a reification, an abstraction that is convenient for political discourse, academic study, and social service intervention. Poor people are abstracted from their particular locales and cultures and are counted statistically, analyzed, and turned into "cases" by a variety of well-meaning people. Although some homeless people travel, this study—along with others—finds that the majority of street people are from the local regions in which they are found and that contrary to depictions in some dramatic television and film presentations,[1] they are generally not from the middle class but from low-income or working-class families. Moreover, since much literal homelessness is episodic (see Rossi, 1989), to consign someone to the category of homeless can be very misleading since he or she may be homeless one week and housed the next. As several social scientists have noted (Blau, 1992; Katz, 1989; Rossi, 1989), any solution to the problem of homelessness lies with solutions to the broader problems of low-income communities throughout the United States. The homeless are not cases or numbers but are part of a low-income community, whether in North City or New York City. Their fate is bound up in the broader economic and social trends that are reducing the standard of living of working-class and poor people. Although they are part of the broader culture of the poor, as I have shown, homeless people do also form their own communities on the street while maintaining links with other segments of the low-income community.

The individualist paradigm of U.S. culture greatly dictates the pathos and disempowerment that are evident when people like our subjects are presented out of context. As human interest stories in the media, they all tell heartrending stories of poverty. As people labeled not only as homeless but sometimes as criminals, alcoholics, or mentally ill, their very labels produce pity, compassion, or anger. Yet when viewed over time within their context as a group, these same people are capable of engaging in strong patterns of association, political organizing, and other cooperative ventures. Both the process of categorization and the damning labels ("homeless," "substance abusers," "mentally ill") tend to negate the essential humanity and commonality of people like our subjects.

What if the Checkerboard Community Were Treated as a Community?

I have suggested throughout this book that the street people of Checkerboard Square are a community, as well as being part of the broader low-income community. However, none of the systems that govern the lives of poor people—from private employers to landlords to social workers to charity officials to health care providers—think of the homeless in this way. The structure of our society—both private markets and the public sector—forces individual homeless people (or families) to present themselves as atomized biographies, to differentiate themselves to those in power as "worthy cases," and to separate themselves from their broader group in order to gain any resource that is necessary for survival.

I discussed in Chapter 5 the fact that assistance to subjects in North City, when available, usually carried the price of humiliation and subordination. More subtly, most chances for improvement in these subjects' lives also required that they separate from the broader community. The social networks and subcultures among the poor discussed here were either ignored or were seen as barriers to the personal changes in street people's lives that were felt to be necessary by service workers.

Almost 50 years ago, Whyte (originally 1943; 1966 here) found a similar process occurring in Cornerville. Settlement workers showed the most interest in and involvement with those relatively few Cornerville residents who were prepared to leave the slum and to take advantage of education or services in order to gain upward mobility. Whyte suggests that the workers looked upon the others who "were going nowhere" with either pity or contempt. Indigenous social networks and social relations were also ignored or actively fought. I suggest, however, that such a logic of separation is not just a prejudice among middle-class caregivers but is a response of all of us to the individualistic structure of both private markets and government benefits.

To secure a tiny SRO hotel room, the street people of North City must often leave the part of town they call home, leave their street friends (who, if they obtain housing, are unlikely to be placed near them), and submit to control by government—such as workfare and personal scrutiny—in order to get a rent check from welfare. To get into detoxification programs, alcohol or drug rehabilitation, or many mental health programs, the homeless person has to leave his or her street friends, discontinue an autonomous life to submit to a form of institutionalization, and often go to a different geographic area. Employment possibilities (when extant) or referrals to job training inevitably mean traveling some distance, changing the patterns of daily life (in a way that often makes going to soup kitchens or getting into shelters impossible because of scheduling and restrictive shelter rules), and often submitting to new sets of harsh rules (such as at a Job Corps site).

Most of the public and most advocates and social workers see this process of individuation and separation as unproblematic because, after all, any improvement in a homeless person's life—a tiny room somewhere or a minimum wage job—is considered worth sacrificing for. Yet the basic tenets of our culture— "strive to get ahead," "leave the dysfunctional peer groups of the slum," "if you get something, it will lead to something better"—are not so clear to the denizens of Checkerboard Square, as we have seen. First, their own experience with work, landlords, state services, and similar institutions suggests that one step does not lead to something better and that the sacrifice entailed comes at a high price and often goes unrewarded. Second, as I have discussed, their feeling of group solidarity often places collective interest and group interaction ahead of personal gain. Subjects frequently wanted to know, "Why can't we all get housed?" or "Why can't we all have services?" not just when would *they* get something.

What if homeless people like those in Checkerboard Square were offered the opportunity of *collective mobility* and *collective resources* rather that individual scrutiny, surveillance, and treatment? What if the dense social networks and cohesive subcultures that constitute the homeless community were utilized by advocates, social workers, and others? What if housing could be provided near the geographic areas in which street people congregate, decent housing that does not require leaving the group but that could be shared by street friends? There is no structural reason why obtaining shelter should entail separation from friends and community, except for the scarcity of adequate housing in U.S. cities and the refusal of the service system to acknowledge ties other than traditional families in making housing placements. If apartment buildings were taken over by the homeless or made available for rehabilitation by government for the entire community, provision of centralized space would be a tremendous gain for the Checkerboard Square community, freeing its members from the dangers of the elements on the one hand and from isolation and dispersal on the other.

In a similar vein, the scarcity of work or other productive options for the use of time has traditionally meant that homeless people must scatter to job referrals in distant places, migrating across regions, and that they must face the individualized assignment of a few available training slots to the "cream of the crop." In contrast, the many current calls for the re-creation of the 1930s public works camps, such as the Civilian Conservation Corps, have the advantage of providing some meaningful projects for poor people that they could do together, potentially without leaving their home areas. Joint work projects or even volunteer service would link the community together rather than disperse it. The street people of North City, as we saw in Chapter 4, most liked the work they did together, such as at the fish piers or in carnivals. When collective ties and solidarity are built upon and arbitrary employer control and surveillance are weakened, productive work (it need not be wage labor) could certainly be done by the Checkerboard Square community.

What if social benefits were distributed not individually but collectively so that income maintenance or resources for food, shelter, and other goods were given to an entire group of people, not to individuals? That is, one would not need to wait for hours, provide all aspects of one's personal life, and come into a welfare office continually to be recertified, but would obtain a collective grant as part of a co-hort of homeless people (or other group of poor people). The individual would no longer be the locus of treatment or reform; that locus would be a broader community to be aided. Although this idea seems radical in an individualist soci-ety, a few glimmers of it are found in our history. At the height of the social unrest in the Great Depression, the New Deal provided open-ended grants through the Federal Emergency Relief Administration program (see Jansson, 1988; Piven & Cloward, 1971), which in some cases went to groups of starving farmers or to groups of unemployed workers to set up work camps and relief stations. To some extent, grants to community action centers during the 1960s "war on poverty"— although not for the purpose of income maintenance—provide a precedent in that monies for job training, community action, social services, and housing were given to a community for disbursement to poor people. The ideal of affirmative action for groups that are discriminated against and for group settlement of American Indian land claims also contains within it the notion of societal redress to a collective group, although it has not always been implemented in this fash-ion.

Recognition of the homeless as a community and as part of the larger poor community would also entail recognition that, as was done in the 1960s, a com-mitment of resources for community organizing could help stimulate collective empowerment and political power. This too would be highly controversial. Even limited efforts of the government to assist in organizing the poor during the war on poverty in the 1960s led to tremendous criticism and antagonistic reaction among both liberals and conservatives (see Marris & Rein, 1982; Moynihan, 1970). The subjects of North City had a strong respect for community organizers and seemed to need some outside help since suspicion about the motives of indige-nous leaders (and the possibility of self-interest and partiality) was often high in Checkerboard Square, as we saw in Chapter 6.

These ideas seem radical not just because of the current array of political forces in the United States today but also because of the historical cultural view of the problems of poverty that is generally shared by most Americans. Only during very exceptional times—the height of the Great Depression in the 1930s and the height of civil rights agitation in the 1960s—have Americans briefly deviated from this attitude. It is unlikely that a collective orientation toward the problems of the poor will occur without very dramatic events causing a paradigmatic shift in the conceptualization of poverty and homelessness.

Questions for Homeless Advocates and Movements

In the past decade, a wide variety of research studies, advocacy literature, and journalistic reporting has shown Americans the horror of homelessness, has provided statistics about poverty, and has proposed a variety of macro-level policy changes that would alleviate poverty. As I noted in Chapter 1, because the context of the new homelessness of the 1970s–1990s occurred during conservative administrations, and because of the absence of major social unrest among the poor, the "movement" for the homeless was led by advocates who sought to convince public officials and the general public of the need for basic services.

The movement for the homeless has been partly successful in establishing service programs, in gaining increased attention and sympathy for the poor, and in securing increased civil and legal rights for the homeless. It has been far less successful either in stopping the escalation of poverty and homelessness or in placing broader social changes, such as affordable housing or full employment programs, on the national agenda.

Compared with the three dominant views of the homeless and the very poor described in this chapter, the advocacy literature and social scientists who support a social structural approach to issues have stressed a more collective approach. Kozol (1988:11), for example, states that the homeless lack housing and that a solution to homelessness lies first with providing affordable housing; Dunbar (1988:5) notes that the problem of poverty is lack of income and criticizes all approaches that look at the behavior of the poor rather than at increasing their income. Unquestionably, approaches that stress income redistribution and radical changes in the housing market and other free markets begin to address the issues of poverty and homelessness.

Although I applaud the contributions of advocates and social scientists who have raised these issues, in fact few of them have proposed a truly collectivist paradigm for viewing poverty, and few—as noted in Chapter 1—have talked of the poor as actors in their own right. The suspicion within the Checkerboard Square community about the altruism of the state reminds us that the people to be helped may not always be amenable to major government interventions and that this suspicion parallels the broader public's distrust of the government.

The distance between some of the opinions of the subjects from Checkerboard Square and those of homeless advocates is reflected in part in the liberal–social democratic model of many advocates and researchers who have stressed the *collective* causes of poverty and the provision of increased resources through government but who have not take into account the privatized and *individualist* manner of the distribution of resources. "More" of everything—housing, jobs, income—does not address the unbridled role of employers, landlords, and state bureaucrats in controlling the lives of the poor; nor does it address a system of distribution that requires that the poor be humiliated and be separated from communities and that they accept labels based on an individualist paradigm. In this sense, no matter how many new jobs are created or new homes are built, the liberal social structural model of analyzing homelessness tends to lead us back to the individualist social service approach in which government agents assess each person or family, determine what is best for them, and place them in housing or jobs or drug treatment or whatever.

My interpretation of North City's culture of resistance and of the social organization of street people can only be suggestive of what the social science literature on homelessness, poverty, social movements, and the state, as well as political advocates, may need to consider in furthering social action. The subjective orientations of the homeless of North City, although supportive of many liberal-to-leftist social policy proposals, also reveal considerable skepticism about the traditional structures of U.S. society on which advocates often rely for reform (the workplace, the family, the state). I conclude by posing three questions that flow from this ethnographic study, the answers to which I believe are key to achieving major social changes in the political and socioeconomic structure in the United States.

"Can Major Social Change Occur Without Indigenous Social Movements Among the Poor?"

> They [the system] will move only when we force them [to] and then only as much as we force them to change.
>
> —Mitch

Mitch's statement, although it is about North City in particular, represents an accurate reading of the history of social change and social movements that affect the poor. Whether one reflects on the local situation in North City, in which the changes that did occur followed the tent city protest (see Chapter 5), or on the national trends and the effects of the social unrest of the 1930s and 1960s (see Piven & Cloward, 1971, 1977), only indigenous social movements among groups of poor people have substantially altered the social welfare system, the national political balance of power, and government policy generally.

Charity officials, social service leaders, and advocates often seem to work on the assumption that educating the public to a variety of conditions and social problems will produce not only financial support but also political change. Although the history of advocacy movements (middle-class "claims makers" and experts demanding changes in conditions that affect the poor) is a long one, dating back to the abolitionists and the temperance movement, the post-1960s period has seen a veritable mushrooming of professionalized advocacy (see Zald & McCarthy, 1987). Despite the success experts may enjoy in influencing the public on selected social issues (the environment, child abuse, drunk driving, consumer rights), social issues such as poverty, which are deeply embedded in the organization of capitalism, are not easily amenable to the influence of professionalized advocates. In many ways, the 1992 Los Angeles riots may do more for the poor—at least in putting the issues of urban America on the political agenda—than have all the years of fundraising, press releases, and academic monographs about poverty and homelessness.

Street people in North City tended to view politics as reflective of class self-interest rather than as a superordinate common ground in which all Americans could be moved by compassion or rational argument. Perhaps unfortunately, their view more accurately represents political and social reality in the United States. If things do change for the poor, it is usually because the broader public fears social disorder in the slums, businesses fear the negative impact of violence, and political leaders fear a loss of legitimacy.

In this book I cannot answer the critical question of how to develop and nurture indigenous social movements of the poor, but I call attention to the possibility of the poor once again being historical actors in their own right. I question what has been a rather broad exclusion of their opinions and their social movements from much of the literature on the poor and much of the strategy of advocates.[2]

Is Social Change Possible Without Altering Control of Resources by Private Elites or Public Authorities?

A second and related issue, which has also received little attention in the social science literature or within advocacy circles, is the contradiction between the efforts of advocates to increase state services and the distaste consumers of these services often have for the "system" that provides such services and resources. As discussed in Chapters 4 and 5, the homeless of North City resisted control by private employers and by public shelters and welfare systems. Generally, their experience convinced them that "the system" was exploitative or coercive in nature. Although they recognized individual employers, landlords, or social workers who were exceptions, on the whole they were critical of both private authority and public bureaucracy.

The conservative domination not only of political power but of social discourse in the last decade and a half has generally forced out of the public eye any critique of authority and bureaucracy from a left-wing rather than a right-wing perspective. As noted in Chapter 5, most liberal advocates have been reduced, like Sam Gompers of the old AFL, to having only the slogan "more." More jobs, more training, more shelters, more benefits, more programs, and so forth are needed, but just as Gompers called for more wages and benefits but not for changes in the wage system, the advocates do not usually deal with the fundamental problem of control over resources.

The subjects I have studied remind us that the problems of the poor are not simply those of insufficient work, insufficient housing, and insufficient social benefits but also include the structure of institutions such as the workplace and government services. More minimum wage jobs at workplaces at which employers completely dominate unorganized employees, more wretched flophouses from which landlords make large profits from the poor, and more service workers to run large warehouse shelters are clearly not answers to the problems of the poor. The vast power of employers, landlords, and governmental officials over the poor was resented as much by our subjects as was the lack of affordable housing, good jobs, and adequate social benefits.

As with the question of indigenous social movements, there are no easy answers to this dilemma. Historically, the power of employers, landlords, and government bureaucracies has been challenged successfully only at times in which labor movements, tenant movements, welfare rights movements, and other movements of the poor have been strongly organized and vocal. Advocates, social scientists, and political leaders have a limited ability to catalyze such movements, much less to actually lead them. Moreover, the failure of the state to serve as an instrument of the people, which was at the center of Marxist and socialist strategies of social change, has only recently been widely recognized by the Left. The disorientation following the collapse of communism in Eastern Europe is not unrelated to the issues raised here. The failure of the state to truly serve as an instrument of power for citizens generally is a problem felt from the United States to Russia, yet nothing else seems to have replaced the state as a vehicle for popular control.

Although on paper one can propose all sorts of ideas for new services or programs that include the poor and provide consumer control, new vehicles of popular control can ultimately only be developed by the poor themselves through social action and experimentation.

Can Major Social Change Occur While Advocates Affirm the Dominant Social Norms?

I began by arguing that the widespread consensus about the family and the work ethic obscured the degree to which these dominant ideological tenets do not reflect reality. The experiences of the subjects in their families (Chapter 3) and at the workplace (Chapter 4) hardly support a glorification of "family values" or the nobility of low-paying work.

Yet both conservatives and liberals frame their world views around these values, and the basic difference between them, we are told, lies in their conception of how to better support "family values" and the "work ethic." The Republicans' firm insistence on the traditional forms of family and business domination clearly makes them the more believable ideologues. To the extent that the Democratic party includes liberal and radical feminists and others who have challenged the traditional family, as well as advocates for the poor who defend welfare, its members will be suspect as using these norms as tactical slogans rather than being true believers.

Regardless of the sincerity of those who advance family values and work as the pillars of society, these slogans do little for people like the subjects of this book. If family values can actually be implemented through social policy, what will this mean for the millions of the single poor, childless couples, or nontraditional family units? At least in the state in which North City is located, families have preference in public housing, in obtaining shelter space, in income maintenance benefits, and in obtaining heath care. If family values are emphasized even more, what will this mean for abused children who want to leave their homes, battered women who seek to flee their husbands, or those who are distraught after divorce or separation? And the enforcement of the work ethic, either by liberals or conservatives, usually means a retreat from social benefits as "encouraging dependency" and a crackdown on the effort of the poor to survive through underground or casual work.

It appears that historically, the family and work ethics are useful cultural myths that have long been used against the poor (as well as against immigrant and minority cultures). Historians suggest that the poor were attacked for failing to abide by the work ethic as early as the sixteenth century (Michielse, 1990), then throughout the seventeenth, eighteenth, and nineteenth centuries, as well as during the twentieth century (see also Katz, 1986). If the poor have been charged with indolence and vice when unemployment was high and when it was low, when the workforce was agricultural and then when it was industrial and now when it is postindustrial, why would social policy changes revive the allegedly flagging work ethic of the poor, as liberals often claim? Those who for whatever reasons cannot work, cannot secure work, or whose work appears to differ from that upheld by the dominant work ethic will still be held out as object lessons, whether the official unemployment rate is 3 percent or 10 percent.

Many poor people, particularly racial minorities and immigrants, have been criticized for centuries by dominant elites because their families (extended family ties, inclusion of nonrelated people) either seemed different from the preferred Yankee model or because the patterns of migration, innovative work patterns, or the disruption of old ties led to breakdowns in their families. Once again, it is hard to see social policy changes affecting the family ethic both because much of the current ferment is as cultural as it is economic (the impact of feminism, for example) and because, as with the work ethic, violation of the family ethic will continue to lead to political scapegoating and exclusion from the social welfare system.

Advocates need to consider whether they can simultaneously advance funding for the poor while reaffirming societal myths and slogans without helping to inflict further harm upon those excluded from the fruits of the work ethic and family values. Despite the mythology, to what degree do private families and individual paychecks really provide a source of cohesion or community in the United States? Will a broader, more collective notion of rights and of collective labor ever be possible in our society if the language historically employed to scapegoat the poor continues to be used by those who presumably want reform?

Putting homeless people back into the issue of homelessness is a complex task since, as Marcuse (1988) notes, it raises many broader, complex issues about our society and culture. As he suggests, this is what attracts us to the issue to homelessness and yet equally repels us. The people of Checkerboard Square force us to see the limits of modern society to control people or to satisfy human needs, but they do not provide any easy answers to help us to resolve these problems. Although it is hoped that under U.S. capitalism the poor will not "always be with us," it is also hard to see the day when homelessness and poverty will disappear.

Notes

1. The media's tendency to obscure the major issues of homelessness includes presentations of the very affluent becoming homeless. My favorite example is an episode of the television show "St. Elsewhere," in which Dr. Mark Craig, a noted cardiac surgeon, becomes homeless and is forced to stay in a shelter. Another recent example occurs in the movie *The Fisher King,* in which Robin Williams plays a professor who has become homeless. Although it is possible for anyone to become homeless, I suggest that, if you visit your nearest homeless shelter, any effort to find current or former doctors or professors there will probably be fruitless.

The media, particularly liberal writers and producers, have reconstructed a variety of social problems that overwhelmingly affect the poor as middle-class issues in an effort to arouse the sympathy of the public. Although well-meaning, I am not certain how helpful these efforts are in developing true understanding of the causes and experiences of homelessness or other problems in our society.

2. For a fuller discussion of the exclusion of the social movements from the literature on homelessness and the exclusion of the poor from the literature on social movements, see Wagner and Cohen, 1991.

Bibliography

Abramovitz, M. *Regulating the Lives of Women.* Boston: South End Press, 1988.

Addams, J. *Twenty Years at Hull House.* New York: Signet, 1961.

American Psychiatric Association. *Diagnostic and Statistical Manual of Mental Disorders.* Washington, DC: APA, 1987.

Anderson, E. *A Place on the Corner.* Chicago: University of Chicago Press, 1978.

_____ . *Streetwise: Race, Class and Change in an Urban Community.* Chicago: University of Chicago Press, 1990.

Anderson, N. *The Hobo.* Chicago: University of Chicago Press, 1923.

Arce, A. Tadlock, M., Vergare, M., & Shapiro, S. "A Psychiatric Profile of Street People Admitted to an Emergency Shelter." Hospital and Community Psychiatry, 34, 1983:812–817.

Armstrong, L. *The Home Front: Notes from the Family War Zone.* New York: McGraw-Hill, 1983.

Aronowitz, S. *False Promises.* New York: McGraw-Hill, 1973.

_____ . "Why Work?" Social Text, 4(3), Fall 1985:19–45.

Auletta, K. *The Underclass.* New York: Random House, 1982.

Awalt, C. "Brother, Don't Spare a Dime." Newsweek. September 30, 1991:13.

Bachrach, L. "Interpreting Research on the Homeless Mentally Ill: Some Caveats." Hospital and Community Psychiatry, 35, 1984:914–916.

_____ . "Chronic Mentally Ill Women: Emergence and Legitimation of Program Issues." Hospital and Community Psychiatry. 36(10), 1985.

Bahr, H. *Skid Row: An Introduction to Disaffiliation.* New York: Oxford University Press, 1973.

Bahr, H., & Caplow, T. *Old Men Drunk and Sober.* New York: New York University Press, 1974.

Bassuk, E. L., & Rosenberg, L. "Why Does Family Homelessness Occur? A Case Control Study." American Journal of Public Health. 78, 1988:783–788.

Baxter, E., & Hopper, K. *Private Lives/Public Spaces: Homeless Adults on the Streets of New York.* New York: Community Service Society, 1984.

Bellah, R., Madsen, R., Sullivan, W., Swidler, A., & Tipton, S. *Habits of the Heart: Individualism and Commitment in American Life.* New York: Harper & Row Publishers, 1985.

Blau, J. *The Visible Poor: Homelessness in the United States.* New York: Oxford University Press, 1992.

Bluestone, B., & Harrison, B. *The Deindustrialization of America.* New York: Basic Books, 1982.

Blum, J., & Smith, J. *Nothing Left to Lose: Studies of Street People.* Boston: Beacon Press, 1972.

Boelen, W. A. "Street Corner Society: Cornerville Revisited." Journal of Contemporary Ethnography. 21(1), 1992:11–51.

Boston Globe. "Poll Shows Family Life Still Vital." November 24, 1991:1, 24.

Brake, Michael. *Comparative Youth Cultures.* London: Routledge, Kegan Paul, 1985.

Chamberlin, J. *On Our Own.* New York: McGraw-Hill, 1978.

Cherniss, G. *Staff Burnout: Job Stress in the Human Services.* Beverly Hills, CA: Sage Press, 1980.

Clifford, J., & Marcus, G. *Writing Culture: The Poetics and Politics of Ethnography.* Berkeley: University of California Press, 1986.

Cloward, R., & Piven, F. "Hidden Protest: The Channeling of Female Innovation and Resistance." Signs. 4, 1979:651–659.

Cohen, C., Teresi, J., Holmes, D., & Roth, E. "Survival Strategies of Older Homeless Men." Gerontologist. 28, 1988:58–65.

Cohen, M. B. "Interaction and Mutual Influence in a Program for Homeless Mentally Ill Women." Unpublished Ph.D. dissertation. Brandeis University, Florence Heller Graduate School, 1988.

Cohen, M. B., & Wagner, D. "Acting on Their Own Behalf: Affiliation and Political Ideology Among Homeless People." Journal of Sociology and Social Welfare. 19(4) 1992:21–40.

Coulson, M., Magas, B., & Wainwright, H. "The Housewife and Her Labor Under Capitalism—A Critique." New Left Review. 89, 1975.

Crystal, S. "Homeless Men and Homeless Women: The Gender Gap." Urban and Social Change Review. 17(2), 1984.

Dalla Costa, M., & Dalla Costa, J. *The Power of Women and the Subversion of the Community.* Cambridge, MA: Falling Wall Press, 1973.

Davis, J., & Smith, T. *General Social Surveys 1972–1988.* Storrs, CT: Center for Public Opinion Research, 1988.

DeParle, J. "Study Digs Deep to Find Poverty's Roots." New York Times. July 26, 1992.

Dubofsky, M. *When Workers Organize: New York City in the Progressive Era.* Amherst: University of Massachusetts Press, 1968.

Dunbar, L. *The Common Interest.* New York: Pantheon, 1988.

Edelman, M. *Families in Peril.* Cambridge, MA: Harvard University Press, 1987.

Edwards, R. *Contested Terrain.* New York: Basic Books, 1979.

Eisenstein, Z. (ed.). *Capitalist Patriarchy and the Case for Socialist Feminism.* New York: Monthly Review, 1979.

Fischer, P., & Breakey, W. "Homelessness and Mental Health: An Overview." International Journal of Mental Health. 14, 1986:6–41.

Foucault, M. *Madness and Civilization.* New York: Pantheon. 1965.

⸻ . *Discipline and Punish: The Birth of the Prison.* New York: Pantheon, 1977.

Galper, J. *The Politics of Social Services.* Englewood Cliffs, NJ: Prentice-Hall, 1975.

Gans, H. *The Urban Villagers.* New York: Free Press, 1962.

Garfinkel, H. "Conditions of Successful Degradation Ceremonies." American Journal of Sociology, 61, 1956:1956:240–244.

⸻ . *Studies in Ethnomethodology.* Englewood Cliffs, NJ: Prentice-Hall, 1967.

Gaylin, W., Glasser, I., Marcus, S., & Rothman, D. *Doing Good: The Limits of Benevolence.* New York: Pantheon, 1981.

Giroux, H. *Theory and Resistance in Education.* London: Heinemann Educational Books, 1983.

Glasser, I. "The Culture of a Soup Kitchen: Sanctuary." Unpublished Ph.D. dissertation. University of Connecticut, Anthropology Department, 1986.

Golden, S. *The Women Outside: Meanings and Myths of Homelessness.* Berkeley: University of California Press, 1992.

Grigsby, C., Baumann, D., Gregorich, S., & Roberts-Gray, C. "Disaffiliation to Entrenchment: A Model for Understanding Homelessness." Journal of Social Issues. 46(4), 1990:141–156.

Gutman, H. *Work, Culture and Society in Industrializing America.* New York: Alfred A. Knopf, 1976.

Harrington, M. *The New American Poverty.* New York: Holt, Rinehart and Winston, 1984.

Hoch, C., & Slayton, R. *New Homeless and Old.* Philadelphia: Temple University Press, 1989.

Hope, M., & Young, J. *The Faces of Homelessness.* Lexington, MA: D. C. Heath, 1986.

Hopper, K., & Hamburg, J. *The Making of America's Homeless: From Skid Row to the New Poor.* New York: Community Service Society, 1984.

Horowitz, R. *Honor and the American Dream: Culture and Identity in a Chicano Community.* New Brunswick, NJ: Rutgers University Press, 1983.

Hudson, C. "The Development of Policy for the Homeless: The Role of Research." Social Thought. 14, 1988:3–15.

Jansson, B. *The Reluctant Welfare State: A History of American Social Welfare Policies.* Belmont, CA: Wadsworth, 1988.

Jencks, C. *Rethinking Social Policy: Race, Poverty, and the Underclass.* Cambridge, MA: Harvard University Press, 1992.

Johnson, A. "Is Mental Illness a Cause or Result?" New York Times. July 29, 1990

Johnson, A. K., & Kreuger, L. W. "Toward a Better Understanding of Homeless Women." Social Work. 34, 1989:537–540.

Jones, L. "The Full Employment Myth: Alternative Solutions to Unemployment." Social Work. 37(4), 1992:359–364.

Journal of Contemporary Ethnography. Special Issue. "Street Corner Society Revisited." 21(1), 1992.

Katz, M. *In the Shadow of the Poorhouse.* New York: Basic Books, 1986.

————. *The Undeserving Poor.* New York: Pantheon, 1989.

Klatzky, S. *Patterns of Contacts with Relatives.* Washington, DC: American Sociological Association, 1972.

Kornblum, W. *Blue Collar Community.* Chicago: University of Chicago Press, 1974.

Kornblum, W., & Williams, T. *Growing Up Poor.* Lexington, MA: Lexington Books, 1985.

Kozol, J. *Rachel and Her Children.* New York: Fawcett, 1988.

Kramer, M. *Reality Shock: Why Nurses Leave Nursing.* St. Louis: C. V. Mosby Company, 1974.

La Gory, M., Ritchey, F., & Mullis, J. "Homelessness and Affiliation." Paper presented at the 84th annual meeting of the American Sociological Association, San Francisco, CA, August 11, 1989.

Lefkowitz, R., & Withorn, A. (eds.). *For Crying Out Loud.* New York: Pilgrim Press, 1986.

Levitan, S. *Programs in Aid of the Poor.* Sixth ed. Baltimore: Johns Hopkins University Press, 1990.

Liebow, E. *Tally's Corner.* Boston: Little, Brown, 1967.

———— . *Tell Them Who I Am.* New York: Free Press, 1993.

Lipsky, M., & Smith, J. "When Social Problems Are Treated as Emergencies." Social Service Review. 53, 1989:5–25.

Lipton, F., Sabatini, A., & Katz, S. "Down and Out in the City: The Homeless Mentally Ill." Hospital and Community Psychiatry. 34, 1983:817–821.

Macarov, D. "The Concept of Unemployment in Social Welfare Programs: The Need for Change in Concept and Practice." Journal of Sociology and Social Welfare. 9(1), 1984:1–24.

———— . "Reevaluation of Unemployment." Social Work. 33(1), 1988:23–28.

MacLeod, J. *Ain't No Making' It.* Boulder, CO: Westview Press, 1987.

Magnet, M. "America's Underclass: What to Do?" Fortune, May 11, 1987:130.

Marcuse, H. *One Dimensional Man.* Boston: Beacon Press, 1964.

Marcuse, P. "Neutralizing Homelessness." Socialist Review, 18, 1988:69–96.

Marin, P. "Why Are the Homeless Mainly Single Men?" The Nation. July 8 1991:46–51.

Marris, P., & Rein, M. *Dilemmas of Social Reform: Poverty and Community Action in the United States.* Chicago: University of Chicago Press, 1982.

McCarthy, J., & Zald, M. "Organizational Intellectuals and the Criticism of Society." Social Service Review. 46, 1975:344–362.

McChesney, K. Y. *Characteristics of the Residents of Two Inner-City Emergency Shelters for the Homeless.* Los Angeles: Social Science Research Institute, University of Southern California, 1987.

Mead, L. *Beyond Entitlement: The Social Obligations of Citizenship.* New York: Free Press, 1986.

Merton, R. *Social Theory and Social Structure.* New York: Free Press, 1968.

Michielse, H.C.M. (trans. Robert van Krieken). "Policing the Poor: J. L. Vives and the Sixteenth Century Origins of Modern Social Administration." Social Service Review. 64, 1990:1–21.

Miller, H. *On the Fringe: The Dispossessed in America.* Lexington, MA: D. C. Heath, 1991.

Mills, C. W. "The Professional Ideology of Social Pathologists." American Journal of Sociology, 49, 1943:165–180.

———— . *The Sociological Imagination.* London: Oxford University Press, 1959.

Morrissey, J., & Goldman, H. "Cycles of Reform in the Care of the Chronically Mentally Ill." Hospital and Community Psychiatry. 35, 1984

Moynihan, D. P. *The Negro Family: The Case for National Action.* Washington, DC: U.S. Government Printing Office, Department of Labor, 1965.

———— . *Maximum Feasible Misunderstanding.* New York: Free Press, 1970.

Murray, C. *Losing Ground: American Social Policy 1950–1980.* New York: Basic Books, 1984.

New York Times. "Poverty Is Perceived as Increasing and State of Poor Unimproved." August 23, 1989:32.

Newman, K. "Culture and Structure in the Truly Disadvantaged: An Anthropological Perspective." Unpublished paper, 1989.

(North City newsweekly). "Advocates Leave Homeless Group." May 3, 1990:1, 5.

Patterson, J., & Kim, P. *The Day America Told the Truth.* Englewood Cliffs, NJ: Prentice-Hall, 1991.

Pearce, D. "The Feminization of Poverty: Women, Welfare and Work." Urban and Social Change Review. 11, 1978:28–36.

Piliavin, I., & Sosin, M. "Tracking the Homeless." Focus. 10, 1987:20–24.

Piven, F., & Cloward, R. *Regulating the Poor: The Functions of Public Welfare.* New York: Vintage, 1971.

————. *Poor People's Movements.* New York: Pantheon, 1977.

Ringenbach, P. *Tramps and Reformers: The Discovery of Unemployment in New York.* Westport, CT: Greenwood Press, 1973.

Roberts, S. "Reagan on Homelessness: Many Choose to Live in the Streets." New York Times. December 23, 1988.

Roedlinger, D., & Foner, P. *Our Own Time: A History of Labor and the Working Day.* New York: Greenwood Press, 1986.

Ropers, R. *The Invisible Homeless.* New York: Human Sciences Press, 1988.

Rosenthal, R. "Worlds Within Worlds: The Lives of Homeless People in Context." Paper presented at the 84th annual meeting of the American Sociological Association, San Francisco, CA, August 11, 1989.

Rossi, P. *Down and Out in America: The Origins of Homelessness.* Chicago: University of Chicago Press, 1989.

Roth, D., Bean, J., & Johnson, E. *Homelessness in Ohio: A Study of People in Need.* Columbus: Ohio Department of Mental Health, 1986.

Rothman, D. *The Discovery of the Asylum.* New York: Little, Brown, 1971.

Rubin, L. B. *Worlds of Pain.* New York: Basic Books, 1976.

Russell, B. *In Praise of Idleness and Other Essays.* New York: W. W. Norton, 1935.

Ryan, W. *Blaming the Victim.* New York: Random House, 1971.

Safety Network (newspaper of the National Coalition for the Homeless). Hopper, K. "Circles of the Mad and the Homeless: Overlap, Not Identity." April 1991:4.

Schmalz, J. "Miami Police Want to Control Homeless by Arresting Them." New York Times. November 4, 1988:1.

Schorr, L. *Within Our Reach: Breaking the Cycle of Disadvantage.* New York: Anchor, 1988.

Scull, A. *Decarceration: Community Treatment and the Deviant—A Radical View.* Englewood Cliffs, NJ: Prentice-Hall, 1977.

Sennett, R., & Cobb. J. *The Hidden Injuries of Class.* New York: Vintage, 1973.

Shinn, M., Knickman, J. R., & Weitzman, B. C. "Social Relationships and Vulnerability to Becoming Homeless Among Poor Families." Paper presented at American Psychological Association, New Orleans, LA, 1989.

Shinn, M., & Weitzman, B. "Research on the Homeless: An Introduction." Journal of Social Issues. 46(4), 1990:1–11.

Sidel, R. *Women and Children Last.* New York: Viking Press, 1986.

Silverman, C., Segal, S. & Anello, E. "Community and the Homeless Mentally Ill: The Structure of Self-Help Groups." Paper presented at the 84th annual meeting of the American Sociological Association, San Francisco, CA, August 1989.

Snow, D., & Anderson, L. "Identity Work Among the Homeless: The Verbal Construction and Avowal of Personal Identities." American Journal of Sociology. 92(6), 1987:1336–1371.

Snow, D. & Anderson, L. *Down on Their Luck.* Berkeley: University of California Press, 1992.

Snow, D., Baker, S., Anderson, L., & Martin, M. "The Myth of Pervasive Mental Illness Among the Homeless." Social Problems. 33(5), 1986:407–423.

Sosin, M., Piliavin, I., & Westerfelt, H. "Towards a Longitudinal Analysis of Homelessness." Journal of Social Issues. 46(4), 1990:157–174.

Stack, C. *All Our Kin: Strategies for Survival in the Black Community.* New York: Harper & Row Publishers, 1974.

Struening, E. L. *A Study of Residents of the New York City Shelter System.* New York: New York State Psychiatric Institute, 1987.

Struening, E. L., & Susser, E. *First Time Shelter Users of the New York City Shelter System.* New York: New York Psychiatric Institute, 1986.

Susser, E., Struening, E. L., & Conover, S. "Childhood Experiences of Homeless Men." American Journal of Psychiatry, 144, 1987:1599–1601.

Susser, I. *Norman Street: Poverty and Politics in an Urban Neighborhood.* New York: Oxford University Press, 1982.

Suttles, G. *The Social Order of the Slum.* Chicago: University of Chicago Press, 1968.

———— . "Culture and Lifestyle Among the Minority Poor." (In) K. Gronbjerg, D. Street, and G. Suttles (eds.), *Poverty and Social Change.* Chicago: University of Chicago Press, 1978, 93–114.

Trattner, W. *From Poor Law to Welfare State.* Fourth ed. New York: Free Press, 1989.

Uzelac, E. "Compassion for Poor Burns Out Across Nation." Baltimore Sun. December 1, 1990.

Wagner, D. *The Quest for a Radical Profession: Social Service Careers and Political Ideology.* Lanham, MD: University Press of America, 1990.

———— . "Social Work and the Hidden Victims of Deindustrialization." Journal of Progressive Human Services. 2(1), 1991:15–38.

Wagner, D., & Cohen, M. B. "The Power of the People: Homeless Protesters in the Aftermath of Social Movement Participation." Social Problems. 38(4), 1991:543–561.

Watson, S., & Austerberry, H. *Housing and Homelessness: A Feminist Perspective.* London: Routledge, Kegan Paul, 1986.

Weitzman, B., Shinn, M. B., & Knickman, J. R. "Mental Health Problems as Risk Factors for Homelessness." Paper presented at American Public Health Association meeting, Chicago, October 1989.

Wellman, B., & Leighton, B. "Networks, Neighborhoods, and Communities: Approaches to the Study of the Community Question." Urban Affairs Quarterly, 14(3), 1979:363–390.

Whyte, W. F. *Street Corner Society: The Social Structure of an Italian Slum.* Chicago: University of Chicago Press, 1966.

Willis, P. *Learning to Labor.* Aldershot: Gower, 1977.

Wilson, W. J. *The Truly Disadvantaged.* Chicago: University of Chicago Press, 1987.

Wineman, S. *The Politics of Human Services.* Boston: South End Press, 1984.

Withorn, A. *Serving the People: Social Services and Social Change.* New York: Columbia University Press, 1984.

Wright, J. "The Worthy and Unworthy Homeless." Society. 25(5), 1988:64–69.

Zald, M., & McCarthy, J. *Social Movements in an Organizational Society.* New Brunswick, NJ: Transaction Books, 1987.

About the Book and Author

During the past decade, homelessness became a widespread phenomenon in the United States for the first time since the Great Depression. The public frequently blamed the poor for their plight. Journalistic and academic accounts, in contrast, often evoked pathos and pity, regarding the homeless primarily as objects of treatment and rehabilitation. David Wagner challenges both of these dominant images, offering an ethnographic portrait of the poor that reveals their struggle not only to survive but also to create communities on the streets and to develop social movements on their own behalf. Definitely not passive victims, the homeless of *Checkerboard Square* survive within an alternative street culture, with its own norms and social organization, in a world often hidden from the view of researchers, journalists, and social workers.

Checkerboard Square reveals the daily struggle of street people to organize their lives in the face of rejection by employers, government, landlords, and even their own families. Looking beyond the well-documented causes of homelessness such as lack of affordable housing or unemployment, Wagner shows how the poor often become homeless through resistance to the discipline of the workplace, authoritarian families, and the bureaucratic social welfare system. He explains why the crisis of homelessness is not only about the lack of services, housing, and jobs but a result of the very structure of the dominant institutions of work, family, and public social welfare.

David Wagner has written on social welfare issues in journals such as *Social Problems, Social Service Review, Social Work,* the *International Journal of Health Services, Contemporary Drug Problems,* and the *Journal of Sociology and Social Welfare.* He is author of *The Quest for a Radical Profession: Social Service Careers and Political Ideology* (1990) and is assistant professor of social work at the University of Southern Maine. He holds a Ph.D. in sociology from the City University of New York.

Index